Subaltern Historiography

A Reader

Subaltern Historiography

A Reader

Editors

C.I. David Joy

Ebenezar Shinekumar

HMI/KUTS

2020

Subaltern Historiography: A Reader – Jointly published by the Indian Society for Promoting Christian Knowledge (ISPCK), Post Box 1585, Kashmere Gate, Delhi-110006 and Henry Martyn Institute (HMI), Hyderabad-500052 and Kerala United Theological Seminary (KUTS), Kerala-695011.

ISBN: 978-81-947592-7-0

Laser typeset by

ISPCK, Post Box 1585, 1654, Madarsa Road, Kashmere Gate, Delhi-110006 • *Tel:* 23866323

e-mail: ashish@ispck.org.in • ella@ispck.org.in
website: www.ispck.org.in

Contents

Foreword

Many Earnest Christians reject any positive relationships between Christianity and other faiths. They make exclusive claims for the superiority of Christianity and the finality of Christ based on such New Testament texts as 'there is no other name given under heaven', and the alleged dominical words of Jesus in the Fourth Gospel that no one can come to the Father except through him. Let me state at the outset that I believe that Jesus Christ is indeed the full, perfect and final revelation of God. I will yield to no one on that point. But that does not then give me the right to ride roughshod with muddy boots on what a person of another faith considers to be her holy ground nor to denigrate and belittle what she believes is a revelation from a transcendent divine reality by whatever name it is called and however it may be conceived and described. To dismiss other faiths is not only unforgivable arrogance but is a position that flies in the face of reality. It is unreasonable and indeed unbiblical. When we assert that it is only through Christ that humans have access to God and thereby mean the incarnate Logos, we land in an untenable position. Is there any Christian who would doubt that, for example, Abraham had an encounter with God so crucial that he should be regarded as the founding father of three of the major monotheistic faiths? And what about Moses? We could extend the list. Clearly Christians do not in fact jettison all the religious experience of those who encountered God in the pre-Christian dispensation.

Some of the most sublime Christian teaching is based on what we call the Old Testament, which we read as an indispensable part of our Bible. The New Testament would in large measure be incomprehensible if we did not assume much of what is taught in the Old Testament. If it comes only through Christ and if it is true, as we clearly have to acknowledge, then we must postulate a pre incarnate Logos/Word as the means of the access to God, the source of all goodness, love, life and truth.

The Fourth Gospel in which the apparently exclusivist verse occurs of people coming to the Father only through the Son asserts right at its beginning that the Word enlightens everyone who comes into the world. St Paul claims in Romans that Gentiles can be adjudged blameworthy because they have a law written in their hearts and so like the Jew to whom has been vouchsafed a direct revelation from God, they too can be accused of having fallen short of the glory of God.

God is alone the source of all goodness, truth, life and love. Whoever possesses these attributes has received them from God, otherwise we have to postulate several sources of these things and thereby administer a fatal blow to monotheism. Obviously, Christians do not have a monopoly on these qualities. Often in fact they are shown up conspicuously by people of other faiths or of none. We cannot, if we want to be taken seriously, assert that Mahatma Gandhi was not a very good man, nor that the Dalai Lama is not transparently holy and serene. Is God any less glorified that these people are not Christian? Albert Einstein was a brilliant scientist. Is what he propounded any less true because he was a Jew and not a Christian? It surely would be preposterous to claim that it was.

I do not know of any major religion which at its best teaches that it is morally right to oppress or to exploit fellow human beings, or that injustice and war are to be preferred to their glorious counterparts, or that it is a worthy goal to pursue development of a harsh, cruel and uncaring society that should degrade the environment and be wantonly wasteful of scarce and irreplaceable natural resources.

There is so much that conspires to separate and alienate us from one another. There is the growing intolerant fundamentalism and a resurgence of xenophobia and ethnic chauvinism. We are face to face with daunting problems that threaten us with catastrophe — Aids, poverty, disease, the population explosion, human rights violations and ignorance. We need to build coalitions with those who share our values.

The religions of the world, whilst certainly different, do in fact share some important values. Let us celebrate our diversity in culture, faith, ethnicity, etc., so that we can show that we are indeed the rainbow people of God.

Though this book is written in a clear way for the general public and for students who wish to learn about the world's world views, it does rest on some theoretical foundations which may be of interest to historians of religion and others concerned with the analysis of human values. We use a seven-dimensional framework to analyse the religions—in terms of ethics, ritual, narrative or myth, experience, institutions or society, doctrine and art. Religions are placed in a historical context, and viewed in relation to their periods of formation and re-formation. I stress to the ways in which they blend with other movements such as modern nationalism.

I am most grateful to Rev. Dr. David Joy, Principal KUTS, for proposing this book, and also to HMI, to collaborate and partner, who notably helped in the execution of the work.

Packiam T. Samuel
Director - HMI

Introduction

Martin Luther King Jr, the herald of the liberation movement of the subalterns in the North America who inspired and continues to empower millions of subalterns in the history of the world visited Trivandrum in 1959. A seminar was organized by the Kerala United Theological Seminary and Henry Martin Institute to remember gratefully his contributions and remind our society about the message of liberation for establishing a better world. In this connection the Kerala United Theological Seminary celebrated the visit of Martin Luther King Jr. on 13th August 2019. Since Martin Luther King Jr. empowered the people of the margins, it is noted that the people of the margins in our society can learn lessons from his life.

A public lecture on that day on "Interfaith and Subaltern Historiography" had been delivered by Rev. Dr. Packiam Samuel (Director, HIM, Hyderabad). A workshop on subaltern historiography was conducted and prominent people in the field such as Sri. M.A. Baby, Dr. Dyron Daughrity (Pepperdine University, USA), Dr. Donald Schweitzer (St. Andrew's College, Canada), Dr. V.V. Thomas (UTC, Bangalore) and many others presented papers.

This edited book is a collection of essays written by Rev. Prof. Dr. C.I. David Joy (Christian Mission and Postcolonialism), Rev. Prof. Dr. Don Schweitzer (Dalit Theology and Evangelical Freedom) ,Rev. Prof. Dr. Dr. V. V. Thomas (Interfaith, Subaltern historiography and the self-perception of the church through the centuries), Rev. Ebenezer Shinekumar (Śabarimala: A Syncretic Religion and Model for Interfaith Relations),Rev. John Davidson Johnson (Exclusion: A Human made SIN in God's own Cosmos), Dr. Jayasree (Postcolonial Reading of Nazareth Manifesto: Socio-Political Explosion), Shri. M.A. Baby (The 60th Anniversary commemoration of the visit of Martin Luther King Jr.), Rev. Ninan Jacob (Rich and Poor in Pauline Understanding), Rev. Prof. Dr. M. Stephen (The Interfaith Understanding and Subaltern Historiography), Dr. Supongmayang Longkumer (The Oral Lore in Luke and in the North East Indian Tribal Context: An Interpretation through Tribal Biblical 'Reoralizing' Hermeneutics), Dr. Sajitha Varghese (Women Property Owners in the Book of Acts), and Dr. Dyron B. Daughrity (Donyi-Polo: New Challenges to Christianity in Arunachal Pradesh and Northeast India). These essays indeed present a clear picture of subaltern historiography applied in theology and hermeneutics.

As you already probably know, the Kerala United Theological Seminary (KUTS), established in 1943, is a premier theological and ministerial education center of the churches in Kerala State, affiliated to the Senate of Serampore College/University, West Bengal, India. It was established through a joint effort of missionary societies and churches- the London Missionary Society, the Church Missionary Society, and the Basel Mission and The Church of God in South India. At present, the seminary is run by the six dioceses/regions (About 4000 congregations) of the Church of South India (CSI) Kerala State, with an ecumenical outlook. Through its teaching, scholarship, life and community services, the Seminary seeks to nurture the formation of a Christian identity, which is ecumenical in outlook, which remains intrinsically Indian. Its customized curriculum with its basis in Indian spirituality, resources and challenges seeks to transform classroom academics into faith in action in the real world, both within India and in the global context.

This publication is an attempt from our side to actualize the vision and mission of theological education. I sincerely thank my friend Rev. Prof. Dr. Packiam T. Samuel (Director, HMI) for the support and encouragement. I also thank Mr. Sundeep Chawdhry of ISPCK for his willingness to publish the work. Rev. Ebenezar Shinekumar, co-editor of the book has painstakingly arranged the conference. I am sure this book will enable many people to creatively think in tune with subaltern hermeneutics.

Rev. Dr. Prof. C.I. David Joy
Principal, KUTS.
Board Member SBL-ICI

Christian Mission and Postcolonialism

C. I. David Joy

The extraordinary context of Christian mission today due to the well-structured studies in the field of post colonialism, demands a broader and deeper understanding of mission. In terms of the currently assumed borders of mission, it is noted that many models and patterns emerged during the colonial era and imposed by the colonial powers. In order to propose a possible paradise for Christian mission in a post colonial period, it is important to analyze the solo-cultural and religion political structure of the post colonial period. In the same way I should evaluate new patterns of mission in postcolonial era and propose new directions in this regard.

Revisiting Postcolonial context

Immediately after the end of colonial rule across the globe, there were many free nations formed under the leadership of native leaders. Shashi Tharoor in his 2017 book *Inglorious Empire: What the British Did to India* is a systematic analysis of   the colonial rule in India.[1] One of the shocking revelations made by

Tharoor in his book is about extend of economic exploitation by the British Raj. As a result, Independent India had to struggle a lot to rebuild its economy. For many new nations, it was not a simple obstacle to overcome, but a serious issue which had to be addressed by using all their resources. There were many other encounters that shaped the free nations when they were growing up. Among them, issues of democracy, migration, displacement, civil wars, ethnic violence, racial discrimination and gender violence played key roles in determining the new life location of the people during the postcolonial context. Since the scope of this article is to define Christian mission and postcolonialism, I will only present the most significant ingredient of the postcolonial history with special reference to the contexts where Christian mission encountered new horizons of experiences. Tinyiko Sam Maluleke explains the emerging context of Christian mission in his 2007 article "Postcolonial Mission: Oxymoron or New Paradigm?" in a relevant manner. He argues:

> Postcolonial mission takes place in the midst of the so-called 'knowledge economies, 'globalisation' and the 'information highway'. These developments will be considered with a keen eye for new forms of imperialism, new forms of false and violent deals between modem day Rahabs and modem day invaders. Above all, postcolonial mission will not hesitate to be critical of the project of economic growth carried out without regard to the earth and the poor.[2]

Changes in socio-cultural indentify of native people are an ongoing process. It is significant to identify major dements that have challenged the world order in a postcolonial world. They are mainly centralization of power, Exploitation of non-renewable resources, displacement of people for development refugee crisis and forced migration, Gender discriminations and emergence of new religion identities.

Centralization of power

When the colonial rulers conquered native cultures and people, they tried to bring them under one umbrella namely colonial power. Even after the emergence of free nations, that nation of centralization of power continued in many ways. Frances Hutchison and Brian Burkitt in their 1997 book *The Political Economy of Social Credit and Guild Socialism* argued that there were colonial political reasons behind the shaping of oppressive economic policies in a postcolonial context.[3] Their arguments offered a dear picture about the postcolonial scenario which controlled the political and cultural governance in today's postcolonial contexts. A major issue that had to be addressed by the rulers of the free nations was poverty.

It was part of the political engineering process during the colonial era and many postcolonial contexts continue the same uncritically. Even in strong and huge democratic nations such as India, Brazil, Nigeria and soon, "large classes of people became mere employees, engaged in tasks on the primary inducement of money, obeying orders and taking no personal responsibility for the outcome of the enterprise"[4]

Such a centralization of power is a mainly due to the concentration of power in one major system of governance. Colonial powers never allowed multiple voices to emerge to support the major power center and in postcolonial contexts the ruling class uncritically adjusted same pattern of governance.

Albert Tuaopepe Wendt is a Samoan poet and writer who

carefully analysed the postcolonial situations and redefined the term post colonial. He says "For me, the post in post- colonial does not just mean after, it also means around, through, out of, alongside, and against."[5] When this definition is considered genuine, the socio-cultural context of postcolonial period seem to be broader and wider that the popular understudying. Therefore, it is important to understand the multiple layers of postcolonial contexts with the help of available resources and tools today. Rajeev S Patke elucidated Albert Wendt's poetry and stated "Wendt's remembering is an antidote to the anxiety of succumbing to neo-colonial influences".[6] Thus, it is observed that in order to comprehend postcolonial context, neo-colonial realms may also be understood.

Exploitation of Non-renewable resources

During the colonial era, the colonizers expected non-renewable resources from the native lands without any control or reservation. As a result, many native cultures suffered a lot of disability in terms of ecological balances. In continuation to the colonial policies, free nation too followed the attitude of exploiting non-renewable resources without any intention to protect the earth. It is noted that as many governments in the newly formed free nation could not address the issue of development in a proper manner, former colonial powers remained ink free nations in the form of corporate giants in exploiting non-renewable resources for making economic profit. Saral Sarkar in his 1999 book *Eco-socialism or Eco-capitalism: A Critical Analyses of Humanity's Fundamental Choices* , argue:

> But since the early 1970's, we have been hearing of absolute scarcity of resources. One would suppose that at least as far as minerals – Which are non-renewable –are concerned,

there could be no doubt that they would be exhausted sooner or later.[7]

It is noted that, such a conflict creates an atmosphere of problem of poverty and development struggle in postcolonial nations. I observe that many postcolonial nations could not develop their own policy of sustainability due to the interventions of the corporate giants and multinational companies mostly following the ideology of neo-colonialism. Peter Marshall proposed a new philosophy for a new age after having evaluated the complexities of today's world. He writes in his book *Riding the wind*:

> While politics is usually defined as the art of government, in its widest and original sense it is the common pursuit of the good life. The good life covers all areas of social interaction- production and consumption, work and play, ritual and celebration, the social and the spiritual. It enables people to read life in their potential as individuals and social beings.[8]

When the non-renewable resources are exploited uncritically this common pursuit of the good life will not be possible. In order to remain in a society of well being and equality, a just use resumes should be promoted.

Gender Discrimination

In contemporary society, the domination of patriarchy and male hegemony seems to be a ruthless tool for subjugating women. In most of the ancient societies, through they were patriarchal in nature, women enjoyed a respectable place in terms of experiencing their spaces and roles. However, the colonial hegemonies of gender created huge gap between men and women. Martin Brokenleg in his 2006 article "LAKOTA HCA" explain this phenomenon by citing the example of Lakota people he argues:

The philosophical and social changes, which had an intense impact on Lakota culture came with the physical presence of people, including missionaries. Three institutions-thechurch, the federal government and education-created profound cultural change for the Lakota Society .... The missionaries particularly rejected Lakota sexual ethics.[9]

In postcolonial context, there are many attempts to revisit the sexual ethics imposed by the colonial missionary ethics, in order to accommodate people with different sexual orientation. Aruna Gnanadason explores this issue further and accuses, "The legacy of British intolerance" which provided "unjust legal sanctions".[10] Moreover, for a variety of reasons, women have been sexually assaulted during the process of geographical and cultural domination. Reflecting on the records of colonial history, it is noted that the military during the colonial era 'legitimized' rape as weapon to dominate the other. Unfortunately, it continues in postcolonial contexts as well. 2018 Nobel prize for peace has been given to two crusaders against sexual violence namely Nadia Murad and Dr. Denis Mukuwege. It happened in the midst of a global reckoning over sexual violence. In awarding the Nobel Prize to the activists the committee decided to expose the perpetrators who are responsible for the atrocities.

Colonial legacy in Historiography

Across the globe, historiography is based on the available written sources of history. It emerged "from the European encounter with the unknown other".[11] It is noted, "the West, as the apparent maker and custodian of history in both geopolitical and scriptural terms, was the site of "truth".[12] In their context, it is suggested to assess the events in history which have been misguided by the socio political reasons caused by colonialism. It is significant to do so as these are exoduses of migrants in every context due to known and unknown reasons. A proper assessment of historiography may counterintuitively serve the purpose of enhancing and developing new horizons of study of history for establishing new societies. It is not an easy task to remove all colonial elements form history, but at least, one can bring back the overlooked voices in terms of accommodating unrepresented communities. Lain Chambers defines historiography:

> Historiography did not merely study the past: it registered, transmitted and translated it. Its truth was the faith and mission of the West. So, the recent irruption of others into the heartland of European savoir poses disturbing questions about the status of our knowledge and the particulars protocols of historiography. For this intrusion rewrites the conditions of the West: its sense of truth, its sense of time, its sense of being.[13]

Since, this seems to be a major issue in many postcolonial contexts, it is suggested to decolonize the colonial historiographies by applying postcolonial historiographic tools in order to understand the real data behind the events. One of the major challenges today in a postcolonial context is to recognize and listen to the silenced people during the colonial era. Historiography therefore becomes "reworking the very sense of history, culture, society and language that had previously excluded or silenced such voices, such a presence."[14] In order to create a society of justice and freedom, it is significant to explore the location of such silence voices and communities. There are many colonials and missing achievers across the globe where data is gathered by colonial bureaucracy. However "history is more than a matter of obtaining information, as any historian knows, and historical knowledge is as much a result of methodology as anything else."[15]

Therefore, selecting an appropriate methodology and applying the same in a relevant manner shared be the starting point of reading the postcolonial context. It is interesting to read the observation of Niell Ferguson as he describes the beginning of British empire from a different viewpoint:

> It should never be forgotten that this was how the British Empire began: in a mad storm of seaborne violence and theft. It was not conceived by self-consciousness, imperialist, aiming to establish English rule over foreign lands, or colonists hoping to build a new life overseas.[16]

Later, perhaps, they stated offering imperial structure in colonized nations in order to execute their politics and intents. Thus, the colonized nations primarily became the site of exploitation and oppression.

Colonialism to Globalization

Reflecting on the aftereffects of colonialism, it is important to evaluate the implication of colonial power networks. William H McNill's 1963 book *The Rise of the West: History of the Human community* is a pioneering volume that exposed the reason behind the social change in a postcolonial world. Only through a careful analysis of his arguments, one can arrive at some conclusion about the route of colonialism to capitalism and Globalization.[17] This book is a perspectival analysis of historical data since 500 B.C to 1950. It is vital to note that the author expresses that there has been the era of Western dominance from 1500 A.D to the present.[18] The concept of dominance is linked with colonial expansion and economic capitalism. Willian H McNeill describes the European colonialism as the spread of European settlement. He after a careful study of history explains the data in the following manner:

> In diverse parts of the earth, European settlers produced a series of mutations from the social patterns of their homelands. The rigorous slavery of a West Indian sugar plantation and the rude egalitarianism of a New England frontier community represent extremes of a spectrum along which many intermediate social forms may be discerned.[19]

This analysis may not be a perfect one as far as the postcolonial historiography is concerned. However, one can surely trace out the elements of truth from his analysis. However, the claim of western domination is part of a brazen attempt by dominant historians to divert the focus of debate from the native voices to the dominant voices. Despite the development and education, why only still same are maintained as dominant custodian of power is a question to be debated. W.H. McNeill responds well:

> Ideas also spread throughout the world with increasing velocity and volume as communications increased. To be sure, political and language barriers sometimes obstructed the flow of ideas; religions or sectarian commitments likewise checked their infiltration into particular groups; and differences of local or class customs of an central cultural tradition, or of personal taste.[20]

The era of globalization is also known as an era of neo-colonialism. It is in this scenario that the interpretation of history has to be seen. At the dawn of colonialism, there was an alliance between state and religion in Europe and they could continue their corporation ever at the time of colonizing the nations. W.H. McNeill clearly expresses this:

> In such confusion and contrariety, perhaps all one can say by way of general summary is that both religion and secularism acquired a new energy from their mutual jostling.[21]

One of the observations made by the native/postcolonial historiographers was kind of unholy alliance between the colonial powers and missionaries in most of the contexts. Therefore, the rise of the globalization across the globe, specifically in the West should be seen as an outcome of colonialism and capitalism. Daniel Jeyaraj in his 2005 article, "The first Lutheran missionary Bartholomäus Ziegenbalg: His Concepts of Culture and Mission from a postcolonial perspective" argues:

> Postcolonial studies are based on a particular kind of understanding and interpretation of historical events and their consequences. In this paper, close attention is paid to the life experiences, wounded memories and resistances of the colonized and exploited people. The normative claims of histories, which were written by the colonizers are rejected because these histories assumed the racial and moral superiority of the colonizers and treated the colonized as non-entities. Categories of abusive power, political violence, economic subjugation, racial dominance and feminist ideologies are used to interpret the dislocation and destruction of the identity of the oppressed people.[22]

This is stated because of the power networks and the continuation of social institutions with colonial nature in postcolonial contexts. Victor Roudomet of and Roland Roberson in their 1995 article, " Globalization, world-system theory, and the comparative study of civilization : Issue of theoretical Logic in world – Historical Sociology" propose that all four sources of social power had been connected with colonialism. They are ideological, economic, military and political.[23] In post colonial contexts their relationships could be defined with the help of overlapping and interesting power networker.[24] However these power networker and basis and basics of globalization advocate unprecedented violence as the grammar of socio-political structures of our world. I think most of the seeds of violence, some during the colonial era and in postcolonial period, continues. Since the colonial hegemonic powers created a brutally violent political culture in the colonies, the free nations had to live with such a culture in postcolonial period.

In order to enter into a culture of just and meaningful life, I suggest that there should be new debate on public policies including political networkers. Peter Frankopan's 2015 book *The Silk Roads: A New History of the World* is a myopic view of the history of the world, both informative and reflective. He evaluates the channels of flow of money in postcolonial contexts very well and locates the weapon industry as a prime location.   While reflecting on the history he exposes that "the age of the west is at a crossroads".[25] This is an indication about the new responsible role of the postcolonial natures. However, the atmosphere of globalization and economic liberalism worked in a varied manner in postcolonial contexts. Francis Fukuyama supports this observation.

> Just as culture affects ability of countries to establish and sustain political liberalism, culture affects their ability to make economic liberalism work. Just as in the case of political democracy, the success of capitalism depends on some measure on the survival of pre-Modern cultural tradition into the Modern age. Like political liberalism, economic liberalism is not totally, self- sustaining, but depends on a degree of irrational thymos.[26]

It might have happened due to the "restriction on trade" during the colonial and postcolonial era.[27] Thus, a gap between nations in terms of economic policies and sustainability of the issue of global power network has to be noticed as " the objectives of liberalism and of democracy were once again however, in conflict".[28] Thus it is clear that the colonized and the colonizer interacting over the centuries produced a composite political culture in postcolonial contexts and mostly fostered a hybrid political culture and globalization is only a byproduct.

Key Works on the topic

It is not very easy to identify the key works on the topic as there are a number of significant contributions on the topic across the globe by the scholars who take the postcolonial mission seriously. 2008 book *Remapping Mission Discourse* is a well-crafted volume which could offer new directions and guidelines to the issue of postcolonial Christian mission in a systematic manner.[29] It also offers new paradigm for Christian mission in the context of socio-political changes in India. This book could identify the key issue in doing mission especially in the context of shifting horizons of theological education and social changes across the globe.

Paul G. Hiebert's 2009 book *The Gospel in Human Contexts: Anthropological Explorations for Contemporary Mission* is a survey of various dimensions of anthropological issues based on ethnosciences.[30] It is a clear introduction to the basic understanding of mission with a general description of various significant topics. The last part of the book is the most comprehensive understating of Christian values in mission, claiming mission as intercultural mediation. Another significant volume is *Christ and Caesar in Christian Missions* which could be a resource book for understanding the political locations of current Christian mission.[31] This collection of essays explores multi-faceted political shifts in a contemporary world, addressing socio-political questions in a deeper manner.

I consider Vinoth Ramachandra, a Sri Lankan theologian to be a trend-setter in terms of defining Christian mission in a postcolonial and pluralistic world. His 1996 book, *The Recovery of Mission: Beyond the Pluralist Paradigm* is an in-depth study of mission by considering various aspects of multiculturalism and religious pluralism in Asia.[32] The uniqueness of his work is that it could accomplish the hypothesis in a way of making a survey of religious conversations and engagements within the framework of political imperialism. In the same year, he published another book entitled *Gods that Fail: Modern Idolatry and Christian Mission* which suggests a broader and wider understanding of socio-cultural dynamics in the world for a legitimate caricature of mission of God. It also explains the unique role of Christian mission in bringing transformation to the complex world order.[33]

2016 book *Reading the Bible Missionally* initiated a number of interesting conversations in terms of using the Bible meaningfully while defining Christian mission.[34] It demands for a contingency planning for a possible interpretation of the Bible from the point of Christian mission by taking postcolonial socio-cultural shifts into account. At the other end of the spectrum, there are interpretations that would minimize the potential of the empowering power of the Bible by building up new humanity. Daniel Jeyaraj in his 2005 article, "The first Lutheran missionary Bartholomäus Ziegenbalg: His Concepts of Culture and Mission from a postcolonial perspective" offers a fresh understanding about the mission reading strategies in our context.[35]

Directions in Postcolonial Christian Mission

In order to debate on the direction in postcolonial mission, I should firstly share my experience with the mission activities of the Church of South India and Anglican Communion as I have been part of both of their activities in many ways. The Church of South India need to revisit Christian Mission in a postcolonial context. In the 1990's CSI Published a series of resource materials to address the trajectories of Christian mission. And later it is noted that the Church appointed a full-time person to access the activities.[36] There are a lot of literatures available to look into the issue of postcolonial mission based on the contemporary mission theology. In most of the cases, contemporary mission theory will address the issues and concern posed by political and social institutions through a vibrant and constant engagement. There are many silver lines among the dark clouds as the mission activities have been by many substantial studies of retrospect and introspect in terms of history and politics.

Mission Based on Good News

A major shift in Christian Mission from colonial era to postcolonial period is an understanding of an inclusive Christian community formation. The message of conflict and fear could not be preferred as postcolonial contexts demand a message of reconciliation and peace. In this regard the articulation of Duncan B. Forester is significant:

> But always Christians must remember that the Bible is primarily Gospel, Good news and promise, and only secondarily and derivatively, law. The Gospel is prior to the law. It is about love, forgiveness, new beginnings, grace, fulfillment, abundant life, rather than about condemnation, rejection, repression and the meticulous observances of a battery of rules.[37]

The shift was not an overnight process but a gradual one. However, there are still areas of conflict that need to be addressed.

Michael W. Coheen S2014 book *Introducing Christian Mission today. Scripture, History and Issues* is a well crafted monograph on the above said issues.[38]At the same time, there are many new endeavours to address a relevant mission paradigm for a postcolonial context. While discouraging the postcolonial Christian mission, it is significant to affirm the fact that there is a relationship of the Gospel to human social and cultural contexts. "Which makes a fresh awareness that "the gospel in trans.[39]A new paradigm for postcolonial mission cannot be drafted in a vacuum is the chist event has been their to be a core event in designing the frameworks and activities of the Christian mission in a postcolonial context. Michaul W Coheen Explains:

> Jesus assures him that he is (Lk 7:18-23) and that the works that he is doing are signs that the power of God to never the creations has indeed broken into history. Jesus own disciples also struggle to understand that although the kingdom has already dawned, it has not yet arrived in its fullness. The forces of the age to come are flowing into history but the counter forces of the old age remain a powerful reality.[40]

Contextualization

It is significant to discuss about the legitimacy in the contextualizing of Christian message for adopting it within the framework of local culture and societal paradigms. Andrew walls' 2002 book, *Cross-cultural Process in Christian History* is an outstanding attempt in defining the process of contextualization without diluting the core message of Christ event.[41] Andrew Walls summaries his arguments:

> No one ever meets universal Christianity in itself: we only meet Christianity in a local form and that means a historically, culturally conditioned form. We need not fear this; when God became man he became historically, culturally condition man

in a particular time and place. We need not be afraid of it. There is nothing wrong in having local forms of Christianity provided that we remember that they rare local.[42]

According to Walls, there are four forms of contextualization namely non contextualization, minimal contextualization, uncritical contextualization and critical contextualization. However, all these forms of interpretation and understanding should take epistemology seriously for differentiating or connecting revaluation and theology. Joshua D. Reichard suggests:

> For example, interreligious dialogue may help Pentecostal missionaries to critically examine the ways in which certain theologies may reinforce the structures of empire and seek to consciously contextualize their work on that basis. Pentecostal missionaries are gaining awareness that Latin America has experienced relatively little impact from the European Protestant Reformation and its historical effects in the West.[43]

In a postcolonial context, it is noted that contextual form of the Gospel is significant. Michal W Coheen asserts their endeavours to understand the cross-cultural dimension of Christian mission had been initiated by some missionaries during the colonial period. He writes:

> This process was initially evident with missionaries whose cross-cultural experiences gave them critical distance and new eyes for a fresh look at the church in western culture. They were able to see how the religious belongs of western culture compromised the gospel and the witness of the church. But the dynamic is now taking place at a global level.[44]

It is not only significant for a relevant missionary but also crucial for developing a possible e for particular   living contexts. It demands a number of facilities of a person to meet together to aspire for a multicultural person. Such persons will constitute a multicultural community which can take up the responsibility of Christian mission in postcolonial contexts effectively. Though it is a great challenge in a culturally conditional world, it should be made possible to encourage such communications to emerge for doing meaningful engagement and mission. Auli Vähäkangas suggests:

> Mission organizations and individuals involved in mission search many times for cod, gold and glory but foe way of the cross is not followed. We use rhetoric of liberation and talk of great ideas about partnership etc. But at the same time there is the reality of oppression and well-intending paternalism.[45]

Towards a Missional Hermeneutics

It is noted that a postcolonial reading strategy has been applied very fruitfully in interpreting the Bible by taking the presence of the empire in the text and context by many interpreters of the Bible across the globe. However, it is significant to draw insights from such reading frameworks for a missional hermeneutics. Richard Bauckham in his 2016 article, "Mission as Hermeneutics for scriptural Interpretation" reveals some unknown and hidden dimension of missional hermeneutics by taking mission as hermeneutics. I am moved by the affirmation of Richard Bauckham about the significance of the Bible in Christian mission. He writes:

> That the church's mission in and to the world is the practice of the biblical text in which the text is constantly being interpreted as important. A missionary hermeneutics of this kind would not be simply a study of the theme of mission in the biblical writings, but a way of reading the whole of scripture with mission as its contract interrupt and goal.[46]

I have noticed that many contemporary biblical scholars affirm that there was vibrant and alternate socio-religious life initiated by the early church and the purpose of the Bible was to continue the missional life of the early church. In such a scenario, mission becomes a practice of the biblical text and the Bible should be interested with a clear missional focus. Jiona Havea in his 2011 article, "The cons of contextuality ….. contextuality" affirms the need for taking contextual theology in to account while thinking of a relevant missional hermeneutics in a postcolonial world.

> He writes:

> I do not pretend that contextualization is free of having blind spots. Ecological sensitivities, heightened by the troubles associated with climate change and global warming have made awareness of and care for the environment (context) as a theological obligation. How may we theological in a world that disintegrates, unravels before our own eyes………. Postcolonial consciousness calls attention (with voices coming from the North!) to the causes and interests of the south and enables the relocation of the hype.[47]

It is significant to understand the postcolonial context very well in order to develop relevant missional hermeneutics for a postcolonial context. Shawn B Redfor's 2017 article, "Mission Theology and Postmodern Social Networks" is a study that could offer some fresh direction in terms of undertaking the postmodern social networks for interpreting the Bible in a contextually relevant manner.[48] How do the social networks dictate and design a new context for missional Hermeneutics? Shown B. Redford cleanly explains:

This analysis will examine the role that social networks have in affecting the nations, people of God, and mission of God with the goal of understanding how these system influence allegiance toward God. Social networks are empowered by people, and they their networks are empowered by people, and they have the capacity to be helpful, destructive, wise or thoughtless, and godly or godless.[49]

It is a sensitive and series task to address the role of social networks as most of them are the products of postcolonial world. Craig G. Bartholomew in his article "Theological Interpretation and a Missional Hermeneutic" stands for more deeper and broader interpretation of the Bible by taking the dreams and aspiration of the people of God. He states:

> Christian communities read scriptures from a particular social location. Out of this context, they bring question to the text, in service of the mission of God. Here the focus is on the community and what it means for the people of God to read scripture faithfully in light of their missional context.[50]

Thus, a hermeneutic exercise becomes part of the Christian mission in a postcolonial world. N T Wright further elaborates the context by stating "people around the world, not least in the middle East, see Christianity and the West as synonymous. They think Christianity is about economic exploitation and violent control."[51] This kind of framework may not be helpful in assessing a legitimate picture about the missional hermeneutics. Sathianathan Clarke in his 2014 article, "World Christianity and Postcolonial Mission: A Path Forward for the Twenty-first Century" explores the significance of Christian mission in building up a new paradigm for liberation. He states:

> There is broad acceptance that Christian mission must involve a preferential option to locate, empower, and embrace the reflections of the marginalized. Interestingly, much of the

postcolonial voicing of the marginalized comes from these mission platforms. The representation for these collectives has shifted to include substantial reflections from the churches in the South, especially Africa and Asia. Because these communities are economically deprived, reflections on mission practice from the South also lift high both for the material plight of the poor and for spiritual contribution that such communities can make to postcolonial mission.[52]

Therefore, it can be argued that missional hermeneutics in a postcolonial world must consider the socio-political realities of the world seriously in evaluating the context and then must arrive at a conclusion about the basic credentials of missional hermeneutics. In this regard, Joel B Green Explores:

> If "Mission" is understood with reference to God's agenda in the world, and not merely as an index of individual or churchly outreach on God's behalf, then " missional " refers more broadly to how the community of God's people comes to identify itself with, and to participate in, God's work. [53]

Thus, concept indeed offers us a more legitimate picture about God's mission in today's postcolonial world as it can surely offer a genuine hermeneutical framework for developing a mission.

Subversiveness, Solidarity and Mission

Christian mission has been understood in a postcolonial context as an engagement of solidarity and sub . Scott W. Sunquist affirm this aspect with the help of crystal clear insights from the Bible. He argues that mission has to be understood as evangelism in a broader sense.

> Evangelism requires the death of something – security comfort, relationships – so that new life can be planted. The seed of faith must be planted in broken, aerated and irrigated soil. The work of sowing is just that: work .... Evangelism

> will require a change in calendar- it will mean taking up the cross of Christ the normal Christian life is a life of witness, and a life of witness counts the cost and enters into the struggles of the kingdom. [54]

In a changing world with a clear assessment about the trajectories of mission, it is suggested to understand the major horizons and areas of postcolonial mission by taking the pressure of the neo colonial forces in context securely. In this regard, Paul G.Hiebert's views seem to be very challenging and promising. He argues:

> In a glocal world full of tensions and conflicts, how can we work toward the unity of the church, theology, and mission? One way is to develop global systems from the top down: from centralized institutions built around specialists who define theology, organize the church, and manage missions. Another way is to develop global networks from the ground up: networks that begin at the local level and develop midlevel and global dialogues, partnerships, and networks for fellowship and ministry.[55]

In a postcolonial Christian mission, there is a fresh understanding about God's intervention in the history. It is evident in the formation of ecumenical movement in the 1950's which could propose a new pattern of Christian witness and mission.   In the same way Christian mission has been comprehended as integral to the church by addressing the issues such as problem of missional structure, the spread of the sectarian spirit, the voice of the African revolution and the challenge of resurgent religion. [56]

The era of postcolonialism is described to be a world turned upside down for various reasons. However, Christian mission could survive and continue because of its ability to be subversive and to be in solidarity with the people of the margins. Scott

W Sunquest further states:

> Christianity in the midst of these global transferring was showing a new strength, residency, and adaptability. Christian mission and mission theology took off in different direction in light of these changes.[57]

At the same time, Christian mission could adjust many possible patterns of dialogue and witness in order to sustain its ability for liberation. Postcolonial Christian mission witnessed to many vibrant movements of native voices to nationalist Christian mission to be independent in framing missional agenda by taking the local issues seriously. In the same way, it is noted that there are a number indigenous resurgent of emerging ecclesial voices due to the native versions of Christian mission. As a result Christian mission in a postcolonial world receives a new core and goal. Scott W. Sunquest explains:

> Christian mission is now carried on in a postcolonial, Post-marxist, and postmodern globalized world, no one knows exactly what that means. We do, however, have some hints. It means that the scars of colonial oppression and the deep wounds of community remain with us …. We also know that same of the same issues of secularism, technology, religious, church unity, and the meaning of church have not changed.[58]

This understanding will surely act as a guideline for resisting the world of postcolonial Christian mission.

Contextual Christology as core message of mission

David Hartano is his 2017 article, "Contextual Christology: Carrying the great Commission with Joy" argues that "core message of the gospel has to be sounded grounded in the Bible, a testament to the redemptive activity of God, wrought in Jesus Christ."[59] Among the contextual Christologies, Postcolonial

Christology has a unique place as it seems to be an interpretation of the Christ event in view of the socio-political realities of postcolonial period. It is not an easy task to assess the origin and development of postcolonial Christology, but I consider the womanist expressions of Christ might have played a crucial role in proposing the basic credential of postcolonial Christology. However, a genuine expression of postcolonial Christ could be the starting point for discussing the missional elements in understanding a postcolonial Christ. It should not be at the level of an image but should be at the level of a legitimate conversations for proposing a borderless community of Christ. While talking about contextual Christology, it is important to understand the dimensions of a postmodern anthropology for mission in a postcolonial world. Michael A. Rynkiewich in his 2011 article, "Do We Need a Postmodern Anthropology for Mission in a Postcolonial World?" explains this in a systematic way:

> At the same time, advances in anthropology contributed to mission education and practices. Each refreshed the other, each challenged the other, and each changed. Then, in the 1960s, Mission Studies adopted the modernist anthropological model, but stopped talking with anthropologists. The split has left both disciplines weaker. The newest generation of anthropologists has begun to study local expressions of Christianity. However, missiologists may find it difficult to read their ethnographies, since anthropology as a discipline has advanced but missiologists have not kept up their end of the conversation.[60]

From the above discussion, it is noted that there has been a close link between Christian missions and colonialism in many ways. Therefore, it is significant to find out insights for understanding the impact of postcolonialism in defining a fresh agenda for doing Christian mission in today's context. I am sure, this essay could present a comprehensive perspective of Christian mission from a postcolonial viewpoint. By citing some examples for the colonial era, the essay presented a specific horizon of Christian mission in terms of challenges and encounters in the history. This chapter also introduced the principles and practices of postcolonialism in the context of Christian mission by proposing a wider and broader framework of implications of Christian mission in today's context.

Endnotes

[1] Shashi Tharoor, *Inglorious Empire: What the British Did to India,* (Delhi: Penguin Books, 2017).

[2] Tinyiko Sam Maluleke, "Postcolonial Mission: Oxymoron or New Paradigm?" *Swedish Missiological Themes, 95,* 4 (2007), 525.

[3] Frances Hutchesum and Brian Burkitt, *The Political Economy,* London: Routledge, 1997.89

[4] Frances Hutchuson and Brian Burkitt, *The Political Economy,* 61.

[5] Albert Wendt, *Inside Us the Dead: Poems 1961 to 1974,* (Auckland: Longman, 1976), 6.

[6] Rajeev. S. Patke, *Postcolonial Poetry in English,* (Oxford: OUP 2007), 16.

[7] Saral Sarkar, *Eco-socialism or Eco-capitalism: A Critical Analyses of Humanity's Fundamental Choices,* (London : Zed books, 1999), 93.

[8] Peter Marshal, *Riding the wind,* (London: continuous, 2000), 16 3.

[9] Martin Brokenleg, "Lakota HCA", in *ed.* Terry Brown, *Other voices, Other worlds: the Global Church Speak out on Homosexuality,* (London: Darton, 2006), 10.

[10] Aruna Gnanadasan, "The Struggle to be Human", in ed. Terry Brown, *Other voices, Other worlds: the Global Church Speak out on Homosexuality,* (London: Darton, 2006),84.

[11] Lain Chambers, "Migrancy , Culture, Identity", in *The postmodern History Reader,* ed, Keith Jenkins, (London : Routledge 1997), 78.

[12] Lain Chambers, "Migrancy, Culture, Identity", 78.

[13] Lain Chambers, "Migrancy, Culture, Identity", 78.

[14] Lain Chambers, "Migrancy, Culture, Identity", 78.

[15] Diane Elan, "Romancing the postmodern Feminism and deconstruction" in ed, Keith Jenkins, *The postmodern History Reader*, (London: Routledge, 1997), 66.

[16] Niell Fergusan, *Empire: The Rose and Demise of the British world order*, (New York: Basic Book, 2002), 1.

[17] Willian H. McNeill, *The Rise of the West: History of the Human community*, (New York: Mentor Book, 1963).

[18] Willian H. McNeill, *The Rise of the West*, 619.

[19] W.H. McNeill, *The Rise of the West*, 718-19.

[20] W.H. McNeill, *The Rise of the West*, 893.

[21] W.H. McNeill, *The Rise of the West*, 641.

[22] Daniel Jeyaraj, Swedish Missiological Themes, 93, 3 (2005) The first Lutheran missionary Bartholomäus Ziegenbalg: His Concepts of Culture and Mission from a postcolonial perspective, Swedish Missiological Themes, 93, 3 (2005), 379.

[23] Victor Roudomet of and Roland Roberson, "Globalization, World-system theory, and the Comparative study of civilization: Issue of Theoretical Logic in world – Historical Sociology in Civilization and World system: Studying world –Historical Change, in ed, Stephen K Sanderson, London: Altamira, 1995, 279.

[24] Victor Roudomet of and Roland Roberson, Quoted Michael Mann, *The Sources of Social Power*, (Cambridge: CUP, 1986).

[25] Peter Frankopan, *The Silk Roads: A New History of the World*, 519.

[26] Francis Fukuyama, *The End of History and the Last Man*, (London: Penguin Book, 1992), 233.

[27] Thomas R Metcalf, *Imperial Connection*, (Rankhat : Permaneut Blacks, 2007), 213.

[28] Immanuel Wallers, *After Liberalism*, (New York: The Newpren, 1995), 202.

[29] Simon Samuel and P.V. Joseph, eds., *Remapping Mission Discourse: A Festschrift in Honor of the Rev. George Kuruvilla Chavanikamannil,* (Delhi: NTC-ISPCK, 2008).

[30] Paul G. Hiebert, *The Gospel in Human Contexts: Anthropological Explorations for Contemporary,* (Michigan: Baker Academic, 2009).

[31] Edwin L.Frizen, Jr. and Wade T.Coggins, eds., *Christ and Caesar in Christian Missions,* (California: William Carey Library, 1979.)

[32] Vinoth Ramachandra, *The Recovery of Mission: Beyond the Pluralist Paradigm,* (Carlistle: Paternoster, 1996).

[33] Vinoth Ramachandra, *Gods that Fail: Modern Idolatry and Christian Mission,* (Downers Grove: IVP, 1996).

[34] Micharl W. Goheen,ed., *Reading the Bible Missionally,* (Michigan: WB Eerdmans, 2016).

[35] Daniel Jeyaraj, "The first Lutheran missionary Bartholomäus Ziegenbalg: His Concepts of Culture and Mission from a postcolonial perspective", *Swedish Missiological Themes,* 93, 3 (2005).

[36] The Archbishop of Canterbury, the Church Mission Society and Durham University have become partners in creating an innovative seven year post: Mission Theologian in the Anglican Communion. The purpose is to research, stimulate, connect and publish works of theology in the Anglican Communion, with particular focus on insights from Africa, Asia and Latin America, in their ecumenical contexts. The Rt Revd Dr Graham Kings, currently Bishop of Sherborne, has been appointed and will take up this new post in July 2015. He will be based in London, visiting Durham University, as an Honorary Fellow, and will travel in the Communion. He will convene a series of seminars in Anglican Communion Studies for theologians, particularly in Africa, Asia and Latin America. A new web site, launched today, MissionTheologyAngCom.org, will publish the papers. *(www. https://www.virtueonline.org/bishop-graham-kings-appointed-mission-theologian-anglican-communion).*

[37] Duncan B. Forrester, "Good and fray," in *Terry Brown,* 289.

[38] Michal Coheen, *Introducing Christian Mission today. Scripture, History and Issues,* (Illinois: IVP, 2014).

[39] Paul G Hiebert, *The Gospel in Human Contexts: Anthropological Exploration for Contemporary Mission,* (Michigan: Baker Academic, 2009),31.

[40] Michel W Coheen, *Introducing Christian Mission today. Scripture, History and Issues*, 2014, 49.

[41] Andrew Walls, *Cross-cultural Process in Christian History*, (NY: Orbis books, 2002).

[42] Andrew   Walls, *Cross-cultural Process in Christian History*, 235.

[43] Joshua D. Reichard, 'Mutually transformatige missions' A postcolonial, process-relational Pentecostal missiology", Missiology: An *International Review* 2015, gol. 43(3): 252.

[44] Michael Coheen ,   *Introducing Christian Mission today*, 296.

[45] Auli Vähäkangas, "Postcolonial Mission: Oxymoron or Paradigm Shift" - A Response to Malnleke Auli Vähäkangas *Swedish Missiological Themes*, 95, 4 (2007)."

[46]Richard Bauckham, "Mission as Hermeneutics for Scriptural Interpretation" in ed. Micharl W. Goheen, *Reading the Bible Missionally*, (Michigan: WB Eerdmans, 2016) .2.

[47] Jiona Havea "The cons of contextuality ….. Contextuality" in ed., Stephen B Bevans and Katalina Tahalfe. Williams, *Contextual Theology for the Twenty-first Century*, (Oregon: Pickwick, 2011), 41-43.

[48] Shawn B Redford, "Mission Theology and postmodern Social Networks" in *Contemporary Mission Theology Engaging the Nations* ed, Robert L Gallagher and Paul Hertig, (Maryknoll: Orbis, 2017),252.

[49] Shawn B Redford, "Mission Theology and postmodern Social Networks", 252.

[50] Craig Bartholomew, "Theological Interpretation and a Missional Hermeneutic" in ed. Micharl W. Goheen, *Reading the Bible Missionally*, (Michigan: WB Eerdmans, 2016),69.

[51] Tom Wright, "Reading the New Testament Missionally", in ed. Micharl W. Goheen, *Reading the Bible Missionally*, (Michigan: WB Eerdmans, 2016), 193.

[52] Sathianathan Clarke, "World Christianity and Postcolonial Mission: A Path Forward for the Twenty-first Century" *Theology Today* 2014, Vol. 71(2), 196.

[53] Joel B. Green, "Reading James Missionally", in *Reading the Bible Missionally*, 207.

[54] Scott W Sunquist, *Understanding Christian Mission: Participation in Suffering and Glory,* (Michigan : Baker Academics, 2013), 330.

[55] Paul G. Hiebert, *The Gospel in Human Contexts: Anthropological Explorations for Contemporary*, (Michigan: Baker Academic, 2009),178.

[56] Scott W. Sunquest, *Understanding Christian Mission: Participation in Suffering and Glory,*142.

[57] Scott W. Sunquest, *Understanding Christian Mission: Participation in Suffering and Glory,*142.

[58] Scott W. Sunquest, *Understanding Christian Mission: Participation in Suffering and Glory,*167.

[59] David Hartano, "Contextual Christology: Carrying the great Commission with Joy" ed, Robert L Gallagher on Paul Heritg, *Contemporary Mission Theology: Emerging the Nations,* (Maryknoll: Orbis Books, 2017), 37.

[60] Michael A. Rynkiewich "Do We Need a Postmodern Anthropology for Mission in a Postcolonial World?" *Mission Studies* 28 (2011), 166.

Dalit Theology and Evangelical Freedom

DON SCHWEITZER

In his pioneering essay which began Dalit theology, Arvind Nirmal wrote that "the struggle of Indian Dalits is a story that provides us with a liberative motif that is authentically Indian."[1] In other words, Dalit experiences of caste oppression and their struggles for freedom provide a genuine native space in the Indian context for interpreting the gospel. Following Nirmal's lead a unique, authentically Indian theology and approach to interpreting the gospel, Dalit theology and hermeneutics, has developed here. However, these are not at home in India at present. They work to transform this space. They labour for a future that breaks in wherever Dalits and others experience freedom, dignity, have the necessities of life and room to flourish. They seek an India yet to come, where Indians live together without the divisions and oppression of caste distinctions, and with the necessities of life.

The suffering and pathos that Dalits experience is one source of Dalit theology and hermeneutics. There is also an inner transformation, a freedom already received, that comes through Jesus Christ. Nirmal described this as follows:

> We are not just Dalits. We are Christian Dalits. Something has happened to us. Our status has changed.[2]

Nirmal refers here to a new status given in Christ which brings an inner freedom from the confines of imposed identities. This is experienced paradoxically in the midst of caste oppression, poverty and despair. It makes the liberating message of Scripture a second source of Dalit theology. The new status, the freedom given in Christ that Nirmal refers to can be called evangelical or Christian freedom as it is founded on the gospel. It has been an important theme in Western theologies. In the New Testament it is most prominently expressed in Paul's letter to the Galatians, but also in chapters fourteen and fifteen of his letter to the Romans. It is present in the theology of Augustine and figured prominently in the Reformation theologies of Martin Luther, John Calvin and Ulrich Zwingli. It has been an important topic in twentieth century Western Christian thought, in the theologies of Karl Barth, Gustavo Gutierrez, Jürgen Moltmann, James Cone and Letty Russell. Evangelical freedom is multifaceted. It involves freedom from guilt, anxiety and imposed cultural or religious identities. It has to do with the past, the future and the present. It is the freedom to interpret the gospel in new ways in new or changing contexts, and to live according to the Spirit, guided by the law but not bound by its letter. Evangelical freedom "is a life force"[3] that should seek to actualize freedom for all in every dimension of life. As classically described by Martin Luther, we are free in Christ from any tyranny, and this freedom is to be exercised in love for others.[4]

When Luther wrote his treatise on Christian freedom, the area where he lived, now Germany, was an economic and religious colony of Rome. One reason for the rapid spread of the Reformation in Germany was its appeal to a rising sense of German nationalism. There were postcolonial aspects to his argument that a "Christian is perfectly free lord of all, subject to none."[5] The Christian freedom Luther proclaimed entailed release from Rome's colonial control. It continues to have potential as a resource for postcolonial theologies. But here we will discuss it in relation to Dalit theology.

Dalit theologians are also interested in furthering the increase of freedom, in their case, freedom for Dalits and others from an imposed servitude to others. They sometimes cite Galatians 3:28, "there is no longer Jew or Greek, there is no longer slave or free, there is no longer male or female, for all of you are one in Christ Jesus," in a programmatic way.[6] In the Indian context this establishes a goal of freedom from caste divisions and oppression.[7] Evangelical freedom finds perhaps its boldest but rather abstract Biblical expression in Galatians 5:1: "For freedom Christ has set us free." In the United States the lack of concrete definition here allows this passage to sometimes be co-opted by right wing political interests.[8] Mindful of the methodological exclusivism of Dalit theology, what follows will compare and contrast Dalit theology and hermeneutics, broadly interpreted, with the theme of evangelical freedom as found in Western Christian theology. The methodological exclusivism of Dalit theology is that it is done by Dalits, out of their experiences of suffering, denigration and liberation. It is this rootedness in Dalit experience that provides a genuinely native space for Dalit theology and hermeneutics. This rootedness helps prevent these from being co-opted by theological and hermeneutical concerns originating elsewhere. Yet while Dalit theology and hermeneutics are rooted in Dalit experience, they can be enriched by interaction with other forms of theology and other fields of knowledge.[9] With this in mind, we ask what Dalit theology and hermeneutics have to say to the theme of evangelical freedom as developed in Western Christian theologies, and vice versa.

Dalit Theology as a Form of Evangelical Freedom

We begin by noting commonalities between the two. Dalit theology and hermeneutics can be described as an expression of evangelical freedom in the Indian context. They exemplify in several ways the freedom arising from the gospel that is part of the new identity based on what God has done for humanity in Christ. This divine action overrules the identity imposed by caste distinctions which describes Dalits as by nature polluting and unfit for civilized company or occupations, so that they are denigrated "as lazy, stupid, licentious, dishonest, suitable only for manual labor, unclean and repulsive."[10] As a result of this imposed identity Dalits tend to suffer from a "wounded consciousness,"[11] a sense of inherent inferiority, worthlessness and hopelessness. This ascribed identity also creates a social ethos which tends to trap Dalits in poverty, deny them access to education and health care, renders them vulnerable to exploitation and violence, and makes Dalit women vulnerable to sexual violence. The gospel brings Dalits a new religious identity of being beloved and accepted by God. It states that they have dignity, worth and calling in God's eyes. This effects a change in their status, which as Luther might say, is first experienced in their inner person.[12] For Luther this was a paradoxical identity, as he believed that in our outer person we never live up to our inner status in Christ. For Dalits it is a paradoxical identity because it stands in opposition to the social ethos described above, which afflicts them regardless of their religious beliefs and often permeates the church. Still this status received in faith effects a change in how Dalits view themselves. It helps to heal the wounded psyche created by caste oppression. Even when their external situation remains unchanged or they suffer persecution for being Christians or converting to Christianity, many still treasure this new status. It strengthens them inwardly and helps them live with dignity.[13] The new identity that Dalits receive through Christ is the basis of evangelical freedom.

Both Dalit theology and Western theologies understand this freedom received from Christ as an active disposition that seeks outward expression. For Luther, a person's inner identity as righteous should inspire them to acts of love and service for others.[14] It should give rise to actions that correspond to it. Similarly, in Dalit theology, the new identity received through the gospel and a liberative social vision and praxis go together.[15] The first gives rise to the second and also serves it. The inner identity received by Dalits through Christ seeks outward expression, often through communal action. This can be through the refusal of traditional occupations such as scavenging, through participation in social justice movements aiming at Dalit liberation, or through religious festivals, like the Palm Sunday procession of Paraiyar Christians in Thulasigramam, which functions partly to loudly proclaim their changed status to their Hindu neighbours.[16] Such outward expression is not possible for every Dalit community. But where it is possible it tends to happen. In Dalit theology the freedom received inwardly from Christ is understood as part of an Exodus that aims at a total liberation of the whole person and of all people. As in the notion of evangelical freedom in Western theologies, this freedom received inwardly through Christ has an eschatological goal that embraces the whole of creation. It springs from the new reality and promise brought by Christ and the Holy Spirit. So, there are significant commonalities between evangelical freedom as understood in Western theologies and Dalit theology. What do Dalit theology and hermeneutics have to say about this freedom to Western Christian theologies?

The Dialectic of Word and Spirit in Dalit Christianity

In Western Christian theologies evangelical freedom is typically seen to be based on what God has done in Jesus Christ. The Spirit leads people to this freedom by opening them to faith in Christ and then inspires and empowers them to live out their new identity received in Christ. Christ is the source of this freedom which the Spirit brings one into. But Dalit theologians have pointed out that in the history of Dalit mass conversions to Christianity a more dialectical relationship exists between the work of Christ and the Spirit.

An aspiration for dignity and freedom was already present amongst many Dalits prior to their receiving the gospel. An example of this was their choice of the name Dalits as a self-designation. This was a dismissal of "all other imposed identities,"[17] an assertion of Dalit freedom and dignity that arose as part of the Dalit Sahitya and Dalit Panther movements. In his seminal essay Nirmal mentioned these as deserving theological reflection.[18] Dalit theology and hermeneutics were greatly stimulated by them. Christian theological reflection is driven forward by signs of the times like these two movements.[19] The assertion of Dalit independence and dignity in them was not based on faith in Christ, yet it expressed a sense of dignity, of freedom from imposed identities and a yearning for justice. Where did this come from?

According to the Nazareth Manifesto (Luke 4: 18-19), the Holy Spirit inspired Jesus to proclaim good news to the poor, release to the captives, recovery of sight to the blind and freedom to the oppressed. Nirmal referred to this as a "manifesto for Dalits."[20] On the basis of Luke's description here of how and where the Holy Spirit is at work, we can extrapolate to say that the Holy Spirit is active wherever people struggle against oppression and humiliation, shake off false imposed identities and apprehend a new sense of their own dignity.[21] This extrapolation is in keeping with the Augustinian understanding that every "choice of what is morally good is caused by divine grace."[22] The freedom expressed and created in the choice of the name Dalits can be seen as a Spirit-created freedom that originated apart from faith in Christ. Significant aspects of evangelical freedom are present in it, such as freedom from conformity to the imposed norms of a different culture. This expression of freedom in turn led Nirmal and others to see a new meaning in Biblical texts which convey the message of evangelical freedom.

Looking at Dalit mass conversions to Christianity we see something similar. These mass conversions were frequently expressions of Dalit aspirations for freedom in which they took the initiative to reject the identity imposed on them by using the opportunity that missionary preaching provided.[23] The aspirations for freedom and dignity that existed amongst Dalits prior to their conversion to Christianity and that motivated many to convert to faith in Christ can also be described as Spirit-created. In his study of Dalits in Tamil villages, David Mosse noted how the proclamation of the gospel introduced "a relativizing self-awareness"[24] into the social ethos where they lived, "a reflexive capacity or sociological awareness and self-distancing"[25] from inherited ethos and practices. This disrupted the hegemony of caste teaching and created an opening for change. On numerous occasions Dalits have seen in the proclamation of the gospel an opportunity to escape the prison of caste distinctions. Through individual or mass conversions to Christianity or Buddhism, many have availed themselves of such possibilities on their own initiative. In this way the presence of the gospel in caste-ridden contexts has frequently been a means to an end, an opportunity to actualize the Spirit-created yearning for freedom that existed in Dalit communities prior to faith in Christ. As John Boopolan concludes,

> Already present liberative social visions guided the agency of Dalit converts who had a pre-existing impulse for freedom and dignity. It is such Dalit agency that uncovered liberative insights in what they encountered in Christianity.[26]

The gospel here provided a new footing[27] for human life, a new basis for identity and social interaction, an alternative symbolism which gave subaltern communities the possibility of rejecting "the hegemonic symbolic universe of the dominant communities"[28] and naming another as their own. A Spirit-created desire for freedom led Dalits to take advantage of this new footing that the gospel provides and enter into a new religious identity based upon it.

Jürgen Moltmann noted that freedom in the social sphere does not result simply from the new identity received in Christ. He observes instead that the Spirit working through faith in Christ "effects in us the raising of new energies through the word of the gospel,"[29] while the Spirit working in nature and society opens new possibilities that these energies can take advantage of. This pattern is present in the history of Christian Dalit communities. As Mosse notes:

> But if Christian experience opened up such alternatives, the deployment of these in social struggles was dependent upon other social and political changes that occurred in Tamil society only in the twentieth century. Religious change has rarely (if ever) been an independent source of social transformation. Becoming Christian was certainly never sufficient to free Dalits from the subordination they experienced in village society.[30]

But what Dalit theologians lift up with their emphasis on the agency and initiative of Dalits in mass conversions is that a converse dynamic also occurs. The Spirit can create new energies and freedom within people, which then take advantage of the new possibilities that the presence of the gospel in Indian society creates.

The Spirit creates aspirations and movements for freedom. Christ, as present in Christian worship and through objects of Christian tradition like the Bible, provides a new footing in the Indian context that can be of service to these aspirations. The Spirit moves people to actualize the possibilities and gifts that Christ makes available. Conversely, the encounter with Christ may ignite a Spirit-created drive for freedom that previously lay dormant. Either way, in these dynamics the work of Christ and that of the Spirit are complimentary. Neither does the work of the other. It would be a mistake to downplay the contribution of either. Both are needed. It is Christ who provides the transcendent footing for a new self-understanding that people, however inspired by the Spirit they may be, cannot create for themselves. This transcendent footing is the source of a new status that grants one an inner freedom and dignity over against externally imposed identities, even when one's options to actualize this are limited. Yet it has frequently been a Spirit-created yearning for freedom that came into being apart from faith in Christ that has led Dalits to recognize and appropriate this as such. Dalit theologians agree with Western theologians like Moltmann that the gospel is the source of a new identity that brings an inner freedom and dignity, and the energy to further express this socially when possible. But they also point out that this saving dynamic can run in the opposite direction to the pattern Moltmann identifies. Through its presence in society the gospel can be a means by which a Spirit-created freedom can find expression and enhancement. The unique social location of Dalit theology in a culture deeply formed by Hindu caste distinctions helps to make apparent this role of the Spirit in the creation and shaping of aspirations for freedom that see in the gospel a basis for their realization.

Appreciation of the dynamic that Dalit theologians lift up when they focus on the agency and initiative exercised by Dalits in mass conversions deepens when one notes how once Dalits have entered into this new identity of being in Christ, they have sometimes worked to transform it, re-orienting the goals and strategies of Christian missions towards enhancing their dignity and social status. For instance, as a result of such work by Dalit Christians in Andhra Pradesh, Christian mission was re-conceived there as "the reconstruction of the identity and dignity of Dalits, where they begin to affirm their selfhood as a gift from God by being inclusive and open to receive and accept all as created in the image of God."[31] Here Dalits re-oriented the mission goals of the church that they entered into, and used their "new religious identity as a political weapon and an agency for liberation in their social struggles."[32] The transcendent footing that Christ provided did not remain unchanged here once Dalits appropriated it. They exercised their evangelical freedom to re-configure its meaning, stretching the image of Jesus they received so that he took on a new, liberating effect in their context. We see here an instance of how the Holy Spirit can lead the church to a new understanding of Jesus Christ that is more efficacious in a new context than what it had before. Canadian theologian Gregory Baum developed a theory of dialectical doctrinal development that described how the Spirit works to this effect.[33] The development of Dalit theology and hermeneutics is an example of this kind of doctrinal development. For Baum this work of the Spirit meant that the church is not trapped in its past, that it can be a sign of hope to the world. In Dalit theology this dynamic is about how the Spirit works to further the liberation of the oppressed by re-configuring the church's understanding of Jesus and its mission.

A similar pattern can be noted in Dalit hermeneutics. The Bible has been described as "the foundation of Dalit theology."[34] It becomes a source of freedom for them, conveying a message of judgment and liberation when read in the light of their experience.[35] This reading is generally done on the basis of a preunderstanding that running through the Bible is a liberating message that needs to be appropriated in their context and that surfaces when read in light of their experience.[36] Here again, a Spirit-created aspiration for freedom that exists prior to reading Scripture is frequently at work. This Spirit-created aspiration turns Dalits to Scripture to find a promise and source of hope that grounds, enlightens and amplifies their desire for freedom.

The Spirit-created aspiration at work here is both consonant with evangelical freedom given through Christ and yet has a relative independence in regard to it.

By attending to this Dalit theologians provide a corrective to Western understandings of evangelical freedom that only stress its basis in Christology or how the Spirit enables it to be appropriated or expressed in action. Dalit theologians emphasize that what can become evangelical freedom may be inspired by the Spirit apart from explicit faith in the gospel. Dalit hermeneutics note that the Spirit not only inspires and empowers one to actualize what Christ makes possible, but also to re-configure this so as to unleash the liberating power of the gospel in one's context. Both demonstrate that evangelical freedom has two sources, not one. It is created, shaped and sustained by the Spirit and Christ, each playing different roles but both working together.

This dialectical relationship of Christ and the Spirit is key to the creative dimensions of evangelical freedom and to extending it to others. While the Spirit working in nature and culture creates new possibilities for the actualization of freedom in Christ, Spirit-inspired aspirations for freedom can lead to new understandings of the meaning and dimensions of this freedom.

American theologian Mark Lewis Taylor has observed that the philosophical liberalism prevalent in North Atlantic societies proclaims, "freedom for all while believing only in freedom for some."[37] This liberalism is an ideology of freedom. But historically it has been implemented in restricted ways, so that in many instances freedom has only been granted to select social groups, typically privileged white men, and withheld from others. Taylor sees that this restriction of freedom has repeatedly been challenged in history, sometimes successfully, by what he terms prophetic spirit, which focuses on the underside of history and seeks to broaden the extent to which the freedom liberalism proclaims is realized in history.[38] Prophetic spirit engages contractual liberalism over how its rhetoric of freedom is applied and to whom it should be extended.

A similar pattern can be discerned in the Indian church regarding evangelical freedom as freedom from cultural domination. Indian Christian theologians proclaimed the freedom to receive the gospel in their own vessels, "not in the European cup."[39] Yet as Nirmal noted, they remained obsessed "with the Brahmanic tradition"[40] and did not extend to Dalits this freedom from cultural domination that they rightly demanded for themselves.

Evident here is how the freedom to worship and follow Christ within one's own cultural tradition has been proclaimed in Indian churches, but often only permitted to a limited extent, essentially among members of the same social group. It was generally extended only to a privileged few, until Dalits joined the church through mass conversions, or until this restriction was challenged by theological reflection spurred on by the Dalit Sahitya and Dalit Panther movements. These Spirit-created signs of the times challenged the restriction of evangelical freedom to non-Dalits, and inspired the extension of it beyond this through Dalit theology and hermeneutics. One can see similar patterns in Western Christianity. Evangelical freedom was proclaimed and practiced in Western Protestant churches, but often only extended to white, middle class men. In frustration with this, peoples of colour often created their own denominations where they could live out the freedom that was theirs in Christ but generally denied them in white churches. It was only when the appropriateness of this restriction was challenged that it eventually came to be extended within white denominations, often still partially, to women and people of colour. Gustavo Gutiérrez noted a similar dynamic in relation to Paul's message of evangelical freedom in Latin America. Evangelical freedom came to be understood there as including liberation from unjust social structures and economic oppression through social transformation as a result of aspirations to liberation amongst the poor and oppressed being accepted as a sign of the times which required a fresh interpretation of the gospel and commitment to the liberation of the poor on the part of the church and its leaders.[41] In many instances, on the basis of their experience of freedom in Christ, Christians have worked to secure freedom for others not of their social group. But it is also true that in many instances group and individual bias have prevented this, and freedom has only been extended to others in response to challenges from Spirit-created aspirations for freedom.

That the Spirit creates aspirations to freedom and dignity outside or within the church that are at odds with the church's official teaching and mission goals is amply demonstrated by Western church history in the modern era, where these aspirations have often been at first denied or denigrated, and then later aspects of them have become integrated into church teaching.[42] Through the creation of such aspirations the Spirit may re-configure the church's understanding of freedom and love, so that its mission is changed to better serve the poor and marginalized. In this way the Spirit works to increase the range of social groups within the church to which evangelical freedom is extended. Jesus Christ remains for many Christian

Dalits a distinctive source of evangelical freedom and dignity. Yet the Spirit is also a source of a freedom that has continuities with what Christ brings, that moves the church to live out this freedom in new ways, and that broadens the range of those to whom this freedom is extended. The Spirit works here as the disrupter of ecclesial or social institutions and ethos that restrict the freedom people have in Christ. These insights into the creative role of the Spirit in the coming into being and shaping of evangelical freedom can enrich Western theological understandings of it.

Love and freedom

Implicit in the above is the idea that the understanding of love in the church has a history. Through the protests of the poor and marginalized, the Holy Spirit may challenge the church's understanding of love, or its restriction of who love and freedom are extended to. The church has not always understood love in the same way. For instance, in Canada, from roughly 1880 to 1996, Protestant and Roman Catholic churches believed that running residential schools for Indigenous children was an expression of love for them. Now, in response to protests and activism by former residential school survivors, these same churches have apologized for having done this. They now recognize that this was a colonial work of cultural genocide. Through a complex shifting in prevailing social attitudes in Canada, what was once proclaimed to be an act of love, running residential schools, is now seen to have been a sin that the churches have apologized for.

The churches' understanding of evangelical freedom is tied to its understanding of love, as evangelical freedom is freedom for love. This helps to explain the pattern noted previously, where evangelical freedom is often not extended by one social group within the church to others. Our understanding of love is often bound up with our sense of cultural normativity. When we exercise evangelical freedom through love for others, what we do out of love is often shaped by what we believe to be culturally normative. As a result, Christian love is often an expression of the cultural norms of the relatively privileged, extended to those who are culturally other in colonizing or restricted ways. This was the case with residential schools for Indigenous children in Canada. Christians often extend what they consider to be charity to others, but not so often the evangelical freedom that they cherish for themselves.

This shaping of our understandings of love and freedom by what we hold to be culturally normative is part of what Luther described when he spoke of the self as being curved in upon itself.[43] For Luther this is part of the condition of original sin which is never fully overcome in history. Being curved in upon oneself leads one to use everything, including the gospel, in the service of one's own distorted sense of self-interest. This tendency to idolize one's sense of self and its attendant cultural values leads to an elevation of the latter as universally valid. When this happens Christian love and freedom become more an expression of these values than of the teachings of Christ. Luther thought that the state of being curved in upon one's self could be overcome only by suffering which leads one to throw one's self unreservedly upon God's mercy. But it can also be overcome by experiences of joy and beauty, or by witnessing others' experiences of beauty and joy, by dialogue with others, or by witnessing the suffering of others. The distortion or restriction of evangelical freedom and Christian love by a false sense of cultural normativity can sometimes be overcome by encountering Spirit-created aspirations of freedom and dignity in others in these ways. Yet frequently these aspirations require expression through political, economic, legal or discursive power in order to gain the recognition they deserve.

The freedom we receive through Christ is always situated in a cultural context. When this freedom becomes equated with our cultural norms in idolatrous ways it is often Spirit-created aspirations for freedom and dignity on the part of those who are marginalized, oppressed or culturally other that can lead us to recognize the idolatrous nature of this, so that we can move beyond it to a deeper experience of love and freedom for both ourselves and those who are culturally different to us. Such Spirit-created movements often have "a focus on marginality and sites of oppression."[44] By bringing injustices into the civil sphere so that they become the focus of theological reflection, such movements give theology an ethical direction that extends the range of evangelical freedom and transforms the ethical concern of the church. Dalit theology and hermeneutics, through their emphasis on the role played by Dalit experience and agency in the transformation and shaping of the understanding of the gospel in the Indian context, lift this up in a powerful way.

The basis and telos of evangelical freedom

If Dalit theology and hermeneutics lift up the role of the Holy Spirit in the creation and shaping of evangelical freedom, what do Western understandings of evangelical freedom have to say to Dalit theology and hermeneutics in return? First, let us begin with Paul Ricoeur's observation that the gospel does not initially speak of freedom. Instead, it speaks of something else and it is through the interpretation of this that it speaks of freedom.[45] The gospel speaks of Jesus, his ministry, his calling of the disciples, his last supper with them, his death on the cross, and then the transforming event of his resurrection. All this requires interpretation to discern its meaning. It is the truth attained through interpreting this that makes one free. Between the proclamation of the gospel and Paul`s injunction to the Galatians, "for freedom Christ has set us free,"[46] stands a wealth of doctrinal reflection that defines and defends his understanding of justification by grace summarized in Galatians 2:16. Galatians 3:28 summarizes a central meaning of this. As John Calvin noted, "freedom is especially an appendage of justification."[47] Doctrinal reflection, seeking an understanding of the gospel's meaning in terms of the thought forms of one's context, is required to get from the story of Jesus to the notion of evangelical freedom. There are doctrinal developments in the history of Christianity that every generation must either renounce or make and appropriate for themselves, and in their own way.[48] Doctrines like the Trinity and justification by grace are handed down in the church from generation to generation, but each generation must work through the interpretive process by which these came to be if these are to continue to be living understandings of the meaning of the gospel that guide the church's worship and mission. Here Western theologies may have something to say to Dalit theology and hermeneutics about the underpinnings of evangelical freedom. To date, the "wounded psyche and battered consciousness of Dalits do not seem to invest their subjective energies in evolving unified conceptual edifice of theological doctrines."[49] However doctrinal reflection can lead to or justify insights that are liberating for the oppressed and reorient the church's vision. For instance, the doctrines of the Trinity and the Chalcedonian Definition seem to underlie or at least be implied in Nirmal's assertion that it "is the dalitness of the divinity and humanity that the Cross of

Jesus symbolises."[50] As evangelical freedom is situated "in the horizon of redemption, justification, and sanctification by God through Jesus Christ"[51] and the Holy Spirit, doctrinal reflection is required to preserve and render contextually appropriate the theological basis on which it rests. Each of these doctrinal areas needs to be cultivated to unfold the many facets of evangelical freedom. Doctrinal reflection is also necessary to discerning the parameters of evangelical freedom in a given context and how it should relate to other liberation movements, emancipatory projects and religious communities.

Second, earlier we noted that in the United States Paul's injunction in Galatians 5:1, "for freedom Christ has set us free," is sometimes co-opted by right wing political interests. Freedom is always partially defined by its goals. In Western societies evangelical freedom has to be differentiated from political interests bent on preserving a certain culture and standard of living regardless of the cost to others. It also has to be dialectically related to modern Western notions of autonomous freedom which have no higher purpose than overcoming every barrier to setting and achieving one's own goals. While there is important resonance and congruence between the latter notions and evangelical freedom, there are also important differences.

The story of the Exodus has been a touchstone for many liberation movements, particularly those with Jewish or Christian associations. But in the Exodus, the initial movement from captivity to freedom is predicated upon a change in masters, from servitude to humans to servitude to God. The former enslaves, the latter sets free.[52] The Exodus is not a movement to autonomy, but to communion with God and others. As appropriated by Martin Luther King, Jr. during the American civil rights struggle, it is a journey towards the beloved community characterized by justice and peace, which has room for every race, ethnicity and religion. Similarly, the freedom for which Christ sets free is the fruit of communion with God that Christ makes possible, and it exists for the sake of deeper communion with others.

As the gospel provides a new footing for liberation, it has a field of meaning that needs to be respected to prevent the church becoming curved in upon itself and so that it can be addressed on the basis of this by Spirit-created movements for freedom when it does. The gospel as narrated in the New Testament and proclaimed by Paul and others, like the story of the Exodus, has a concreteness rooted in the underside of history and a dynamic that aims at the emancipation of the oppressed.[53] This helps the protests of Spirit-created liberation movements achieve resonance within the church when they address it from within or without.

Western Protestant theologies often point to the Barmen Declaration as an important benchmark for contemporary theology. Here the Confessing Church differentiated itself from an idolatrous spirit of destruction that had possessed most of Germany and much of the German Protestant church. Dalit theology and hermeneutics rightly emphasize the role of the Spirit in creating aspirations to freedom which make use of the gospel to fulfil these and of how empowered and guided by the Spirit Dalits have re-shaped the church's understanding of Jesus and its mission so as to better serve the poor and oppressed. Barmen is an ecclesial memory figure with a different emphasis. It reveals the importance of continuously listening to the Word and allowing it to shape one's self and the church. Both emphases are needed. As the face of evil changes from age to age, the church needs to listen to the signs of the times and re-interpret the meaning of the gospel in light of them. But as it does so it needs to respect the gospel's field of meaning and allow this to also determine the church's message and mission.

Third, the telos of evangelical freedom is determined by its basis in the crucified and risen Christ and the work of the Holy Spirit. Dalit theology demands that the gospel and its message be understood concretely that Jesus be recognized as a Dalit and that his message is one of liberation for the oppressed. It represents an Indian version of the preferential option for the poor. But evangelical freedom is also about the recognition of others, acceptance of their differences and making space for them. "The struggle with differences is always an intertwined yet distinctive aspect of the struggle for liberation amid oppression."[54] This is important, as the "pluriformity of the Dalit world is to be acknowledged."[55] The term Dalit embraces many sub-castes and jatis, which are sometimes in conflict with each other. There are also important differences within Dalit communities between men and women, etc. While Dalit theology and hermeneutics have focused on liberation, there is also a need to unfold how evangelical freedom includes making space for those who are other and accommodation for differences. The liberation that evangelical freedom aims at is one where there is room and respect for differences, and no one religious or cultural identity is imposed on others. Evangelical freedom often has to be asserted, particularly by the marginalized and oppressed. But the doctrine of justification by grace, which is the root of evangelical freedom, is also the basis for reconciliation with former enemies after liberation is achieved, and for accepting and respecting those who are different.

Justification by grace also lays the basis for a capacity for self-critique and openness to the critiques of others, in addition to being a source of self-assertion in the quest for liberation. Finally, it provides a basis for self-acceptance when one is confronted by irreparable guilt. In any liberation struggle there are failures and mistakes that incur guilt. Justification by grace enables one to continue working for liberation despite the burden of decisions or actions that caused harm and cannot be undone. Evangelical freedom, as it is based on justification by grace and the work of the Spirit, enables one to act responsibly and undertake the risk of guilt, in the knowledge that one's identity is ultimately based on what God has done in Christ and not one's own actions.

As a relatively privileged Western theologian whose appreciation of the role of the Spirit in creating and shaping evangelical freedom has been greatly enhanced by Dalit theology and hermeneutics, I offer these last three reflections in what is hopefully a spirit of critical appreciation, ecumenism and solidarity.

Conclusion

Evangelical freedom is a gift and a task.[56] It is a gift received through faith in Christ that seeks outward expression, and to be established for all, and so it becomes a task that the Holy Spirit guides and empowers us to fulfil. Dalit theology and hermeneutics highlight the work of the Spirit in creating aspirations of freedom and dignity that play a vital role in the extension and establishment of evangelical freedom in society. By linking it to concrete experiences of injustice and suffering, they concretize it as the liberation of the marginalized and oppressed. They refuse to allow the church's understanding of evangelical freedom to remain abstract. They remind middle class Western theologies that notions like freedom need to be understood from the underside of history, in relation to the dalitness of God and God's people and creation, if they are to remain faithful to the crucified and risen Christ.

Endnotes

[1] Arvind Nirmal, *Heuristic Explorations* (Madras: The Christian Literature Society, 1990), 143.

[2] Ibid, 148.

[3] Eberhard Jüngel, *The Freedom of a Christian* (Minneapolis: Augsburg Publishing House, 1988), 19.

[4] Martin Luther, *The Freedom of a Christian* (1520), in *Luther's Works Vol. 31,* edited by Harold Grimm (Philadelphia: Muhlenberg Press, 1957), 344.

[5] Ibid.

[6] James Massey, *Dalits in India* (Delhi: ISPCK/Manohar, 1995), 81.

[7] L. Jayachitra, "Jesus and Ambedkar," in *Dalit Theology in the Twenty-first Century* edited by Sathianathan Clarke et al. (New Delhi: Oxford University Press, 2010), 128-30.

[8] See for example, http://www.valuesandcapitalism.com/four-things-christian-libertarians-believe/.

[9] J. Jayakiran Sebastian, "Interrogating the Methodology of Dalit Theology: 'Can We Now Bypass That Truth?'," in *Revisiting and Resignifying Methodology for Dalit Theology* edited by James Massey and Indukur John Mohan Razu (New Delhi: Centre for Dalit/Subaltern Studies/Bangalore: United Theological College, 2008), 102-3.

[10] Nathaniel Roberts, *To Be Cared For: The Power of Conversion and Foreignness of Belonging in an Indian Slum* (Oakland, CA: University of California Press, 2016), 3.

[11] A. Maria Arul Raja, "Dalit Theology Methodologies: Breaking New Grounds," in Massey and Razu, *Revisiting and Resignifying Methodology for Dalit Theology,* 72.

[12] Luther, *Freedom of a Christian,* 344.

[13] Bonita Aleaz, "Of Conversions and non Conversions: Varied forms of Dalit life and living today," *Asian Journal of Theology* 28/1 (April 2014), 90.

[14] Luther, *The Freedom of a Christian*, 359.

[15] Penial Rajkumar, *Dalit Theology and Dalit Liberation* (Burlington, VT: Ashgate Publishing Company, 2010), 41.

[16] Anderson Jeremiah, *Community and Worldview among Paraiyars of South India* (London: Bloomsbury, 2013), 138.

[17] Raja, "Dalit Theology Methodologies," 73.

[18] Nirmal, *Heuristic Explorations*, 142.

[19] Elizabeth Johnson, *Creation and the Cross* (Maryknoll, NY: Orbis Books, 2018), 225.

[20] Nirmal, *Heuristic Explorations*, 153.

[21] José Comblin, "The Holy Spirit," in *Mysterium Liberationis* edited by Ignacio Ellacuría and Jon Sobrino (Maryknoll, NY: Orbis Books, 1993), 463-5.

[22] George Tavard, *From Bonaventure to the Reformers* (Milwaukee: Marquette University Press, 2005), 120.

[23] Joseph Prabhakar Dayam and Peniel Jesudason Rufus Rajkumar, "Mission At And From The Margins," in *Mission At and From the Margins* edited by Peniel Jesudason Rufus Rajkumar et al. (Oxford: Regnum Books International, 2014), 7.

[24] David Mosse, *The Saint in the Banyan Tree* (Berkeley: University of California Press, 2012), 272.

[25] Ibid.

[26] Sunder John Boopolan, *Memory, Grief, and Agency: A Political Theological Account of Wrongs and Rites* (Cham, Switzerland: Palgrave Macmillan, 2017), 13.

[27] Erving Goffman, *Forms of Talk* (Philadelphia: University of Pennsylvania Press, 1981), 128.

[28] Raja, "Dalit Theology Methodologies," 77.

[29] Jürgen Moltmann, *The Spirit of Life* (Minneapolis: Fortress Press, 1992), 103.

[30] Mosse, *The Saint in the Banyan Tree*, 275.

[31] Bethel Krupa Victor, "Revisiting the Missional Engagement at Parkal: A Recovery of the Role of the Dalit Christian Community," in Rajkumar, *Mission At and From the Margins*, 157-8.

[32] Ibid, 158.

[33] Gregory Baum, *The Credibility of the Church Today* (New York: Herder and Herder, 1968), 151-76.

[34] James Massey, "Revisiting and Resignifying the Methodology of Dalit Theology," in Massey and Razu, *Revisiting and Resignifying Methodology for Dalit Theology*, 61.

[35] Philip Vinod Peacock, "Dalit Identity and Textual Tradition, in Massey and Razu, *Revisiting and Resignifying Methodology for Dalit Theology*, 147.

[36] Y.T. Vinayaraj, "Envisioning a Postmodern Method of Doing Dalit Theology," in Clarke et al., *Dalit Theology in the Twenty-first Century*, 98-9.

[37] Mark Lewis Taylor, *Religion, Politics, and the Christian Right* (Minneapolis: Fortress Press, 2005), 75.

[38] Ibid, 97-102.

[39] Sadhu Sundar Singh, "The Living Christ," in Sugirtharajah and Hargreaves, *Readings In Indian Christian Theology* Vol. I, (London: SPCK, 1993), 76.

[40] Nirmal, *Heuristic Explorations*, 141.

[41] Gustavo Gutiérrez, *Gustavo Gutiérrez: Essential Writings* edited by James Nickoloff (Maryknoll, NY: Orbis Books, 1996), 192.

[42] Gregory Baum, *Theology and Society* (New York: Paulist Press, 1987), 129-33.

[43] Martin Luther, *Luther: Lectures on Romans* edited by Wilhelm Pauck (Philadelphia: The Westminster Press, 1960), 159-60.

[44] Boopolan, *Memory, Grief, and Agency*, 14.

[45] Paul Ricoeur, *Essays on Biblical Interpretation* (Philadelphia: Fortress Press, 1980), 157.

[46] Galatians 5:1.

[47] John Calvin, *Institutes of the Christian Religion* (Philadelphia: The Westminster Press, 1960), 833; III.19.1.

[48] Rowan Williams, *Arius: Heresy and Tradition* (London: Darton, Longman and Todd, 1987), 236-7.

[49] Arul Raja, "Dalit Theology Methodologies: Breaking New Grounds," 72.

[50] Nirmal, *Heuristic Explorations*, 155.

[51] Tavard, *From Bonaventure to the Reformers*, 121.

[52] Jan Assmann, *The Invention of Religion* (Princeton: Princeton University Press, 2018), 79.

[53] Taylor, *Religion, Politics, and the Christian Right*, 160.

[54] Ibid, 162.

[55] Vinayaraj, "Envisioning a Postmodern Method of Doing Dalit Theology," 99.

[56] Gutiérrez, *Gustavo Gutiérrez: Essential Writings*, 235.

Interfaith, Subaltern Historiography and the Self-Perception of the Church Through the Centuries

V. V. THOMAS

Most of us today are familiar with the quest for Christian unity. We have discussed this topic for a long time now. The fact that we as Christians must accept each other is a foregone conclusion, although there are Christians even today who disagree. Our views on these issues have been impacted by different forums such as the World Council of Churches (WCC), National Christian Council of India (NCCI), World Evangelical Fellowship (WEF), Evangelical Fellowship of India (EFI), etc. Most of us agree that we must seek unity amidst profound diversity. However, in our present-day context, we have moved from a strictly *Christian* concept of unity to a *broader* understanding of unity. Therefore, the question today is whether this Christian model of unity should be extended to other religions. Is it possible for us to say that there is a plurality of religions that can co-exist in relationship? Must we seek collaboration with people of other faiths? Of course, this topic has been studied in detail by scholars like Paul Tillich, Wilfred Cantwell Smith, John Hick, Stanley Samartha, and numerous others, and they have proposed various theories.

The real problem that all of us face is the *legitimacy* of different religions. The most fundamental question is why there are many religions if God is one? Shouldn't there be just one religion? Why do I belong to only the Christian religion? Why am I still a Christian? Are all religions equally true? Or equally false? Do all religions share something in common? If yes, then what? How should we relate to other religions? *Why* must we relate to other religions? Can we learn from other religions? Is Christianity the only true religion? Is Christianity the fulfilment of other religions? Is Jesus the full, absolute and final revelation of God? Are all humans saved in and through the sacrificial death of Christ on the cross? In other words, is Christianity meant for all people everywhere? These are all crucial questions that we have faced and are still facing as we relate with our friends in present-day Indian society..

Historical Understanding of Christian Attitude towards other Religious Faiths

In the history of Christian apologetics there have been many different approaches to people of other faiths. The various attitudes that Christians have taken toward other religions do not allow simple classification. Nevertheless, scholars have for years attempted to do so. Exclusivism, Inclusivism, and Pluralism are three different approaches that many scholars have proposed. Another approach is the attitude of aggressive condemnation of all other religions as unworthy. Then there is the attitude of sympathetic appreciation and co-operation. There has also been the attitude of proclaiming a unique and final Gospel without a complete denial of values in other religions. There is famous Theo-centric approach; however, in this approach the term *God* is not defined or pronounced clearly. Then there is the Kingdom-centric approach which is more or less a value based approach; but what values are we talking about? Value-based theologies have problems; they are like having a kingdom without a king. Finally, there is the Christo-centric approach, where the uniqueness of Christ is proclaimed without any ambiguity. Christ is the sole saviour of all. We can say that all these different approaches have their negatives and positives, but they all fall short. None of them are complete.

Subaltern Historiography

In the field of history, the historian is always sensitive about his primary written sources. The commonly held view is that the quality of the end product depends on the quality of the sources use. However, *subaltern* historians look at the written sources in very different ways. While they use written sources, of course, they use them with great caution, even a hermeneutic of suspicion is involved. From the subaltern perspective, primary sources includes the people themselves. They (the people) still write their history in the form of stories, songs, etc. This has been neglected in the modern, professionalized discipline of historical studies.

The subaltern historians believe that there is a vast difference between what a Dalit writes about a particular event and what non-Dalits tend to write. A close examination of the two will reveal a chasm of difference: differences in perspective, outlook, and competing biases.

Raymond Schwab, in his *The Oriental Renaissance,* proposes that texts are the result of an encounter between familiar and novel ideas; yet such an encounter is eminently circumstantial and material. He contends that texts are produced in time and in society by human beings who are themselves agents of their actual history.[1] Modern subaltern historians agree with Schwab on these points.

The whole subaltern methodology has gained a lot of attention in the last few decades in the context of the struggle by subaltern people to re-interpret and re-read their histories. Those histories have been written *for* them, not *by* them. And this is a crucial difference. It was the so called 'others' who defined who Dalits / subaltern were. It was similar to the case of the Occidentals defining who the Orientals were. Of course, it was for the benefit of those Occidentals who were making the decisions on behalf of the Orientals.

The term Subaltern: Its meaning and relevance

To the question who or what is subaltern, Donna Landry in the *Spivak Reader* puts it as follows: "Loosely derived from the writings of the Italian Marxist Antonio Gramsci, the term "subaltern" designates non-elite or subordinated social groups"[2] According to Ranajit Guha, the word 'subaltern' means 'that of inferior rank'. He has used the term "people" and the subaltern classes as synonymous throughout his work.[3] According to him subalternity represents the "demographic difference between the total Indian population and all those whom we have described as the 'elite'[4]. Guha acknowledges that there is some ambiguity about these terms, classes and groups, such as the lesser rural gentry, impoverished landlords, rich peasants and upper middle classes peasants. Guha argues that there is ambiguity in these terms. He leaves this issue to the historian to sort out on the basis of a close and judicious examination of the evidence.[5]

Felix Wilfred, another scholar who is deeply interested in subalternity talks about three elements in subaltern religion in India. According to him, in subaltern religiosity as practiced in India, we can distinguish three strands: (a) The world of spirits, (b) The emergence of gods and goddesses from the contexts of social life, (c) The superimposition of religion by the dominant castes and classes. These three streams mix and mingle to form the world of the religious experience of the subaltern. Of these three, the third—superimposed religiosity upon the subaltern by the dominant castes and classes—silenced the subaltern. The lower castes were forced to believe things they did not necessarily believe. This is true also in the case of subalterns who accepted the Christian religion when it was given to them. (In certain cases imposed upon them.)[6] Wilfred also gives a further clarification with regard to the differences between subalterns and the so called 'folk religion'. He says that these two are very different concepts. According to him, the subaltern religious experience is completely different from the experience of the dominant castes and classes. Subaltern religiosity represents an important social factor in the contemporary situation in India.[7] Some argue that subaltern religion is the same as the folk religion or popular religion. But this is not, in fact, the case. Felix says although there may be elements of similarity, subaltern religion is different from folk religion; Subaltern religiosity refers to a religious *experience,* and its expressions derive from being marginalized.[8] Popular or folk religion can be also practiced by the elite or the high caste, and the elements of it can be fashioned by the upper castes, too. Subaltern religion, however, emerges from the experience of being subjugated and dominated. The religious experience of the Dalits, Tribal people, and women are full of subaltern experiences.

Subalternity is what the Dalits of this country have been pushed into. This subalternity has been caused by various factors, the major one being the caste system, where the majority of the people are considered to be outside the 'varna' system of Hinduism. That has pushed them into economic, social, and cultural disabilities.

Therefore, when we utilize a subaltern methodology, we attempt to emphasize subaltern contributions and experiences. It is a methodology through which the subalterns do not just become the *objects* of history but the very *subject* themselves. Unfortunately, in interfaith dialogue, the people from the lower strata of society are typically not included. This situation must change.

There is also a difference between subaltern religion and subaltern history. When one says *subaltern religion* it means the religion of the majority of this country although it may not have the so called 'great' tradition that philosophical Hinduism talks about. It is mainly the folk religion. Subaltern history is the history of a suffering people. It is the history of the oppressed and the marginalised. It is the history of the sons/daughters of the soil; the working class; the less fortunate ones. However, finally, their history is being told. Now they are moving from the periphery to the centre. They are now mainstream in our cities, in our businesses, in our politics, and in our religions.

As far as India is concerned, this term subaltern was brought to the centre of critical scholarship by a group of thinkers referred to as the 'Subaltern Studies Collective'. They have now published numerous substantial volumes on South Asian history and society from a 'subaltern perspective.'[9]

Self-understanding of the Church through Centuries

I would now like to talk about the self-understanding of the Church through the centuries, and how it became so exclusivistic. Like the frog in the well, the church hardly recognized the reality of other religions, and interactions with other faiths were rare and relatively scarce.

The primitive Church held its identity in the Jewish world. The Church was the 'new Israel." It was a reform movement within Judaism in contrast to the 'old Israel' and this attitude made them to see themselves not 'in relation to' but 'over-against' the Jews. However their self-understanding—that they were the 'new Israel'—led to tensions not only with the Jews but within the Church itself. The early Christians felt that they were the Easter community of the exalted Messiah. The Church faced the same situation again when it left the fold of Palestinian Judaism and entered into the wider world of Greek and Roman religion and culture. The Church entered into Graeco-Roman society with the understanding that "there is no longer Jew and Greek" (Eph 2:13-16, Rom 10:12, 1 Cor 12:13, Gal 3:28 etc). As far as the Church was concerned it was a fatal proclamation because it suddenly abolished its old identity as part of the chosen people, the old Israel. This was almost the end of toleration by the Jewish people within Israel of this new sect called Christians. It was the launching of the Church's mission to the larger world. It was a kind of relocation of Christianity from one world to another. It was the beginning of Church's world mission. Now the major question was with regard to the Church's identity and mission in a society of pagan religions and Greek philosophies. Where will the Christian teachings fit in the philosophical traditions of the Greeks? Here again there was no one single approach. Many Christians held on to Paul's instruction "not to be yoked together with unbelievers". 'What has Athens to do with Jerusalem' was the attitude of many within the Church. At the same time, there were those in the Church who saw Christianity and Greek philosophy not in terms of opposition but in terms of similarity. They held to the Johannine understanding that Jesus Christ is the 'light that lights every human being' coming into the world. Justin Martyr, for example, was very positive in his evaluation of Greek philosophy. He says "Christ is the Logos of whom every race of men partakes and those who live rationally are Christians even if thought to be atheists… Whatever things have been rightly said by any one belongs to us Christians".[10] This approach was in a sense a positive way of defining Christianity in relation to Greek philosophies and cultures. For such people Christian identity was not 'over against,' rather, it was relational.

Moving on from the early part of the Church into the period following the conversion of Constantine, in the early part of the fourth century, the whole face of Christianity was changed from that of the lowly into an affluent people in the society. The Jesus that we encounter in the Gospels is one who came into the world as 'Good news' to the poor. He himself says that the Spirit of the Lord is upon me because he has been anointed to preach the good news to the poor. We read that Jesus always lived his life in solidarity with the poor. He was accused by the Pharisees and the Sadducees that he was a friend of sinners. He was comfortable with the poor, the disabled, and so on. We could say that Jesus spent much of his time with the subaltern people of the age. This Jesus was spat upon, mocked, smitten, arrested, tortured, and finally crucified. Throughout his earthly life he demonstrated that he was a 'servant king' (Mk 10:45), a suffering servant (Mt 8:17), and a king with crown of thorns. Even his disciples had to face the same fate. According to tradition, except for one disciple, the other eleven became martyrs for their master.

In fact, the Church that was founded by Jesus Christ was persecuted severely until the early part of the fourth century. Starting with Nero in AD 64, the persecution continued until the time of Constantine in 312. However, the situation radically changed when Constantine declared himself a Christian after his victory over Maxentius in 312 and at the age of twenty four, Constantine was the supreme leader of the West- the first Christian emperor. In the same year he published what is known as the Edict of Milan, which gave the Church freedom of worship and returned to the Church all her properties that had been confiscated. Constantine made Christianity the official religion of the Roman Empire. He aided the Church and the clergy with public grants. He sought the peace of the Church; The Church came under the umbrella of the state—a change that was to radically change the entire history of the Church from then on. However, with all what he did for the Church, we must not forget that Constantine prolonged his baptism until AD 337 believing that if he waited to get baptised on his death bed he was in less danger of polluting his soul with sin and not getting to heaven. In fact, many have doubted his conversion because of his attitude towards baptism. However, he was now at the helm of the Church, and the once-persecuted Church became the protected Church; The Church that was hitherto insulted now became a powerful Church; it became rich with the blessing of the emperor himself. The Church had ceased to be regarded as an enemy of the state and was now in alliance with it. If being a member of a Church was dangerous, now it became advantageous. The Church had become an accepted and important part of the richest and most powerful empire in the ancient world. The Jesus of Nazareth who could not find a place to lay his head was now residing in massive cathedrals. The humble image of Christ the Good Shepherd was replaced with Christ the King. The "thorn-crowned Christ became the golden-crowned Christ". The Christ whose only possession in the world was his garment, was now having followers with costly costumes and golden crown. The Church now attained a very high position in the Roman Empire. However, it was not without consequences.

As far as my thinking goes, probably the single most issue that the Church struggled with for about one thousand years, almost till the Reformation, was the Church-state relationship following the conversion of Constantine. Of course, the Church state issue has always been there from the time the Romans crucified Christ, but, more technically, it became more pronounced from the time of Constantine. In fact, the Church must have been grateful that the persecution had come to an end, but they were not aware of the dangers of the state getting into the affairs of the Church. The new situation into which the Church 'fell' began to deeply influence every part of its existence in the world. Although Christians remained as the people of God even after the conversion of Constantine, they lived, thought, worshipped, governed and conducted themselves very differently from those Christians who had to pass through the shadow and the fiery period of persecution. Three areas in which these changes appeared most notably were: a) The government of the

Church; b) The Church's relationship with the state; c) The way in which the worship of the Church was changed.[11]

Before the Church came under the state, there was no empire-wide structure of government for the Church. The Church had more of a congregational character and its authority tended to be local. There were monarchical bishops in larger cities, and they had significant influence on the Churches that came under their spiritual care. There was fellowship and interaction among the Churches in different places. However, there was no common government, no common Church law, no one 'head' of the Church other than the founder of the Church, the Lord Jesus Christ.

As the Church came under the state, the above-mentioned characteristics of the pre-Constantine Church changed drastically. Now with the emperor beginning to take control of the situation, he began to call for synods and councils to deal with different issues in the Church. From now on the holding of major Church councils became common in the life of the Church. These councils became important events in creating common belief systems for the universal Church; it promoted unity of the Church and to some extent it brought order and regulations within the larger set-up of the new imperial religion. Another major factor during the post-Constantine period was the development of a clear distinction between the laity and the clergy. The laity who were the majority in the Church had no office; the clergy were Church officials who were set apart from the laity by ordination. As time went by the entire function of the Church fell into the hands of the clergy, a situation that made their office more 'powerful' with lasting implications. There were now lower clergy, higher clergy, and the episcopate.

The lower clergy consisted of those who would help in worship services, visitation, and other tasks. They were the sub-deacons who formed the secretarial staff to the bishop. The higher clergy were the deacons and presbyters. The care of the poor, originally entrusted to the deacons, was now discharged by the lower clergy. Deacons became the chief administrative assistants to the bishops. Presbyters conducted services and administered sacraments; they were the spiritual arm of the bishops. Later these presbyters were named priests.

The episcopate consisted of the bishops of the Church. The lowest in rank was the country bishop. Next in order was the city bishop. Both the country and the city bishops were subject to the archbishop, called metropolitan in the east, who was the bishop of the capital city of the province. The archbishops, in turn, were under the authority of the patriarchal bishops.[12] At the beginning of the 4th century there were three patriarchal bishops: the bishop of Rome, Antioch, and Alexandria. Later, when Constantine made Constantinople the capital of the eastern empire, the bishop of that city became a patriarch. At the Council of Chalcedon in 451, the bishop of Jerusalem was similarly honoured and became a patriarch. The patriarchs of Rome and Alexandria are both given the title of "Pope."[13] This has been the hierarchical order of the Church that was developed which turned into powerful offices that mostly became corrupt as the Church entered into the medieval period.

The Church after the conversion of Constantine (especially after the 6th century) gained not only spiritual but the actual responsibility to run the government, especially in the Western part of the Roman Empire. However, when the tribal chiefs rose to power in Europe, they were called kings. These kings were not happy that the Church was governing the state. They wanted to regain the power not only over the state but even over the Church which became wealthy. In fact, by the time of Reformation, the Church owned more than half of the land in Europe. Power was based on the amount of land that was owned. By the time of the Reformation, there was lot of corruption within the Church. The reformers were convinced that the only way corruption could be removed was to remove the state from having power over the Church. In fact, it was secular kings who appointed officials to the Church. The reformers argued that the officials for the Church should not be made by laypeople. As I mentioned before, probably the single most issue in the post-Constantine period was this Church state issue.

In the same way there were a number of changes taking place within imperial Christianity. The councils that were held one after another in the post-Constantine period gave rise to a number of doctrinal definitions. There was of course the influence of Greek philosophy. God began to be referred as 'Supreme Being', 'Substance' and so on. God's being became more important than God's deeds in history. The idea of the knowledge of God through experience was increasingly replaced by that of rational knowledge. The Ecumenical councils were more bothered about the nature of Christ than what he did during his earthly ministry. Unfortunately, little has changed.

It is unfortunate that the body of Christ became so degraded throughout history. When it started in Jerusalem it was as a fellowship of believers. They were together, simply as a community of fellow believers. When they moved out of Jerusalem into Antioch (Acts 11:26), the disciples were called "Christians". It is interesting to note that they did not call *themselves* Christians; rather, they were called Christians by others. As it moved into Athens, the centre of philosophy, people tended to look at Christianity as a philosophy. They tried to unite Greek philosophy with Christianity. As it moved into Rome, especially after the Church came under the umbrella of the state, the Church began to become more institutional. When it moved to Europe during the medieval period and even later, Christianity became more of a *culture* in Europe. Europe was Christianity and Christianity was Europe.

In present-day India, Christianity is now overcome with 'projects and programs' rather than a ministry or a fellowship. Every leader of any Church or denomination has a project or program as he or she goes out of the country in name of 'ministry' or even within the country. The way some so-called Christian leaders in India do ministry or mission work is to function as if they were on a contract—as a kind of business deal with God. But Christian ministry is not contract work; rather, it is a commitment. Similarly, in North America today, ministry is like a business. The gospel is being sold. We can label this the commercialization of the Gospel! Indeed, the Church is for 'sale' today. The church has become compromised. This is a very sad situation.

The Church is not primarily an institution. Ecclesiastical power structures do not create the Church or our identity. As it is said "the orange robes does not make a sanyasi, it is the experience behind it that creates it". The Church happens and manifests itself in mission in the world. The self-defining of the Church is a process. Today the question is not whether there is salvation outside the Church or not; the real question is whether the Church will be there where salvation takes place. Where is the real Church found today? Is it in the air-conditioned cathedrals and chapels, or in our massive buildings? I think the real Church is found outside the 'official' Church where it stands with the poor on the foot paths, at the construction sites, in the refugee camps, among the migrant communities, the people in transit, where people from different cultures and traditions worship the risen Lord with their everyday experiences of pain and pathos.

Unfortunately, the Church and its many workers today are in the "business" of Christianity. The more one sells it, the more glorified one becomes. "When Reinhard Bonnke[14] makes ten thousand people speak in tongues in half a minute, or when he stages miracle after miracle in his services, then religion is marketed like a new shampoo or a disco song. That is neither the renewal of the Church nor of society."[15] Unfortunately some of the basic values of the Gospel like love, grace, mercy, and relationship are now replaced under such marketing mentality with words like 'prosperity' and 'success'. In the urge to become famous some 'labourers' of the Gospel use whatever means are available at their disposal. For many, the end justifies the means, not knowing (or intentionally ignoring) that in God's kingdom both the ends *and* the means matter. What we see here is a commoditization of the Gospel, a degradation of human relationships, and a compromising of values. A lot of emphasis is laid on Church growth, not realizing the fact that all that grows is not the Church. (Cancer grows too!!!)

Another major struggle that the Church has faced throughout its history is the issue of its identity. There are two positions here that are typically offered. 1) Sometimes the Church understood itself *in opposition* to other faith communities. 2) At other times the Church understood itself relationally to others. It must be said here that whenever the Church understood itself in relation to other people and culture, there was a positive dialogue with the people and religions around them. When this happens, creative and dynamic movements arose in the life of the Church, causing renewal and a vibrant sense of mission.

On the other hand, whenever the Church saw itself *in opposition to* the other or over against the other, it had very damaging and negative results: painful and lasting schisms, crusades, and inquisitions. These are but a few examples of how the Church saw itself over against the other.

Even when we look at the Church and her mission in our own country of India, we see that when the Western missionaries came to this land, whether they were Roman Catholics, or Protestants, their approaches to the Indian people tended to be quite damaging. In fact, many missionaries wanted their converts to be separated from their Hindu and Muslim friends and neighbours. The Christian literature that came out in the nineteenth century reflects a very negative attitude of the missionaries towards Indian religions and cultures. Unfortunately, the identity that the Christian community inherited in this country was one of 'over–against' all other religious traditions existing in the nation. Such an attitude kept the Christian community away from the mainstream of Indian cultural and political life, while trying to enjoy a 'false security' under the missionaries and colonial powers. This situation prevented the Indian Christian community from understanding its own identity in relation to its people. Missionaries created a "fortress mentality" that isolated Christian converts from the society around them. The main problem here is that the new converted Christians were now separated from the people they once called friends. These divisions were coercive and have caused lasting damage between Christians and non-Christians.

This unfortunate situation made the Indian Christian community to live in an atmosphere of mistrust and the fear of the majority community. This, in turn, led to a 'minority consciousness' among the Christians in India. Of course, this situation has rapidly changed in the post-colonial context of independent India.

The Indian context is strongly pluralistic today. I think the need of the hour as far as Christian witness is concerned is that we need to develop an identity which is positive and relational. We need not become hostile and defensive toward people of other faith. We must take into account the religious experiences of our friends from other faiths, while helping them to experience the supreme love of Christ. People of other faiths should not simply become *targets* of our Christian agenda, but they should become our *partners* in establishing God's kingdom on earth. Our theology has to become 'cross referential' and not 'self-referential'—where ministry becomes 'God's ministry' and not 'our ministry,' where mission becomes 'God's Mission' and 'not our mission,' where the *kenosis, necrosis* and *theosis* of Christ become indelible parts of our Christian witness.

We must understand that before we can witness to Christ, we have to become a witness ourselves. What do I mean here? What I mean is this: we need to be first reconciled to God before we can reconcile other people to God. Christian witness must avoid the language of "you" and "them". Witness must become a language of "we and "us". Witness will not become possible with other people if we isolate the other person from our spirituality and religiosity. Before we can do any meaningful witness, we must be willing to renounce our own secret and shameful ways.

As pointed out earlier, we have commercialized the Gospel. Christian witness must prompt us to go to our friends of other faiths and cultures and ask for forgiveness. Imagine how things may change if some of our Bishops, Pastors and other Christian leaders ask forgiveness to our fellow human beings for misunderstanding them, their faith, their culture, etc.? Who knows what will happen if such humility is found among us? In our witness with people from other faiths and cultures, it is important that we remain committed to them *as people*. They are human beings and they deserve our very best; they deserve the profound *agape* of Jesus Christ.

Let me cite a few helpful suggestions on Christian witness from the late Metropolitan Geevarghese Mar Osthathios. He says every missionary's lifestyle must be that of the master if our witness is to be effective. We must show solidarity with the poor; as Paul said, we must become all things to all people. Exorbitant spending on buildings and infra-structure must be stopped, and more resources should be shared with people in need. As Gustavo Gutierrez once wrote, we must have a preferential option for the poor, and it must be practiced by empowering them, and not just by hand-outs. The public as well as the private life of the missionary should be blameless and exemplary, and s/he must make a definite effort to practice what is preached. We must live simple so that others may simply live.[16]

I believe we as Christian scholars must renew our commitment to servanthood as portrayed by Christ, for surely this is a way of making Jesus visible in our pluralistic society. We must examine and prayerfully work out being a servant among our family, friends, and colleagues. We must also become more aware of what being a servant looks like in our personal and professional lives if our Christian witness is to be authentic. How can we be a servant to our Hindu or Muslim or any other friends if we are unwilling to express to them the love of Jesus Christ? We must be willing to take "off" our shoes when we stand on a new ground, in a new culture, or among a new community. In doing this we are showing that the ground we are standing on is "holy" ground! What God has made holy let us not make unholy! What is evangelism after all? It is making a bridge between our hearts and the other person's heart so that Jesus can walk into their lives. May we all understand how to be a disciple of Christ in a world of religious pluralism.

Endnotes

[1] Raymond Schwab, *The oriental renaissance*, Paris: Payot, 1950, Cited in Jacob Dharmaraj, *Colonialism and Christian Mission: Post-Colonial Reflections*, (ISPCK, New Delhi, 1993), 5.

[2] Donna Landry &Gerald Maclean (eds.), *The Spivak reader*, London: Routledge, 1996,23.

[3] Ranajit Guha (ed), *Subaltern Studies 1: Writings on South Asian History and Society*, (Delhi: Oxford University Press, 1982), (Preface).

[4] Ibid., 8.

[5] Ibid.

[6] Felix Wilfred, "Subaltern Religious experience", *Journal of Dharma*, 23 (No.1, 1998), 5.

[7] *Ibid.*, 58.

[8] *Ibid.*

[9] The subaltern group of scholars have produced a ten volume work which is scholarly and from a subaltern perspective on Indian history. This ten volumes are available at the U.T.C library. It was primarily their effort to bring out a historiography which would be basically subaltern in its perspective. The outstanding figure of this group whom one can

consider as the pioneer is Ranajit Guha. He made innovative techniques to read the presence of an insurgent consciousness from what were most often English language colonial accounts. There are others like Partha Chatterjee, Gyanendra Pandey, David Arnold, David Hardiman involved in the development of the Subaltern Studies. Following is a bibliographical detail of the ten volumes.

Guha, Ranajit (ed). *Subaltern Studies I: Writings on South Asian history and Society*. (Delhi: Oxford University Press, 1982).

Guha, Ranajit (ed). *Subaltern Studies II: Writings on South Asian history and Society*. (Delhi: Oxford University Press, 1983).

Guha, Ranajit (ed). *Subaltern Studies III: Writings on South Asian history and Society*. (Delhi: Oxford University Press, 1984).

Guha, Ranajit (ed). *Subaltern Studies IV: Writings on South Asian history and Society*. (Delhi: Oxford University Press, 1985).

Guha, Ranajit (ed). *Subaltern Studies V: Writings on South Asian history and Society*. (Delhi: Oxford University Press, 1990).

Guha, Ranajit (ed). *Subaltern Studies VI: Writings on South Asian history and Society*. (Delhi: Oxford University Press, 1992).

Chatterjee, Partha & Pandey, Gyanendra (eds). *Subaltern Studies VII: Writings on South Asian history and Society*. (Delhi: Oxford University Press, 1993).

David, Arnold &David Hardiman (eds) Essays *in Honour of Ranajit Guha. Vol. VIII*, (Delhi: Oxford University Press, 1994).

Shahid, Amin & Dipesh, Chakrabarthy (eds). *Subaltern Studies IX: Writings on South Asian history and Society.* (Delhi: Oxford University Press, 1996).

Bhadra, Gautam & Prakash Gyan (eds), *Subaltern Studies X: Writings on South Asian history and society.* (Delhi: Oxford University Press, 1999).

[10] Justin Martyr, *Apology* 11, 3.

[11] Harry R. Boer, *A Short History of the Early Church* (Grand Rapids, Michigan: Eerdmans, 2001), 134.

[12] Boer, *A Short History of the Early Church*, 136.

[13] Boer, *A Short History of the Early Church*, 136.

[14] Reinhard Bonnke is a popular itinerant German evangelist who attracts tens of thousands of people for his evangelistic crusades all around the world but mostly in African countries.

[15]   Roswith I. H. Gerloff, "Der Heilige Geist und die afrikanische Diaspora. Spirituelle, kulturelle und soziale Wurzeln und Traditionen schwarzer Pfingstkirchen," *Pastoraltheologie* 84/4 (1995): 185-98 here 198 cited in Hollenweger, *Pentecostalism*, 364. English: "The Holy Spirit and the African Diaspora. Spiritual, Cultural and Social Roots of Black Pentecostal Churches" (SPS and EPTA Conference, Mattersey, England, July 1995).

[16] Metropolitan Geevarghese Mar Osthathios, *Salvation through Grace by Faith Manifested by Work,* An Inaugural Sermon at the National consultation on Evangelism at Yeagiri Hills, Jalapet, Tamil Nadu.

Śabarimala:
A Syncretic Religion and
Model for Interfaith Relations

EBENEZER SHINEKUMAR

Simply, religion is a set of beliefs and practices. But study of religion leads one to an amazing treasury which is related to our history and culture. Also, it is interesting to look into the history of each religion to understand its past, which reasoned many influences with compulsion and persuasion. Because of 'syncretism', it is difficult to conclude that any religion is 'pure' or developed without any influence from neighboring religions. The history testimonies the development may be honorable or rotten. It is remarkable to look into the religion of Śabarimala and to understand how syncretism changed a subaltern deity and how it affects its original representatives. Also, this article lightens to the elements in the religion precious to Interfaith Relations.

Syncretism in Religion

Oxford Dictionary defines syncretism as "the mixing of different religions, philosophies or ideas."[1] In its simplest sense, religious syncretism refers to the fusion of different beliefs or practices.[2] It is a common phenomenon which can be found all over the religious world. In the history of religion 'syncretism' denotes generally an unconscious, widespread tendency, due to or fostered by some readjustment of political relationship or by some clash of civilizations. There is a blending of religious ideas and practices, by means of which either one set adopts more or less thoroughly the principles of another or both are amalgamated to a more cosmopolitan and less polytheistic shape. Such movements in the religious world are often preceded and accelerated by a new philosophical synthesis as well as by a political re-arrangement. But the outcome invariably is a unification of deities, which, as J. Toutain has pointed out, precedes one or other of two lines: either two deities of different religions are assimilated by comparison or several deities are grouped together in a fresh synthesis. The intentions for this re-statement are drawn from the awareness that any particular form of religion is no longer sufficient by itself, that others possess like features, possibly of superior efficacy and appeal. Such features can be incorporated without being detrimental to the essential principles of the particular religion in question. The study of comparative religion exhibits this phenomenon in a variety of shapes and stages. But it is especially prominent during the first four centuries of the Christian era.[3]

According to Lee A. Belford, "Syncretism in philosophy and religion is an attempted reconciliation or synthesis of opposing principles or practices. On the unconscious level philosophies and religions are syncretistic to the extent that they have absorbed elements from a culture not completely consistent with a core of beliefs.[4] However, syncretism usually refers to the conscious effort to select from various sources. According to him, in religion an attempt at syncretism can lead to a reduction of beliefs of diverse groups to a common core, such as "response in feeling to the infinite," a feeling of goodwill, or a simple ethical code. Nevertheless, this becomes reductionism and not syncretism. Most attempts at syncretism fail because a religion is related to a culture, and this fact is in part the secret of its success, the "price of its existence." If justice is done to the particularities, diversity remains. If the particularities are denied, what emerges has no roots and evokes no commitment.[5]

Syncretism and *Sanskritization*

Hinduism is a highly syncretic religion that developed and spread through different parts of the Indian subcontinent. In Hinduism, Syncretism appear mostly in the form of "Sanskritization." The development of Hinduism can be interpreted as a constant interaction between the religion of the upper social groups, represented by Brahmans (the priestly class), and the religion of other groups. From the formation of Vedic religion (1500 BCE) the non-Vedic inhabitants of the subcontinent have been enforced to adapt their religious and social life to Brahmanic norms. This has developed from the desire of lower-class groups to rise on the social ladder by adopting the ways and beliefs of the higher castes. This process, sometimes called "Sanskritization," began in Vedic times when non-Aryan chieftains accepted the ministration of Brahmans and thus achieved social status for themselves and their subjects. It was probably the principal method by which Hinduism spread through the subcontinent and into Southeast Asia.[6]

Thus, the history of Hinduism can be interpreted as the imposition of orthodox custom upon wider and wider ranges of people and, complementarily, as the survival of features of non-Aryan religions that gained strength steadily until they were adapted by the Brahmans.[7] The science of religion introduced the distinction between 'Great' and 'Little Traditions.'[8] The local village traditions called 'little,' in fact, constitute most of Hinduism and are a significant source of the so-called pan-Indian traditions (such as the *Puranas*), called as 'great' tradition.[9] Nevertheless, the village tradition, sometimes called the little tradition, comprises extremely diverse folk rituals and devotional practices, often only tenuously connected to the Sanskritic tradition.[10] 'Little' tradition is polytheistic, sometimes animistic, religious though with an emphasis on the local community, caste-inclusive celebrations or forms of worship, and predominantly countless oral texts in the local language. In many cases these religions have their own priests, as most of the devotees worship only regional deities (*kuladēvatā* or *grāmadēvatā*).[11] The social structure of the little traditions however consists of its own role incumbents such as folk artists, medicine men, tellers of riddles, proverbs and stories, poets and dancers. The social structure of this kind of civilization operates at the level of folk or unlettered peasants and is closely connected with orthogenetic evolution though at times homogenous interaction can play a role as well.[12] So for Alex Michael, folk religions and sects are interpreted as 'Little Traditions.'[13] Sanskritization still continues in the form of the conversion of tribal groups and it is reflected by the persistent tendency of low-caste customs, such as wearing the sacred cord and becoming vegetarians. [14]

Śabarimala: The Syncretic Religion

Śabarimala Sree Ayyappa Temple is an ancient mountain shrine located in the Pathanamthitta district in Kerala. This beautiful temple is situated on the virgin Śabarī Hills in a deep, dense forest. Since 21st November 2016, Śabarimala shrine in Kerala is officially called the "Śabarimala Sree Ayyappaswamy Temple." It was previously named as the "Śabarimala Sree Dharma Sastha Temple." But the temple is better known by its first name, Śabarimala.[15] Śabarimala means the *mala* (hill) of Śabarī, the name of a woman which connects the temple to Lord Rama, in the *Rāmāyaṇa*. According to a legend Śabarī is a tribal devotee of Lord Rama mentioned in the Ramayana.[16] While searching for Sītā in the forest, consequent to her abduction by Rāvaṇa, Rāma and his brother Lakṣmaṇa met a demon named Kabandha, who extolled the virtues of Śabarī and asked them to visit her. Accordingly, they went to the hermitage of Sage Mātaṅga, where Śabarī received them with traditional hospitality.[17]

There are three elements in the concept of the *deity* in Śabarimala, Śāstha. One is related to the primitive deities. These deities called *chata*, *machata* and *kandan chatha* were also known in *Pandinadu* by the names of *Ayyan* and *Ayyanar*. The second is made up of the forms of worship and the customs introduced under the influence of Buddhism in the second century before Christ. The third element consists of the concepts adopted from the *Arya Brahmins*. *Sāstha* may be described as Dravidian deity around whom later developed elements of Buddhism and Brahminism.[18]

Adi-Dravida Tradition

According to another tradition Ayyappan was not a Hindu deity of Vedic or Puranic origin, but a hero of the *Mala Arayans*, a hill tribe who may have been the builders of Śabarimala temple. The *Mala Arayans* are literally, the kings of the hills: *mala* is Malayalam for 'hill' and *arayan* comes from *arachan*, chief or more distantly from *raja*, king. The term means "Hill Kings" or chiefs and has nothing to do with "Aryan" as applied to the Sanskrit people.[19] Samuel Mateer, describes them as prosperous rice cultivators living in houses scattered on steep hillsides.[20] As for religion, Mateer says they worshipped their ancestors, or spirits residing in rocks or peaks. In particular, Mateer narrates a *Mala Arayan* legend about Talanani, "a priest or oracle-revealer of the hunting deity, Ayyappan, whose chief shrine is in "Śabarimala."

According to P. K. Sajeev, founder and general secretary of the Aikya Mala Araya Maha Sabha, Ayyappan the "hunting deity," was a prophesied warrior, born in the early twelfth century CE to fight the invaders during the "Hundred Years War" between the imperial Cholas on the one side, and the second Chera 'empire' and their southern neighbors, the Āy kingdom—supposedly the forebears of the *Mala Arayans*—on the other. He was named Manikandan, or 'little Kandan', after his father, *Kaṇḍan*; bell-necked *Maṇikaṇḍan* was a plausible Sanskritism slipped in at a later date. After defeating the Cholas, Manikandan chose Śabarimala, a hill named after hermits of yore who'd had her ashram there, for his resting place.[21]

But the eminent historians are skeptical of the *Mala Arayan* claim as a whole. M.G.S. Narayanan, the historian and former chairman of the Indian Council of Historical Research, is likewise uncertain, saying this legend of Ayyappan is a "new story" he has not come across before.[22] And yet, Mateer begged to differ, in advance. According to Rajan Gurukkal the community had nothing to do with Śabarimala, and there has been confusion with more local tribes such as the Ulladans, Mannans and Mala Pandarams, some of whom may have had some rights at the temple.[23] In reality we can assume that the origin of Sabaramilala religion is rooted on Dravidian-Adivasi culture.

Buddhist Tradition

Although said to be more recent, the Ayyappan cult is also said to have Buddhist influence. There are scholars like the late P. K. Narayana Pillai who believe that Darma Sastha and Sri Buddha are one and same deity.[24] When Buddhism, which was once prevalent in Kerala, died out in the days of Adi Sankar, Buddha was taken into Hindu theology and pantheon, and people worshipped him as *Sastha*.[25] According to Srivaraham E. V. Pillai, the words 'Dharma' and 'Saranam' connected with the Sastha tradition points to the link with Buddhism. The word 'Dharma' is taken over from Buddhism.[26] Śabarimala is supposed to be a Buddhist pilgrimage due to the severe austerities followed by the Ayyappan devotees, similar to the Buddhist Ashtasilas, also known as the Eight-Fold Path. The Pandalam king who built the Sabrimala temple was also a well-known Buddhist. Additionally, Ayyappa's previous name *Shasta* is also said to have been another name for the Buddha. The similarities of the Ayyappan chants – 'Swamiye Saranam Ayyappa' – and Buddhist chants - 'Buddham Saranam Gachhaami' – and the lack of the word 'Saranam' in any other Hindu context, along with the similarity in appearance of the Ayyappa's right arm's *vajradhara* and the Boddhissattva's *vajras*, all lead to the suspicion that the Ayyappan cult is at least influenced, if not originated through, by Buddhism. Hence, Śabarimala Ayyappa is likened to be the *Potala Lokeshwara* of Buddhism,[27] something that scholars are still debating the consequences over. But some scholars like M. G. S. Narayanan are not in favour to associate Buddha with Ayyappan, because of the lack of evidence.[28]

Brahmanic Tradition

Lord Ayyappa is the presiding deity at Śabarimala residing in the hilly forest in *Naishtik Brahmachari* (eternal celibate) state. There are different versions as to why menstruating women were not allowed to enter the Śabarimala Temple. According to *puranic* and legend, Ayyappan was born as the son of Śiva and Mōhinī (or *Viṣṇumāya*), the enchanting female form of Vishnu.[29] Lord Vishnu took the form of Mōhinī to have destroyed a deadly demon Bhashmasur and acquire the elixir (*amṛt*) for the gods during the great churning of oceans. Legend has it that Lord Shiva got swayed by the charm of Mōhinī and Lord Ayyappa was born of their union. While Lord Ayyappa was still a minor, a lady-demon had created havoc in the down south. She had got a boon from gods that she could only be defeated by the son born out of the union of Lord Shiva and Lord Vishnu. As it happened, Lord Ayyappa defeated her in a battle.

Upon her defeat, it was revealed that the demon was actually a beautiful young woman who had been cursed to live the life of a demon. The defeat set the woman free who, in turn, proposed to Lord Ayyappa. He refused saying that he had been ordained to go to forest and answer the prayers of devotees. But, the young woman was persistent. So, Lord Ayyappa promised to marry her the day *kanni-swamis* (new devotees) stop visiting him with their prayers at Śabarimala. The woman agreed to wait for him at a neighbouring temple. The woman is also worshipped today as Mālikappurathamma at a neighbouring temple. The legend goes further saying that in honour of Mālikappurathamma, Lord Ayyappa does not receive any menstruating woman. Also, the women chose not to visit Lord Ayyappa for it would be an insult to Mālikappurathamma's love and sacrifice.[30] But in reality,

Mālikappurathamma was *Kottavai*, a Dravidian goddess. For the destruction of that tradition that deity was Brahmanized by the new story of Malikappurathamma. *Sastha* or *Chathan* and *Kottavai* are important deities in Dravidian places of worship.[31]

According to the Brahmanic tradition Brahmins are the real custodians of Śabarimala temple. Because the deity related with the temple is *Puranic* origin. But P. K Sajeev encourages us to look into *Puranas* about the absence of *Mohini's* child. So according to him the story mentioned above is a Brahmanic lie.[32] One can assume that this story making was for the possibility of the solution for the Saiva-Vaishnava conflict, and after that the two different sects, *Sivaits* and *Vaishnavaits* came under a single umbrella. Then the story making became one of the reasons for the 'syncretism.' Brahminic tradition added many faiths and customs with Śabarimala temple which reasoned to the destruction of real faith. The renaming of 'Dharma Satha Temple' into 'Sri Ayyappan Temple' was for the implementation of '*naistikabrahmachari*,' a person who refrain from all worldly pleasures and attachments.[33] Because of this, restriction of young women (menstruated women) is implemented with temple beliefs.

There is another story which criticizes the above one. According to the version, Lord Ayyappa is a historical figure. He was born in the royal family of Panthalam, a small kingdom located in the Patthanamthitta district of Kerala. Śabarimala Temple is located in the same district. He grew up in the palace of Panthalam. The relics of the palace still exist. Ayyappa is said to have grown up into a lovable prince for his subjects for he cared for the wellbeing of the people living in his kingdom.

A small continent of intruders led by an Arab commander called Babar or Vāver attacked the kingdom during the time. Ayyappa defeated Vavar, who thereafter turned into his devout follower. As Lord Ayyappa resides at Śabarimala, Vāver lives in spirit in a shrine at Erumeli, a place situated on the 40 km trek to Śabarimala temple. Vāver is said to protect pilgrims going to visit Lord Ayyappa. As per this legend claiming historicity of Lord Ayyappa, the presiding deity of Śabarimala Temple took a vow to answer prayers to every devotee walking up to his shrine.

Given the arduous task that he undertook, Lord Ayyappa shunned all worldly desires including contact with women. Many believe this was the reason why menstruating women were barred from visiting Śabarimala Temple.

Śabarimala and Interfaith Relations

Śabarimala Sree Dharma Sastha temple is one of the few Hindu shrines that welcome people of all faiths. Uniquely, it is a Hindu temple where a Muslim saint has a shrine.[34] A mosque plays host to pilgrims as they engage in the *Petta Thullal*[35] ceremony performed as part of the pilgrimage to the temple. Another model for religious harmony in relation with Śabarimala is a Christian worship centre namely St. Andrews Church. Manju Kuttikrishnan identified it as Śabarimala's 'Secular Credentials.'[36] According to her "Śabarimala proves that secular spirituality cannot be termed an oxymoron."[37]

Śabarimala and Muslim Encounter

With regard to the Vāver tradition it should be remembered that it is difficult to separate the legendary part from the historical. Since Vāver is described as a Muslim, it is natural to assume that Ayyappan lived in or after the 6th century C.

E. But there are no historical evidences to support this view. Even for the Vāver tradition, there is no evidence to support it except some references in old songs. However, the Ayyappan-Vāver episode forms an integral part of the legend. It was on Ayyappan's instruction that Vāver settled down at Erumeli and Ayyappan made arrangements for a Muslim temple to be built for Vāver and his Muslim followers.[38] Erumeli has thus a message for Hindu-Muslim unity and religious amity. People in that place, irrespective of caste and creed, cooperate in the *petta*. The ceremony is arranged on a particular day by the public of Erumeli, Hindus, Muslims and Christians. In the *Chirappu Mahotsavam* (annual festival) the Hindus go in procession to the mosque and make their offerings. In the same way, on the Muslim festival day, *Chandanakudam*, which falls on the day before *petta*, the Muslims go to the *Sastha* temple and make their offerings. Therefore, the mosque at Erumeli is sacred to the Pilgrims. By the time the Pilgrims come to Erumeli the flag would be hoisted at the mosque and the festival would start. The pilgrims worship at both these places. It is believed that the pilgrims should obtain permission from Vāver for the trek through the forests. This religious phenomenon is something unique to Indian culture.[39]

Ayyappa's Muslim friend Vāver is an example of Ayyappa's openness to other faiths, which reflects how a man/woman of any faith can take part in the Śabarimala pilgrimage and traditions. They had such a close relationship that Vāver was not only considered as Ayyappa's best friend, but also his brother, as Ayyappa is said to have asked his father to build a shrine for Vāver by saying 'Consider Vāver as myself.'[40] Often compared to the strong bond of friendship between Krishna and Arjuna in the

Mahabharata, the legend of Ayyappa's celibacy and relationship with Vāver has gone so far that scholars now speculate a possible homosexual relationship between Vāver and Ayyappa. Hence, Vāver now has a shrine in Śabarimala, and a mosque in his name in Kottayam, right next to an Ayyappan temple. Symbolizing a Hindu-Muslim rapport, the temple and mosque even share a wall to show and promote Hindu-Muslim unity.[41]

Śabarimala and the Christian Encounter

A Sixteenth century Catholic Church (St. Andrews) built by Portuguese missionaries in a coastal hamlet is a replica of religious harmony with a tradition of hosting Śabarī pilgrims returning after worshipping Lord Ayyappa.[42] It has been a custom for the church to receive Śabarimala pilgrims from November to January when the *Mandala* and *Makaravilakku* season of the Śabarimala temple takes place. Devotees visit the sea-side church as a stopover to remove their holy beads in a ritualistic manner.[43]

According to local legends, Lord Ayyappa and Fr. Jacomo Femicio, one of the early priests of the church, were friends. The visit of the pilgrims commemorates the bond they shared, especially as the priest was loved by the local people who believed he had healing powers.[44] The relationship between Fr. Jacomo Fenicio and Lord Ayyappa is believed to date back to the sixteenth century. The priest, who was interested in learning martial art forms such as kalaripayattu went to Cheerappanchira Kalari School in Muhamma. It is believed that Lord Ayyappa too was the student there.[45] The church records prove that Fr Fenicio had deep interest in Hindu culture, rituals and martial arts like *Kalarippayattu*. He also penned a book on these subjects in Latin. Though many of these rituals have been given up over the centuries, the spiritual bond between Śabarimala and the Arthunkal Church is still intact.

Śabarimala: The Model for Interfaith Relations

Although there are many things to be criticized Śabarimala is a good resource for Pluralism. Pluralism has been the most important feature of Indian society. 'Swami' is one of the terms which lead us to think about 'polyphony' in Śabarimala worship. One who goes to Śabarimala is named as *Swami*, which means *guru* (teacher), *yajamanan* (lord)[46] and one who goes to Śabarimala for the first time is called 'Kanni Swami' or 'Kanni Ayyappan.'[47] *Swami* is a common name for all devotees who undertake pilgrimage to Śabarimala and the term equalizes all without considering any differences. During the time when many other temples were restricted to low caste people, Śabarimala was opened to all.

In India, preservation of Hindu-Muslim rapport is significant. Over thousand years, Hindus and Muslims have lived together in the subcontinent of India, Pakistan, and Bangladesh. During this time many kinds of conflict—for example, historical/political, socioeconomic, cultural, theological, philosophical, psychological, and personal—have existed between these two religious communities. The nature and number of communal (particularly Hindu-Muslim) riots which have taken place in post-partition India are undoubtedly causes of serious concern to those who would like to see the peoples of this ancient land live together in peace.[48] Also India has witnessed massacres of Christian Missionaries and demolition of churches. This age seeks a good encouragement for the development of dialogue between Hindus with Muslims and Christians for a peaceful life in India. Understanding Śabarimala is fine to compose a good model for polyphony of religions.

According to Raimundo Panikkar, 'the context of any inter-faith dialogue is not the narrowly specific 'religious' fields, but the arena of life, the daily struggle for justice, peace and happiness.'[49] Although Śabarimala is a 'religious field,' it is a 'spontaneous milieu' for dialogue. The Mosque of Vāver and St. Andrews Church create a natural circumstance for the talk. In inter-faith dialogue, the cultural perspective is prominent in the Indian context as the traditional cultures of the continent are integrally related to their religious traditions. In this context Islamism and Christianity are considered as foreign religions. Therefore, inculturation or indigenization has been a major concern.[50] The Vāver tradition and St. Andrews church challenges both communities for dialogue with Hindus.

In the development of the history of Śabarimala Temple, one can witness the destruction of subaltern histories by syncretism and the construction of new history of Brahmanic hegemonies. Even though this is the reality, there are some remnants which cannot be destroyed by assimilation. They remain steadfast for the good future of the society. This model is methodologically sound and is useful for the development of inter-faith relations. Although the rest of India experienced chronic Hindu-Muslim riots, the South Indian Hindu pilgrimage centre "Śabarimala Sree Ayyappaswamy Temple" witnesses a unique festival of communal unity. Moreover, Śabarimala has shrines dedicated to a Hindu God and a Muslim saint. Devotees worship at both these places. No one has seen anything unusual in it. No one has had a problem over it. No one has quarreled over it so far.

For such a rare harmony of faith, Śabarimala has no parallel in the country.[51]

Endnotes

[1] A.S. Hornby, *Oxford Advanced Learner's Dictionary* (New York: Oxford University Press, 2015), 1570.

[2] Daniel P.S. Goh, "Introduction: Religious Syncretism and Everyday Religiosity in Asia," in *Asian Journal of Social Science*, 2009, 5/6, 5.

[3] W. R. Inge, "Syncretism," *Encyclopedia of Religion and Ethics* (New York: T & Clark, 2003), 155 – 158.

[4] For example, Christianity affirmed at one time certain concepts of the mother-goddess derived from paganism. These were not consistent with the professed belief in Christ as sole mediator and redeemer. Lee A. Belford, "Syncretism," in *The Encyclopedia of Americana International Edition*, Vol. 26 (Danbury: Grolier Incorporated, 1992), 180.

[5] Sikhism is called a syncretistic religion because it was founded to reconcile Hinduism and Islam. However, it flourished where most of the people were wither Hindus of Muslims, and the beliefs and practices advocated were not completely alien or without roots., Ibid.

[6] Gavin Flood, *An Introduction to Hinduism* (New Delhi: Cambridge University Press India Pvt. Ltd., 2009), 30.

[7] Brian K. Smith, "Hinduism," in *The New Encyclopedia Britannica*, Vol. 20 (Chicago: Encyclopedia Britannica, 2003), 521.

[8] Axel Michael, *Hinduism: Past and Present*, trans. by Barbera Harshav (New Delhi: Orient Longman Pvt. Ltd., 2006), 25.

[9] Wendy Doniger, "Hinduism," in *The Norton Anthology of World Religions*, vol. II, ed. by Jack Miles (New York: W. W. Norton and Co., 2015), 55.

[10] Arvind Rajagopal, "Hindu Diaspora in the United States," *Encyclopedia of Diasporas: Immigrant and Refugee Cultures Around the World*, ed. by Melvin Ember, Carol R. Ember and Ian Skoggard, vol. I (USA: Springer, 2005): 446.

[11] Axel Michael, *Hinduism: Past and Present*, 25.

[12] Gangadhar V. Shankar Lal, "Great Tradition and Little Tradition," http://legalsutra.com/ 1198/great-tradition-and-little-tradition/ (24 August 2019).

[13] Alex Michael, *Hinduism: Past and Present*, 22.

[14] Gavin Flood, *An Introduction to Hinduism*, 30.

[15] Prabhash K Dutta, "Why Lord Ayyappa shrine is called Sabarimala temple," *India Today*, https://www.indiatoday.in/india/story/why-lord-ayyappa-shrine-is-called-sabarimala-temple-1390621-2018-11-17 November 17, 2018. (30 July 2019).

[16] "What you might want to know about Sabarimala," *The Economic Times*, 18 October 2018b https://economictimes.indiatimes.com/news/et-explains/what-you-might-want-to-know-about-sabarimala/articleshow/66273712.cms?from=mdr (30 August 2019).

[17] M. K., "Śabarī: A Woman median in the RāmāyaGa," in Encyclopedia of Hinduism, edited by K. L. Seshagiri Rao, Vol. IX (California: Mandala Publishing, 2013), 2.

[18] P. T. Thomas, *Sabarimalai and its Sastha: An essay on the Ayyappa Movement* (Bangalore: The Christian Institute for the Study of Religion and Society, 1973), 5.

[19] Samuel Mateer, *Native Life in Travancore* (London: W. H. Allen and Co. 1883), 63.

[20] Ibid., 64.

[21] But the Chola-Chera war is a famously disputed story. The late P.K. Balakrishnan dismissed it as "bhaavanaavyaayaamam," an exercise of the imagination. Rohan Manoj, "The Tribal Ayyappan?" *Outlook*, 22 November 2018, https://www.outlookindia.com/magazine/story/the-tribal-ayyappan/300919 (30 August, 2019).

[22] According to him Sabarimala is not among Kerala's oldest temples. He said, all the Ayyappan song or *Sasthan pattu* (traditional songs on Ayyappan) were written in modern Malayalam. It means they must have been penned only in the sixteenth century at the earliest. M. G. S. Narayanan, "Story and History," in *Sabarimala Sree Dharma Sastha Temple: Ascent to Awakening*, edited by Mukund Padmanabhan (Chennai: N. Ram at Kasturi Buildings, 2016), 44.

[23] Rohan Manoj, "The Tribal Ayyappan?"

[24] P. T. Thomas, *Sabarimalai and its Sastha...*, 20.

[25] Ibid.

[26] Ibid., 21.

[27] *Avalokiteshvara*, in Mahayana Buddhism, the *bodhisattva* ("buddha-to-be") of infinite compassion and mercy, possibly the most popular of all figures in Buddhist legend. Lokesh Chandra. *Lokiteshvara of Potala: The Thousand-armed Avalokite vara* (New Delhi: Abhinav Publications, 1988), 35.

[28] M. G. S. Narayanan, "Story and History," in Sabarimala Sree Dharma Sastha Temple: Ascent to Awakening, edited by Mukund Padmanabhan (Chennai: N. Ram at Kasturi Buildings, 2016), 44.

[29] K. K. R., Encyclopedia of Hinduism Vol.II, K. L. Seahgiri, 77.

[30] Prabhash K Duttahttps, Legend of Sabarimala: Love story that kept women from Lord Ayyappa, *India Today, 28 September, 2018* ://www.indiatoday.in/india/story/sabarimala-legend-women-lord-ayyappa-1351674-2018-09-28.

[31] R. Ramanand, "Sabarimala Kottavai." In *Sabarimalayum Sthreekalum* (Malayalam), edited by Lakshmi Rajeev (Chennai: Ekam, 2019), 144.

[32] P. K. Sajeev, *Sabarimala Ayyappan, Mala Araya Daivam.*

[33] T. S. Syamkumar, *Sabarimala: Hindutva Tanthrangalum yadharthyangalum* (Kottayam: D. C. Books, 2019), 13.

[34] Mukund Padmanabhan, "Forward," in *Sabarimala Sree Dharma Sastha Temple: Ascent to Awakening*, 5.

[35] *Petta Thullal* at Erumeli is a kind of devotional dance. The Pilgrims come to Erumeli by the 26th of *Dhanu* (about 10th January) every year, and on the next day they perform the Petta Thullal. Every *kanni Ayyappan* is expected to participate in the *thullal*. When they dance they sing: "*Ayyappan thinthakathom, Sami thinthakathom... Thinthakathom,thinthakathom – Swamithinthakathom.*" They go to the temple of *Petta Sastha* and *Vavarsamy* and make the customary offerings, which makes the end of the *thullal*. P. T. Thomas, *Sabarimalai and its Sastha...*, 35.

[36] Manju Kuttikrishnan, "Faith in Secularism," in *Sabarimala Sree Dharma Sastha Temple: Ascent to Awakening*, 50.

[37] Ibid.

[38] P. T. Thomas, *Sabarimalai and its Sastha...*, 32.

[39] P. T. Thomas, *Sabarimalai and its Sastha...*, 32.

[40] Roshen. Dalal, *Ayyappa, the Religions of India: A Concise Guide to Nine Major Faiths* (New Delhi: Penguin, 2010), 43.

[41] Ibid.

[42] The parish records say that the church was built by missionaries who reached Kerala following the arrival of explorer Vasco da Gama in Kappad, Kozhikkode, in 1498. Fr. Jacomo Fenicio look charge as a vicar in 1584, It is believed that he installed in the church an idol of St. Seebastian brought from Italy. He is also said to have had a deep interest in Hindu Culture and ritual. Hema Sreekumar, " Love thy Neighbour," in *Sabarimala Sree Dharma Sastha Temple: Ascent to Awakening*, edited by Mukund Padmanabhan (Chennai: N. Ram at Kasturi Buildings, 2016), 52.

[43] T Sudheesh, "Arthunkal church opens doors for Sabarimala pilgrims," *Deccan Chronicle*, 20 November 2017, https://www.deccanchronicle. com/nation/in-other-news/201117/arthunkal-church-opens-doors-for-sabarimala-pilgrims.html (29 August 2019).

[44] "Forgotten tale of religious harmony," *Deccan Chronicle*, 18March 2019. https://www.deccanchronicle. com/131206/news-current-affairs/article/forgotten-tale-religious-harmony (2 September 2019).

[45] Hema Sreekumar, " Love thy Neighbour," 52.

[46] Sreekandhesvaram G. Padmanabha Pillai, *Sabdatharavali* (Kottayam: Sahithya Pravarthama Co-operative Society, 2017), 1750.

[47] P. T. Thomas, *Sabarimalai and its Sastha...*, 24.

[48] Riffat Hassan, "The Basis for a Hindu-Muslim Dialogue and Steps in that Direction from a Muslim Perspective," http://riffathassan.info/wp-content/uploads/2014/03/The_Basis_For_a_Hundu-Muslim_Dialogue 1.pdf (2 September 2019).

[49] Through 'real life,' Panikkar means people's meeting places like streets of cities and places of work. Raimundo Panikkar, "The Ongoing Dialogue," in *Hindu-Christian Dialogue: Perspectives and Encounters*, edited by Harold Coward (New York: Orbis Books, 1990), ix.

[50] Israel Selvanayagam, *A Dialogue on Dialogue: Reflections on Interfaith-encounters* (Madras: CLS, 1993), 19.

[51] Manju Kuttikrishnan, "Faith in Secularism," in *Sabarimala Sree Dharma Sastha Temple: Ascent to Awakening*, edited by Mukund Padmanabhan (Chennai: N. Ram at Kasturi Buildings, 2016), 50.

Exclusion:
A Human made Sin
in God's own Cosmos

John Davidson Johnson

"I have a dream that my four little children will one day live in a nation where they will not be judged by the color of their skin but by the content of their character." [1]
(Martin Luther King Jr.)

Theology is concerned about the question of how God deals with the whole creation. The frontiers of theology have moved from the church and the Christian community to the whole creation. Concerning the Church, with which we must uphold unity, it is the mother of the entire faithful citizen. We can enter the spiritual life through our visible mother Church. The Church is chosen and loved by God Almighty, purchased and purified by the precious blood of Jesus Christ and guarded by the Holy Spirit. Unfortunately, the so-called dominant sections of our society are often accused of being gatekeepers trying to keep people out of God's Reign. Today many of our Church's doors are not open to all due to denominationalism, separatism, human divisions, traditionalism and so on.

God's own Cosmos

"God desires everyone to be saved and come to the knowledge of the truth." [2] God is the source and origin of this beautiful creation and handing over to the humans the responsibility for sustaining and promoting the creation (Gen. 1:26-28, 2:15-17).[3] God cares about the world as one cares about one's body. The world is a body that must be carefully tended, that must be nurtured, protected, guided and loved. The model of the world as God's body encourages holistic attitudes of responsibility for and care of the vulnerable and oppressed in the society.[4]

Exclusion: A Human made SIN

Ecclesial Challenge: Why do we need the so called "sub-centers"[5] nearby certain parishes?

Pastoral Challenge: Rural based people do not get adequate pastoral care. Most of them are excluded from the mainline church related activities.

They are not getting theological opportunities, ministerial aspects and sufficient pastoral concern including the Eucharist experience.

Politics and Economics of Exclusion

Somen Das strongly emphasized that, God is holy and holiness in the Bible includes righteousness and justice. The Church of God must be catholic by her nature – universal in scope and character, transcending barriers of race, caste, color and gender. She must include all - women, children, *Adivasis, Dalits* and the poor people in particular.[6]

- Presence of theologically untrained persons in the sub-centers of the main parish.

- Holy Eucharist: once in a month (Why?)

- Political agenda of majority and minority

- Economic reasons: less number of families, low level of income, insufficiency of ordained pastors, "Salary" of a pastor and so on…

- The problem of 'other people'

- certain point of "caste based identities"

There are still incidents of having separate churches for caste people (*ecclesial* separatism) and this is a shame for the church.[7] Caste oppression among Christians in certain areas has led to the formation of many churches meant exclusively for Dalits. Some of these tendencies in the churches indicate that Christianity in India is not free from the blight of caste. New forms of slavery or a lack of rights for certain minorities or social classes, groups or individuals, leading to increased inequalities and exclusion. Vincent Manoharan wrote that, Dalit pastors are mostly not posted in certain churches where non Dalit dominates.[8]

"Exclusion" is still practiced, particularly in certain areas. Dominant caste groups within the church had more access to education and opportunities for interpreting the Bible. The Scripture is seen as a source of power and comfort in moments of crisis, both personal and communal. Lack of access to Scripture has hindered the so called excluded ones from making a contribution to the interpretation of Scripture.[9]

Issue of Caste

We Commit:

- To be faithful to Jesus Christ and to realize that being born again means to be born against caste.

– To put our energies and resources to work to end caste division, caste discrimination and caste violence in our church and society.

– To make our church courageous and concrete witnesses to the body of Christ free of caste division, caste discrimination and caste violence.

– To our church serving as zero tolerance zones for casteism and caste based discrimination and our church developing policies on social inclusion. That also involves that our institutions become sites that practice preferential option for *Dalits* in admission, employment and in perspective.[10]

Wolfhart Pannenberg says that, the church has been widely understood as a congregation of the faithful (*congregatiofidelium*).[11] Caste discrimination is rampant among Christians in our country. The pain and the shame we feel at the sins of some members of the church ultimately harm us which also limits our values and the new possibilities of the Gospel.

David Joy suggested that,

– Discrimination in the Church in the name of caste is a crime.

– The ministry of the Church will be complete if both women and men participate in the activities of the Church and society.

– The identity of Jesus is not an exclusive one, but universal.[12]

Observations

Jesus Christ becomes ours through the faith in God who provided faith through pastors, teachers and Sacraments. To be a Christian means, to be a follower, a disciple of Jesus of Nazareth.

- The purpose of proclamation is not simply to save people but to build up effective witnessing communities.

- "Sanctify them in the truth; your word is truth." (St. John 17:17)

- From the imposed disempowerment to self-empowerment and emancipation.

- Empowering Leadership.

The leadership must "lead from their knees". Equality develops in practice only where power structures among the people are ended. Focus on the continuously equipping for mission and ministry and building a community rather than running an organization. The ordained ministry understood as a ministry for justice and a ministry for the liberation of the whole creation.

The proof of a good leader is creating another leader, not more followers. Develop servant-leadership by strategically mentoring, teaching and serving the believers. A true leader's measure of success is when they have succeeded in helping others to be successful. Leadership should be about identifying, articulating the vision and giving proper co-ordination and direction, giving expression to, co-ordinating and resourcing the ministry of the whole church.

- The person's hand was withered, but God's mercy had still preserved to him the use of his feet: he uses them to bring him to the public worship of God, and Jesus meets and heals him there. (St. Matthew 12:9; St. Mark 3:1; St. Luke 6:6)

- 1 John 3: 8 says the Son of God appeared to destroy the works of the devil.

- The resurrection of the Christ concentrates the whole of salvation into a single event.[13] Jesus is 'dead' to sin in the sense that He is isolated, separated, only from the system of destructive violence in which the world is caught: He is free from the trap of guilt, oppression and fear.[14]

We need to work together as a team in our parishes, our families and our communities. The communion of saints is immediately followed by the forgiveness of sins, which can only be obtained by the citizens and members of the Church (Isaiah 33:24). The real head of the Church is God who alone should rule in the Church.

The joy of the Gospel (***evangelii gaudium***) is such that it cannot be taken away from us by any person or anything.[15] In light of our gracious and inclusive God who eliminates any type of exclusion. Jesus Christ shows us the ministry of radical inclusion and ministry against false system of exclusion. He offered his invitations to all without requirements or prohibitions.

Recommendations and Suggestions

God gave us this human life as the crown of God's creation which is more precious in the sight of the world. God will provide for those who made in his/her image.

- Christian Gospel has a particular significance in particular place which is one of the important concerns for the Christian Theology.

- Church should be energized by faith and provide worship experiences that are biblically based, Christ-centered, exalt and glorify God.

- Jesus Christ was a bringer of abundant life for all and his offer of life was to all creatures without any discrimination or intolerance.

- Be courageous to take the Cross which has no handle.

- Unexpected Guests at God's Banquet. Dining table is an extension of the Divine table. (Inter-dining among Christians is still a problem in certain areas)

- The oppressed people cannot defend themselves against the powerful. They are the least and the last, the hungry and the thirsty, the unclothed and the strangers, the sick and the captives.

- We, the people of God have to include the last, the least and the lost. Christ and his Good News have influenced many to work for restructuring our society. The mission of proclaiming the Gospel of Jesus Christ has a universal intention.

- Caste or community based positions should be discouraged.

- **Spiritual dialysis** needed through the Word of God which sanctify us.

- Responsibility means literally answerability.[16]

- *'Ecclesia reformata semper reformanda'* means the reformed church should always be reformed.

- Sinless perfection is needed in all aspects.

- **If there is no guilt, there can be no grace.**

- Walking in the light[17] means walking along with the true way of abundant life.

The idea of plurality is essentially an idea of justice, peace and equality. Plurality is a "theological and cultural consciousness" of the wholeness of God's creation and the creative space for the created order.[18] God heals the brokenhearted and binds up their wounds.[19]

The Scripture says: "Happy are those who consider the poor, the Lord delivers them in the day of trouble. The Lord protects them and keeps them alive; they are called happy in the land." [20] For the church the priority is the people of God. The intimacy of sin and death is broken, and the power of God's love is revealed through the Resurrection of Jesus the Christ. Rowan Williams pointed that, where there is salvation, its name is Jesus; its grammar is the Cross and the Resurrection.[21] We need to have a concern for the integral development of society's most neglected members.

Scripture is God's word to those who are oppressed or humiliated. Book of Exodus and other prophetical writings has a base of the transformation of social situation from oppression to liberation. Go to the depths of Scripture exegetically for the purpose of relating that message to human existence. We must clear that the Word of God stands in judgment upon the existing order of injustice. God is not indifferent to suffering and not patient with cruelty and falsehood. God's power and judgment will create justice and order. The preaching of the Gospel and the institution of the preaching ministry are intended to stimulate the faithful and encourage the collective sanctification of the members of the ecclesiastical community.

Repentance means change to what is good. It implies that a thorough change has occurred so that it results in an altered conduct to the Glory of God. The repentant heart has desire to undo the sinful activities. Repentance does not simply express sorrow over sin. It is a change and return to obedience. Being born again means being born from above. This is not a change that comes from human beings, but it is a transformation that comes from God. It comes from hearing carefully the voice of God's forgiveness. God loves humanity like a parent caring for children.

God's merciful and intimate concern is for the humanity and the entire creation. Jesus brings God's forgiveness of sin. Thus sin is taken away and the whole creation reconciled with God. We need repentance that can shape a new vision of how we live together in harmony without any kind of exclusion in the church. "The time is fulfilled, and the Reign of God is at hand, repent you and believe the Gospel" (St. Mark 1:15). Jesus Christ is the eternal light who illuminates human life. Salvation through Christ is a transfer from darkness to light.

Faithful Caretakers

Christ chose his disciples and they were given an intensive training to transform the whole cosmos without any discrimination or bias. The Lord entrusted the precious work of feeding the people to the hands of his disciples. God who has saved us and called us to a holy life not because of anything we have done but because of his own purpose and grace. Those who are in Christ are his missionaries or ambassadors. They are extraordinary people who witness to Christ with supernatural power to accomplish a supernatural task by proclaiming the Good news of Christ to the people of all nations.God is giving a most sobering and serious task to Ezekiel (33: 1-9), to go to Israel and proclaim God's message towards Israel. He was appointed by God to be a spiritual 'watchman' or a faithful 'caretaker'. God had called him to a special ministry in Babylon and to the captive people of Judah during the dark time of their exile from their homeland. It was the task of the watchman or caretaker to position himself/ herself high on the city wall or on a tower, watch carefully, see if an enemy approached the land, and take up his/her trumpet and blow the warning to his/her people. This is a subject of life and death and obviously the caretaker had to be a trustworthy person. It is the caretaker's two-fold duty - firstly need to watch faithfully and see the danger that approaches to his/her people; secondly to blow the warning to his/her people loudly and clearly. The church as a worshipping community, a serving community and a witnessing community has committed to promote a radical social transformation within the society.

The Church is a called out community. The church is one, holy, catholic and apostolic. The church is called Catholic or universal; means all the elect of God are so connected with each other in Christ and grow up together as into one body, compacted together like members of the same body; being made truly one, as living by one faith, hope and charity, through the same divine spirit. The Church will have to practice constant self examination in order to avoid all error and, in matters concerning its own members. The obligation of the Church is to guide and help its members in their sanctification. As David Joy observes, reformation should continue to enable the people of God to experience, explore and expose the meaning of Christ event in a contextually appropriate manner found in our all *ecclesial* situations.[22]

We have to restore to the Church its apostolic nature. The Apostles therefore were missionaries to institute God's reign universally by the preaching of the word of God. They were the first architects of the Church, selected to lay its foundation all over the world. Faithful pastors and courageous teachers are always indispensable to the Church. For Boyd, "the church in India should be fully Indian, fully at home in Indian culture – but firmly based on the Scriptures, and living always in the closest touch with Christ its Head through the power of the Spirit.[23] The church is the part of the Gospel, the church is the fruit of the Gospel, the church is an embodiment of the Gospel and the church is an agent of the Gospel.

Conclusion

Renewal is possible and can be necessary in the structural as well as behavioral areas. It is the responsibility of the church to consider all creation is God's and they have to be properly cared and take care of. We have to recognize the fact that, in a healthy church, there is a clear focus on Jesus Christ. The Church is a multitude gathered from all nations without any barriers. The fellowship with the so called wicked persons is the need of an hour. Theology must be socio-political and prophetic in nature. The called out community are the channels of sharing the Good news and the torch bearers in the midst of darkness situations.

"For I am the Lord your God; sanctify yourselves therefore, and be holy, for I am holy. You shall not defile yourselves with any swarming creature that moves on the earth. For I am the Lord who brought you up from the land of Egypt, to be your God; you shall be holy, for I am holy." [24] 1 John 3:9 clearly says, "No one born of God commits sin." A person born of God has new wants, new desires and aspirations. God works in our lives to bring us into conformity with God's will. God is the ultimate creator who created us to be creative.

The joy of the Gospel is for all people:
No one can be excluded.
Pope Francis.

Bibliography

Boyd, R. H. S. *Khristadvaita: A Theology for India*. Madras: The Christian Literature Society,   1977.

Das, Somen. "Creeds in a Historical and Contemporary Context." In *The Church and the World: Towards a Biblical - Ethical Understanding*. Edited by Somen Das. Delhi: ISPCK, 2006.

Das, Somen. *Christian Ethics and Indian Ethos*. Delhi: ISPCK, 2004.

Garlington, D. "Resurrection of Christ." *New Dictionary of Theology*. Edited by Sinclair B. Ferguson and David F. Wright. Leicester: Inter-Varsity Press, 1988, 582-585.

Joy, C. I. David. *Hermeneutics: Foundations and New Trends A Post Colonial Reading of John 4*. Delhi: ISPCK, 2012.

Joy, C. I. David. "Jesus' Galilee: A Paradigm for a Reforming Hermeneutics." In *Re-imaging Reformation*. Edited by Y. T. Vinayaraj, Dexter Maben and Woba James. Delhi: ISPCK, 2017.

Lapsley, James N. "Responsibility," *A Dictionary of Christian Ethics*, Edited by John Macquarrie. London: SCM Press, 1967, 296-297.

Maben, Dexter S. "Displaced Discipleship: A Paradigm for Interfaith Engagement." In *Re-imaging Reformation*. Edited by Y. T. Vinayaraj, Dexter Maben, Woba James. Delhi: ISPCK, 2017.

Manoharan, Vincent "Reformation and the Sub-altern Communities: A Dalit Perspective." *Religion and Society* 62/ 1, 2 (March – June 2017): 56-70.

Mcfague, Sallie. *Models of God: Theology for an Ecological, Nuclear age.* London: SCM Press Ltd, 1987.

Melanchthon, Monica Jyotsna. "Dalits, Bible and Method." In *Voices form the Margin: Interpreting the Bible in the Third World.* Edited by R. S. Sugirtharajah. New York: Orbis Books, 2016.

Pannenberg, Wolfhart. "The Church and the Eschatological Kingdom." In *Spirit, Faith and Church.* Edited by Wolfhart Pannenberg, Avery Dulles and Carl E. Braaten. Philadelphia: The Westminster Press, ND.

Williams, Rowan. *Resurrection: Interpreting the Easter Gospel.* London: Darton, Longman and Todd Ltd., 2002.

Endnotes

[1] Martin Luther King, Jr. delivered his famous "I Have a Dream" speech on August 28, 1963, at the March on Washington for Jobs and Freedom at the Lincoln Memorial.

[2] 1 Timothy 2:4.

[3] Somen Das, *Christian Ethics and Indian Ethos* (Delhi: ISPCK, 2004), 45.

[4] Sallie Mcfague, *Models of God: Theology for an Ecological, Nuclear age* (London: SCM Press Ltd, 1987), 71-78.

[5] This is an oppressive social order such as the construction of a separate chapel in the same area. Most of the members are from certain subaltern communities and not getting the same space or maximum beneficiaries compared with the urban scenario.

[6] Somen Das, "Creeds in a Historical and Contemporary Context," in *The Church and the World: Towards a Biblical - Ethical Understanding,* edited by Somen Das (Delhi: ISPCK, 2006), 154-155.

[7] C. I. David Joy, *Hermeneutics: Foundations and New Trends A Post colonial Reading of John 4* (Delhi: ISPCK, 2012), 194.

[8] Vincent Manoharan, "Reformation and the Sub-altern Communities: A Dalit Perspective," *Religion and Society* 62/ 1, 2 (March – June 2017), 64.

[9] Monica Jyotsna Melanchthon, "Dalits, Bible and Method," in *Voices*

form the Margin: Interpreting the Bible in the Third World, edited by R. S. Sugirtharajah (New York: Orbis Books, 2016), 116.

[10] An affirmation of faith from the National Ecumenical Conference on Justice for Dalits, Convened by NCCI in partnership with WCC, New Delhi, 22-24, October 2010.

[11]Wolfhart Pannenberg, "The Church and the Eschatological Kingdom" in *Spirit, Faith and Church,* edited by Wolfhart Pannenberg, Avery Dulles and Carl E. Braaten (Philadelphia: The Westminster Press, ND), 108.

[12] C. I. David Joy, *Hermeneutics: Foundations and New Trends A Post colonial Reading of John 4…,* 202.

[13] D. Garlington, "Resurrection of Christ" in *New Dictionary of Theology* edited by Sinclair B. Ferguson and David F. Wright (Leicester: Inter-Varsity Press, 1988), 582-585.

[14] Rowan Williams, *Resurrection: Interpreting the Easter Gospel* (London: Darton, Longman and Todd Ltd., 2002), 55.

[15] John 16:22

[16] James N. Lapsley, "Responsibility," *A Dictionary of Christian Ethics,* edited by John Macquarrie (London: SCM Press, 1967), 296-297.

[17] 1 John 1:7.

[18] Dexter S. Maben, "Displaced Discipleship: A Paradigm for Interfaith Engagement," in *Re-imaging Reformation,* edited by Y. T. Vinayaraj, Dexter Maben, Woba James (Delhi: ISPCK, 2017), 193.

[19] Psalm 147:3.

[20] Psalm 41: 1-2

[21]Rowan Williams, *Resurrection: Interpreting the Easter Gospel* (London: Darton, Longman and Todd Ltd., 2002), 65.

[22] C. I. David Joy, "Jesus' Galilee: A Paradigm for a Reforming Hermeneutics," in *Re-imaging Reformation,* edited by Y. T. Vinayaraj, Dexter Maben and Woba James (Delhi: ISPCK, 2017) 264.

[23] R. H. S. Boyd, *Khristadvaita: A Theology for India* (Madras: The Christian Literature Society, 1977), 314.

[24] Lev. 11:44-45.

Postcolonial Reading of Nazareth Manifesto: Socio-Political Explosion

JAYASREE

Every Reading has a Purpose even after the Book is Closed

> "The Spirit of the Lord is upon me,
> Because he has anointed me
> to bring good news to the poor.
> He has sent me to proclaim release
> to the captives
> and recovery of sight to the blind,
> to let the oppressed free,
> To proclaim the year of the Lord's favor"

The Gospel of Luke is one of the most fascinating areas of study in the New Testament because of the flexibility of the text for interpretations and its content; this can be seen in the literatures which are published year after year.[1] More than other Gospel writers, Luke is aware about the broader context of Roman/ Judean politics and polis. The Roman imperial presence is known to Luke[2]. Deliberately Luke presents the conflict of Jesus with the religious elites, chief priests and scribes together with the elders in the leadership of Sanhedrin. References to governors and military tribunes (22:66-23:25), centurions (23:47) and soldiers (22:63ff) are representing direct presence of the Romans (23:50-53) and the power structure in the colony. The temple treasury was controls by the priestly aristocracy.

Jewish tetrarchs and client kings are dependent on the support of the Romans and the 'native' colonizers were the religious elite like chief priest, priests (Lk 22: 50, 55), officers of the temple, temple guardians (22:52), soldiers who controlled the temple cult of Jerusalem and their hybridity with the Herodians and Romans governors exhibit the power struggle between the colonizers and the colony. Luke seems careful in presenting the Roman officials, there by Rome, in good light against whom neither Christians indulge in anti-imperial activities nor the official played any significant role in placing Jesus in the Cross, an imperial punishment, or any such activities against his disciples. But throughout the Gospel, the subversive voice of the marginals of the colonized is heard.

Gospel of Luke and the Postcolonial Reading

Luke has been "interpreted with passionate persuasiveness both as radically subversive and as skillfully accommodationist in relation to the forces of imperialism and colonialism."[3] The framework of the Gospel includes political and economic context and also the ideological position within the framework of empire and resistance. It is adequately important to analyze the economic and cultural effects of Roman imperialism on subjugated people, like that of Luke and Lukan community and the collusion of imperialism with colonialism in the case of the Roman Empire which is a relevant postcolonial critique of the empire.[4] As per Sugirtharajah, "Postcolonial criticism opens up potential areas for biblical studies to work in tandem with other disciplines".[5] Therefore, the socio-political readings also incorporated into it. As a text, the Gospel of Luke is a postcolonial literature on the basis of its perplexing ambiguities and ambivalences.[6] Ambivalence toward the cultural authority of the colonizer is a condition as well as the sources of its critical and critically transforming power. The work of subaltern reading in its larger frame of liberation theology is a noble achievement, as it stages campaigns against poverty and socio-political injustices. Postcolonial theory builds on these campaigns to enlarge the scope of justice and freedom, whereby the marginal persons recover their dignity. A postcolonial reading of the Bible is a war against sin: colonialism, neocolonialism, dictatorship, corruption and social injustices in every aspect of society, regardless of their agent. The exchange of power between margin and center and periphery and focus such as rich and poor, men and women, urban and rural, Jew and Gentile, religion and politics, under the imperial rule universalized (cf. Acts 1:8) and transcultural (Acts 2: 5-13) social location and the moderate but modified social others and ethic strangers provides ample opportunities for a thoroughgoing postcolonial analysis of the Gospel of Luke.[7]

Colonization generally refers to the process that is perpetuated after the initial control over Indigenous peoples is achieved through invasion and conquest by any imperial power through injustice. Perpetuating colonization allows the colonizers to maintain or expand their social, political, and economic power by subjugating vassals. It is detrimental because the power comes at the expense of Indigenous lands, resources, lives, and self-determination as well as it affects mind, body and indigenous identity. Not only has colonization resulted in the loss of major rights such as land and self-determination, and the present-day struggles are also a direct consequence of colonization (poverty, family violence, chemical dependency, suicide, health deterioration). Colonization is an all-encompassing presence in our lives. Therefore, Postcolonialism is a determination to decolonize, self and other and leading into liberation and to freedom, thus, to transform. At the risk of oversimplification, a postcolonial interpretation concerns with how the center is established at the expense of the other[8] by the philosophical presuppositions, historical excavations and locating and dislocating margin and center. It is an effort that seeks to decenter the center so that there can be either no one fixed center or, more realistically, many centers coexisting simultaneously which is a production of postcolonial hypothesis and reason. Postcolonial Biblical criticism is a critical reading beginning as the mainstream Biblical methodologies by paying attention to the context of the text and going higher to its (text) history, theology, religious, political, cultural world of the text and economics of the colonial milieu out of which the texts emerged and unveils Biblical and modern empires and their impact[9].

The Magna Carta of Jesus: The Nazareth Manifesto

Nazareth Manifesto[10] is a counter-narrative and in conflict with popular spirituality. It is the programmatic presentation of Jesus and a trajectory of the rest of the Gospel. It constructs and presents alternative values, which are in support of the humble and lowly, the marginalized and subaltern. The Nazareth Manifesto[11] unveils an alternative world view of the

Kingdom of God. This worldview creates alternative systems, such as communal sufficiency in shared economic resources, the inclusion of ethnically different groups, the reversal of expectations in eschatology. Content of Nazareth Manifesto that reflects the justice and love of God are contrasted with oppressors, colonialists who intent to secure honor, status and wealth without caring for the well-being of the marginalized, subaltern-'other'. According to Philip F. Esler, there is a response to the social experience of the people within Luke's Gospel[12] which challenges the economic order of the society.

The contrast between the rulers and the humble has a political connotation in (Lk 1: 52= 4:18-19) where it says: he has brought down rulers from their thrones but has lifted up the humble[13] and the prophetic promise is found as release and recovery (4: 18). The rulers here are those who are powerful and oppressing rulers of the people (this rearing leads to 4: 16ff). Here it explicitly refers to the Romans and those like them, who use their power to keep the people of God at bay and whose colonialism has made few rich and sent away large masses hungry (1:53=4:18). They will 'be removed' from their thrones. Here, it literally means "to pull down" or "to tear down" which implies the forceful/ strong action of Yahweh to the oppressive rulers. All the injustices of the ruling class or the rulers against God's people will be reversed as the humble are lifted up by God. This idea of the removal of the rulers (Job 5:11; 1 Sam 2:7; Jdt 9:3) and the exaltation of the humble is expressed in the OT and in Jewish hope and the exaltation of the humble (Ps 147:6; 1 Sam 2:7; Sir 10:14).This kind of political liberation is no less specific and concrete than the great historical act of deliverance in Israel such as exodus event (Ex 15). By bringing this, Luke presents the Messiah who brings the reversal in the political orders of the society.

There are four infinitives used here; to preach good news, to proclaim, to let go free and to proclaim.[14] From the political reversal (1:52='release to the captives' 4:18) the thought moves to socio- economic reversal (1: 53=good news to the poor … let the oppressed free 4: 18) which is one of the important themes from the beginning of the Gospel for our purpose i.e., about the reversal of the rich which says: "He has filled the hungry with good things (which is a good news to the poor) but has sent away the rich empty" comes to the climax in the Nazareth Manifesto. Luke is much concerned of this important issue that has brought stratification in terms of power, prestige, ethnicity, heritage, religious purity etc. in the society.

Messiah the Master Blaster

The Authority of Jesus is expressed as *'The Spirit of the Lord is upon me, Because he has anointed me'*. Luke's frequent indications towards the Holy Spirit are seen in the two volume works. Luke presents Jesus as the anointed (3: 22) son of God and Messiah which leads him to make a political proclamation like a national prophet[15]. God is found not among the colonizers and powerful but desperate poor, the non-elite, and without enough resource for they are in captivity and darkness. It is the reestablishment of justice, a favored time for all not just Pax-Romana. There is a paradigm shift, providing space for the minority (the poor, captives, and blind) and alternative community (which enjoys the Jubilee year) which is literal practice of justice for all. A critique to the privileged community and colonizers as well as indiscriminate establishment of justice to all colonized. The prophetic ministry of deliverance and liberation is messianic in character.[16]

A carpenter's son felt and recognized the need for a manifestation out of the anointment by the power of Yahweh. Jesus could easily be identified with the captives, colonized and subjected other and untouchables as Martin Luther King jr was introduced as a fellow untouchable[17] when he had to address the student community of "untouchables" with a shock of recognizing 'his own identity'. Even in the Nazareth Manifesto, not harmonizing cold comfort of worldly philosophy but in ambivalence,[18] describing the complex attraction and repulsion of the patron-client relationship between colonists and colonized. In such instances, ambivalence is aligned with colonial mimicry. The cultural representation of patron-client, focusing the nature of power Jesus has as an anointed one plays authority to the following proclamation.

Good News to the Poor: Demonetisation

The first century Mediterranean society was made up of two social classes, the rich and poor. The rich or elite in Luke-Acts consists of emperors (Augustus and Tiberius), the Herods, Roman perfects, centurions and the priestly class.[19] The central and local levels of aristocracy constituted less than one percent possessed and controlled vast proportion of the total money and power of the whole population of the Roman Empire. The economy of colonial Palestine was a subsistence one in which the goods were in short supply- 'limited good'. Identification of the socially marginalized are named individually as the orphan, widow, foreigner and slave and collectively as 'the poor'.

The Nazareth Manifesto (Lk 4:18ff) highlights the significance of poor in the Gospel of Luke. The characterization of poor in the Gospel of Luke is motivated and influenced by the social and political constraints experienced by the Lukan community. Luke often adapts Jesus' traditions, which come from a rural setting to suit to the urban socio-economic setting.[20] Those who belonged to the category of the poor are of two groups: those who sought to earn their livelihood such as slaves and laborers and those who lived off subsidy.[21] One may feel that Luke is writing to show that God has a great concern for the poor and the lowly.[22] In the Gospel of Luke,[23] poor are linked with the hungry and weeping (Lk 1: 46f; 6: 20f). They are clearly stated as the prime concern of Jesus in the Gospel of Luke. Jesus proclaims that he is anointed to 'bring good news to the poor' (4:18). Some of the parables in Luke's Gospel are notable for their highly negative attitude to riches (12:16-21; 16:19-31). Luke relates discipleship with embracing poverty[24] (5:11, 28; 9:1-6; 10:1-16). The poor in the Gospel of Luke are the recipients of God's special blessings, because they are poor and needy.[25]

In Palestine, the poor were considered as the humble, whose hope was only in God. In the Hellenistic cities of the Lukan communities, there was social oppression on the part of the rich. Faced with this situation, Jesus preaches not the Stoic renunciation of externals, but God's shocking partnership on the side of those who suffer.[26] The most members of Lukan community belonged to the non-elite class. When one analyses the material of Luke can find that Luke had concern for the marginalized from the beginning of his narrative. "It is reasonable to connect Luke's idealization of the social welfare arrangements in the Early Christian community in Jerusalem with a need in his own congregation for the rich members to help the poor."[27]

Roman imperial power and exploitation is a reality and marginalization and resistance is the attitude. The marginal group is attempting certain form of resistance to the colonizing forces. The Jewish aristocrats and the rich, the promoters of the colonization were in conflict with Jesus and the Gospel is a dualistic discourse targeting the rich and ultimately aimed at the colonizers. The community whom Luke represents might be experiencing a long and extended subordination in the religiously, politically and culturally colonizing imperial power, oppressors and their collaborators and the colonizing ideology. Land was available to be purchase by the rich and it was the loss of small land holder through debt, which resulted in the peasant becoming the new landowner's tenant. There are ample evidences that tenant farmers were subjected to both economic exploitation and physical abuse by landowners and their bailiffs.

In the Greco-Roman society, giving something to someone is not that they must be in need, but based on some pre-existing personal relationship. In response, to give to the poor, the benefactor expected in return either some titles of honor, inscriptions, status or other privileges. Some reciprocity from the person benefited was also expected. The hybridity of poor influences the system of thought placed them as 'other', outcasts/outsider bringing alternative traditions and forcing accommodation. Further, it leads to construction of reality where the colonizer/oppressor in the margin. The ambivalence of social relationship is operated due to the conflict existed in the imperial world. Incorporating this imperial context of conflict is a perpetuation of stereotype for a hopeful program to maintain boundaries with hybridity and ambivalence. The context of the conflict is primarily wealth and poverty. When reading with post colonialist optic, it is central to name the oppressors because colonization of the minds is central to colonialism. It is significant to decolonize the minds of the one who colonized the mind in other words the oppressors or the oppressive regimes and demonetisation[28]. Jesus as the herald of the Good news reverses the popular attitude towards the poor.

Liberation of the Subaltern

The proclamation of Jesus is *He has sent me to proclaim release to the captives and recovery of sight to the blind, to let the oppressed free.* Quoting from Isaiah Luke reserves (61:1 to 58: 6) the word 'heal' for physical cures and adds the words "to set the oppressed free" to emphasize the message of freedom[29] and liberation.[30] Deliverance intended to the crushed, captives, oppressed such as Dalits, tribals, women, children, disabled and poor, displaced and landless people. The proclamation of deliverance and freedom is a powerful tool for the empowerment and liberation even today. A liberated life in Jesus from every subaltern experience is the core of the salvific message Jesus wants to communicate even today through every Christian either individual or community.

Proclamation of liberty is the proclamation of Jubilee. Sending the captives back to their egalitarian society is as God intended for the people of Israel. Providing sight to the blind can mean "the opening of the prison to bound people"[31] or return of sight or opening of eyes. Bound are blind, especially when the captives are in dark dungeons. Those who are alienated from God, bound by the power darkness, which is corruption, exploitation and marginalization at times even religion itself can cause it. It is not manumission but restoration into the equal status of the colonizers.[32] The institutionalization of this liberation is comprehensible only with the jubilee proclamation.

Proclamation and Furtherance of Jubilee

The major theological feature of Jesus' missionary program grows out as constructing new ways of 'release' which includes freedom from bondage including social restrictions.[33]   The audience of Nazareth Manifesto is the subaltern living under the imperial[34] rule reflecting their conflicting perspectives. The text mimics the grand imperial edicts and behavior of the Roman overlords and as well as it is a powerful rejection of their imperial ethos which is a prophetic activity in new directions with new emphasis including geographical[35] and political[36] expansion. The proclamation of liberty to the captives and the acceptable year of the Lord manifest allusion to the proclamation of the year of Jubilee by sound of Trumpet.

In Mesopotamia the year of 'liberty' is proclaimed by raising the golden torch whereas in Israel the proclamation of Jubilee (Lev 25:9) is by blowing of a horn in the Day of Atonement. This serves as an authentic means for the transmission of information to the community. This proclamation was made in order to release the slaves and lands - fields from mortgage and people from enslavement - in consequence of the proclamation of liberty.[37] In the 50th year the Israelites are to make loud music and they must blow trumpets on 10th day of the 7th month which is the Day of Atonement. They must blow the trumpet through all the country (Lev 25:9). This was a year of general release of debts and obligations of bond-wo/men, of lands and possessions which has been sold by families and return to the tribes to which they belonged.

Jubilee is the deliverance from all subjectivity, oppression and poverty, broken, in heart and often in body as well, tied and bound with the chain of physical oppression, marginalization due to caste, class and social standing by the colonizer. It is emancipation from slavery and restoration of lost inheritance. The Jubilee year is a reminder to the community of the need to extend liberation to those who are in bondage of any kind. It declares that the members of the community without freedom deserved the right to experience freedom at some point in their lives.

It is the time for deliverance from physical, moral and economic, imperial, socio-political, military and economic powers. The Roman imperial power was hazardous for people's well being and contrary to God's purpose. Deliverance confronts the destructiveness of Roman order, displays the transformative power of the empire of Jesus and anticipates the final and full establishment of God's purpose for wholeness as the year of the Lord's favor. Jesus proclaims God's imperial work through him by manifesting God's just and liberating purposes for a world saved from imperial power. Jesus' proclamation of deliverance and Jubilee embraces the cosmic, political, societal and individual spheres. It is an exhibition of the manifestation of Jesus in the midst of Roman imperialism.[38]

Jubilee also suggests that human freedom is never to be left to chance or just to the good will of the slave owners. Rather, it was supported by the law which ensured that those who had lost their freedom, or never experienced it, was given a chance to live as free persons. These laws reflect and ensure that every member of the community shared in the benefits produced within the community and that justice was distributed within the community. Derek Tidball opines that the twin ideas 'liberty' and 'return' are focused in this proclamation, and he further maintains that "freedom from labour and freedom from debt were to go hand in hand with restoring broken family ties and repossessing lost family property."[39] Daniel Jones Muthunayagom suggests that "the core and the essence of Jubilee refute the *status quo* of continued oppression and exploitation of people thereby opening up new horizons for just sharing."[40]

Isaiah picturizes the Jubilee year and release of captives and return from Babylonian exile with hope of the messiah which was a pure expectation of political restoration which in fact was the restoration of subaltern Israelites. Jesus applies this messianic language to himself. In Luke's Gospel, the ministry of Jesus is the proclamation of the Jubilee year.[41] It is a breakthrough of the injustice and socio-economic oppression and hopelessness of the common people and for a re-structuring of relations.[42] The picture of the radical teaching of Jesus may be found in the Gospel in which he calls as the sins of economic exploitation and demanding restitution through repentance by bringing a reversal for the community of the Kingdom of God (Lk 14: 33; 16:5-7; 19:8; cf. Lk 3:11). The treatment of the poor and outcast and subaltern becomes their experience of Jubilee. In Luke one could finds the re-distribution of wealth and economic justice as a sign of repentance and integral to salvation.

The phrase of the quotation, "to proclaim the year of the Lord's favour," when understood as a jubilee year, does involve the economic. J. Massynbaerde Ford explains that Jesus may have been inaugurating or proclaiming a jubilee year, in which, according to Jewish law, debts were cancelled, slaves (and prisoners) were released, and people returned to their own land and the land laid follow but the poor were allowed to glean the fields and orchards of the crops or fruits which grew naturally.[43] Among Jesus' contemporaries there were messianic pretenders who used the jubilee year concept and the Isaiah passage, especially the phrase "the day of vengeance of our God," to call their fellow countrymen to fight against the Gentiles for political and religious freedom.[44]

Theological Implications

The Nazareth Manifesto is the challenge to the colonized readers as well as colonizing audience to practice Jubilee 'here and now'. Each follower of this transforming restructuring proclaimer is challenged to proclaim this good news to all, for all are anointed by the Spirit and power of God. The zeal (as Jn 3:17) towards the actualization of Nazareth Manifesto must consume the exploiting power and destructive structure. This anointing must operate to overcome and temptation towards the self stratification, escalation of selfish political power and the energy to subdue any temptation of oppressive system (cf.4:1-12). The readers are sent to proclaim release to the captives in the colony and shed light to those in darkness of corruption, exploitation and oppression. It is an empowerment to let the oppressed of all kind to be free. Ultimately to proclaim Jubilee to every context and in all ages everywhere. Same as the establishment of his mission, the fulfillment of Jubilee is the responsibility of each Christian.

The coming of the kingdom of God brings about a political and social revolution, bringing the ordinary life of mankind in line with the will of God. The revolution described in the Nazareth Manifesto is not simply political but is social as well; for the poor, marginal peasantry thus far exploited to the point that they went hungry themselves in order to render up the tribute and taxation demanded by their local and imperial rulers, now, the Messiah is anointed to bring 'good news to the poor'. A new social order of justice and plenty in hand. The fate of the rich is contrasted with the humble. The rich are going to suffer and crave for food and go hungry because they do not share the food with the hungry now.

There is a call for the church to exercise prophetic ministry for the realization of economic justice. The socio-cultural, political and economic contexts of the early Christianity are closer to Indian context. Exposure to the revolution and globalization have also introduced India to ideologies such as individualism, exploitation, pollution, unemployment, ecological crisis, drug abuse, injustice, moral collapse and corruption. Large groups of people are economically poor and vulnerable with no social security systems and no nets to catch those who fell by the wayside because of sickness, unemployment and exploitation in the Indian society. In India, Dalits[45] are the largest group oppressed in all the aspects of life. They suffer pauperization, indignity and marginalization and they represent all oppressed people of India.[46]

Dalit condition includes destitution and dehumanization, they are degraded, downtrodden, exploited, least educated, subjugated by socio-economic, cultural and political oppression through the history and they are denied individual as well as social identity. In India, economic problems are more than poverty. "There is a system that produces and perpetuates it- a system of exploitation that makes the rich richer and the poor poorer. The present situation is largely the result of inequitable distribution of natural resources, economic wealth and life opportunities."[47]

The announcement of Good News to the poor, captives, oppressed and blind establishes an alternative social system of people without any discrimination of caste, class, gender by which all sphere of life enjoy Jubilee throughout life whereby the binary of center and margin obliterate. Jubilee also suggests that human freedom never to be left to chance or just to the good will of the slave owners. Rather, it was supported by the law which ensured that those who had lost their freedom, or never experienced it, were given a chance to live as free persons. These laws reflect and ensure that every member of the community shared in the benefits produced within the community and that justice was distributed within the community.

Receiving sight is the illumination to view the subjugated condition and oppression of the self and move from darkness to light, darkness to power. Wenham remarks that Jubilee was a time 'to give (the poor) a new start'. Land was returned to those who sold it and those who had been enslaved returned to their families.[48] This verse presents two concepts, 'liberty' and 'return,' which are fundamental to the Jubilee institution. Those who have incurred debts are released and the reuniting of the family on their land in the Jubilee, focuses on the two components of the Jubilee - freedom and restoration.[49]

There is a need for radical transformation of the unjust structures through the revolutionary struggle of the poor and the oppressed.[50] Luke also contributes to the economic struggle on behalf of the poor by proposing that the rich are to be criticized and converted, and by highlighting the conjunction between God, Jesus and the poor. The texts positively affirm the value of riches, appreciating their ability to assist the poor. The Gospel is a radical appeal to the rich readers that demands a clear socio-economic division to place themselves on the side of the poor. In Luke's Gospel Jesus is proclaiming the Jubilee year in the parables.[51] It is a breakthrough of the injustice and socio-economic oppression and hopelessness of the common people and for a re-structuring of relations.[52] In the Gospel of Luke, the picture of the radical teaching of Jesus may be found in which he calls the sins of economic exploitation and demands restitution through repentance by bringing a reversal for the community of the Kingdom of God. "Luke contextualizes Jubilee, presenting a strong prophetic and revolutionary portrait of Jesus' ministry: Jesus announces blessing and good news to the poor, issues warning and even condemnation to the rich and breaks racial and national boundaries."[53]

The kingdom liberates people from the dehumanizing structures of an oppressive poverty which grinds them and the compulsions to possession and power which leads human to oppress one another. This is not to make the poor rich or the rich poor, rather it is to bring a *change of heart*, freedom from the attachment to riches and a *change of structures*, liberation from the oppressive systems. This combination can organize a new community which is the ultimate goal of liberation of the kingdom of God.

Lukan Jesus establishes a new social order which has its ground in 'service' and 'humility'. Both the social and political orders are challenged. Lukan Jesus did not submit to the social practices and also the political pattern of his time. He brings a new order of the society. In this Messiah/kingdom of God, there is no discrimination, disparity, oppression but only egalitarian love is the foundation. He organized a community which is anti-colonial, non- hierarchical. Therefore, the rich are challenged to invite the poor for the banquets, renounce their possessions and give to the poor, show solidarity with the poor, use the resources for the needy and have total trust in God rather than

Mammon (16:13) which in other word, colonial power. The anointing continues by the Spirit of God in every disciple of Jesus to actualize the jubilee in the witness and accomplishment of mission. The target of mission is achieved when jubilee is activated in every context. It is Jubilee – joy of Acquiring liberty, equality and fertility.

Endnotes

[1] François Bovon, *Luke the Theologian: Fifty-Five Years of Research (1950–2005)*, 2nd edition (Waco: Baylor University Press, 2006) provides the most recent definitive and near-exhaustive critical discussion of scholarship on Luke-Acts, from 1950-2005 and covers some seven hundred pages of summaries and assessments on Luke.

[2] The period of the documentation begins with 'in the days of Herod, king of Judaea (Lk.1:5) and the birth of Jesus is places in the time of the first census ordered by Caesar Augustus when Quirinius was governor of Syria (Lk 2: 1-2). The preaching of John the Baptist is 'In the fifteenth year of the reign of Emperor Tiberius, when Pontius Pilate was governor of Judea, and Herod was tetrarch of Galilee, and his brother Philip ruled the region of Ituraea and Trachonitis, and Lysanias ruler of Abilene, during the high-priesthood of Annas and Caiaphas, the word of God came to John son of Zechariah in the wilderness. He went into all the region around the Jordan, proclaiming a baptism of repentance for the forgiveness of sins …' (Lk. 3:1-3). Cf. E.M. Blaiklock, *The Century of the New Testament* (London: Inter Varsity Fellowship, 1962), 11. Cf. R.E. Brown, *An Introduction to the New Testament* (Bangalore: TPI, 2000), 67. Cf. also F.F. Bruce, *New Testament History* (London: Pickering and Inglis, 1982), 4.

[3] Virginia Burrus, "The Gospel of Luke and the Acts of the Apostles", *A Postcolonial Commentary on the New Testament Writings*, edited by Fernando F. Segovia and R. S. Sugirtharajah (A&C Black, 2009), 132.

[4] Cf. Rasiah S. Sugirtharajah, *Postcolonial Criticism and Biblical Interpretation* (Oxford University Press, 2002), 24-28.

[5] Rasiah S. Sugirtharajah, *Postcolonial Criticism and Biblical Interpretation*, 24f.

[6] Virginia Burrus, "The Gospel of Luke and the Acts of the Apostles", 134.

[7] Virginia Burrus, "The Gospel of Luke and the Acts of the Apostles", 133.

[8] In his article, Fernando Segovia provides a comprehensive study on various scholars' different understandings of postcolonialism and its range of applications. Fernando F. Segovia, "Mapping the Postcolonial Optic in Biblical Criticism: Meaning and Scope," in *Postcolonial Biblical Criticism: Interdisciplinary Intersections*, eds. Stephen D. Moore and Fernando F. Segovia (London; New York: T&T Clark International, 2005), 23-78.

[9] R.S. Sugirtharajah, *Exploring Postcolonial Biblical Criticism: History, Method and Practice* (Chichester: Wiley-Blackwell, 2012), 2,3.

[10] Manifesto is *'a written statement of the beliefs, aims and policies of an organization, especially a political party'*. Here the clubbing of two passages are seen (Isa 61:1-2 and 58:6). Omitted Isa 61:1c "to heal the broken hearted" and the "the day of the vengeance of our God". Luke 4:18-19 brings together in modified form verses from the Septuagint (LXX). Cf. Leander E. Keck, *Luke, New Interpreter's Bible 12-Volume Set* (Abingdon: Abingdon Press, 2001), 105.

[11] There are studies which suggest the Gentile mission in the Nazareth Manifesto. Cf. Luke Timothy Johnson, *The Gospel of Luke,* ed. Daniel J. Harrington (Collegeville, Minnesota: The Liturgical Press, 1991), 82. With an anti-Judaic hermeneutic lens and the postcolonial theologies confronts every imperialism, imperialism and supremacism.

[12] Philip F. Esler, "The Socio-Redaction Criticism of the Luke-Acts," *Socio-Scientific Approaches to the New Testament Interpretation* (Edinburgh: T and T Clark, 1999), 124.

[13] It not only refers to the emotional state of a person but also to one's social status and power. This term is used in Hellenistic literatures as "cast down" or "oppressed" and humble, oppressed, poor sick, lame, etc used Biblically. Luke most likely uses this term to show the political oppression of the Jews. R. John Vijararaj, "Human Rights Concerns in the Lukan Infancy Narratives (Luke 1:5-2:52) in *IJT* 46/172 (2004): 1-12.

[14] Leander E. Keck, *Luke,* New Interpreter's Bible, Vol. IX (Abingdon: Abingdon Press, 2001), 105.

[15] Details for prophetical anointing Cf. Joseph A Fitzmyer, *Luke*, The Gospel According to Luke I-IX (London: Yale University Press, 2007), 532.

[16] Frank E. Gaebelein, *Matthew, Mark, Luke,* The Expositor's Bible Commentary: With the New International Version (Michigan: Zondervan, 1997), 867.

[17] Nobel Peace Prize-winning American Civil Rights leader Martin Luther King Jr was accidentally treated to an unforgettable philosophical experience in Thiruvananthapuram on February 22 ,1959. The visit to Kerala 60 years ago provided unique insightful moments for King to strengthen his convictions for the civil rights movement. https://english. manoramaonline.com/lifestyle/news/2019/02/23/martin-luther-kings-tryst-with-truth-in-kerala.html. accessed 11/8/2019.

[18] Like mimicry is a concept developed in psychoanalysis to describe a continual fluctuation between wanting one thing and wanting its opposite. It refers to a simultaneous attraction toward and repulsion from an object, person or action. Homi K. Bhabha, *The Location of Culture* (Routledge, 2012).88. Mimicry is the byproduct of colonial ambivalence.

[19] For details Mary Ann Beavis, "Expecting Nothing in Return: Luke's Picture of the Marginalized" in *Gospel Interpretation: Narrative-Critical & Social-Scientific Approaches,* edited by Jack Dean Kingsbury (Harrisburg, Pa.: Trinity Press International, 1997).

[20] H.J. Cadbury, *The Making of Luke-Acts* (London: ISPCK, 1958), 125. In a number of places Luke had added the word 'city' to proper place names (Lk 4:31; 23:51; 9-19). Villagers made their living through work on the land as tenants, day laborers or servants (17:7-10, 31, 35). There were rich (Lk 7:1-10; 8:3; 23:47) as well as poor (Ch. 1-2, 4:18f) in the Gospel of Luke. Cf also M. V. Abraham, "Good News to the Poor in the Luke's Gospel," *BTF* XIX/1(1987):1ff.

[21] Walter E. Pilgrim, *Good News to the Poor*, 43. Cf also Erick Heen, "Radical Patronage in Lk-Acts," *Currents in Theology and Mission* 33/6 (Dec 2006): 445ff. Concern for poor in the Gospel of Luke has been an interesting area of study. One finds the reversal of fortunes of the rich and the poor (Lk 1:52-53), priority for the poor in Jesus' mission (Lk 4: 18-19), the Kingdom of God belongs to the poor (Lk 6: 20-21), criticism of exploitation of the poor (Lk 21: 1-4). cf. Sam P. Mathew, "The Poor and the Rich in Luke's Gospel," *Religion and Society* 51/2-3 (June-Sep, 2006): 42ff. see also, George M. Soares-Prabu, "Good News

to the Poor, the Social Implications of the Message of Jesus," *Bible Bhashyam* 14/1-2 (Sep, 1978): 202f.

[22] Takatemjen, *The Banquet is Ready: Rich and Poor in the Parables of Luke* (Delhi: ISPCK, 2003), 58.

[23] Jerome H. Neyrey, "Loss of Wealth, Loss of Family and Loss of Honour: The Cultural Context of the Original Makarisms in Q," *Modeling Early Christianity: Socio-Scientific Studies of the New Testament in its Context,* edited by Philip F. Esler (London: Routledge, 1995), 139ff. Cf. also Sam P. Mathew, "The Poor and the Rich in Luke's Gospel," *Religion and Society*: 42-66.

[24] Christopher M. Tuckett, *Luke* (Sheffield: Academic Press, 1996), 95f.

[25] Philip van Linden, *The Gospel of Luke and Acts* (Wilmington: Michael Glazier, 1970), 81.

[26] Eduard Schweitzer, *The Good New According to Luke* (Atlanta: John Knox Press, 1984), 119.

[27] Philip F. Esler, *Community and Gospel in Luke-Acts: The Social and Political Motivations of Lucan Theology*, 186.

[28] Once the good news is experienced as freedom and liberty, the poor attains status equal as the colonizer and the colonial power is ineffective to loot colony when the slaves are demonetisationed.

[29] Takatemjen, "Luke", *South Asia Bible Commentary: A One-Volume Commentary on the Whole Bible*, edited by Brian Wintle (Michigan: Zondervan Academic, 2015), 1342.

[30] Greek words *aphesin* (deliverance) to the captives and *aphesi* (deliverance) to the oppressed, they can render the meanings as *release, forgiveness, loosening, deliverance, redemption and liberation* etc. and it is often translated as *forgiveness* in the Gospel of Luke (cf. 1: 77; 3: 3; 24: 47)

[31] R. C. H. Lenski, *The Interpretation of St. Luke's Gospel 1-11* (Minneapolis: Augsburg Fortress, 1946), 251. The liberation of the oppressed and captives is also an answer to John the Baptist (7:19).

[32] Because the captives may not be subaltern before they were brought as captives but were the brokers of power because they were war captives thus were in political power.

[33] Joel Green, *The Gospel of Luke* (Grand Rapids: Eerdmans Publishing company, 1997), 212.

[34] Imperialism is "the authority assumed by a state over another territory authority expressed in pageantry and symbolism, as well as military power" and colonialism is "the consolidation of imperial power… manifested in the settlement of territory, the exploitation or development of resources and the attempt to govern the indigenous inhabitants of occupied lands". Cf. Elleke Boehmer, *Colonial and Postcolonial Literature* (Oxford: Oxford University Press, 1995), 2.

[35] Expansion of the early Christian communities (Acts 2: 43-47; 8: 1-8; 11:19-26)

[36] The mimicry of imperial power is more obvious since the expansion takes place on a grand territorial scale not just in terms of movements from city to countryside. From a grand style of imperial emissaries Jesus returns to his hometown Nazareth.

[37] Moshe Weinfeld, *Social Justice in Ancient Israel and in the Ancient Near East* (Jerusalem: The Magnes Press, 1995), 157-158.

[38] Israel's traditions offered several paradigms of resistance in negotiating imperial power: armed (1 Maccabees), unarmed (Daniel), strategic accommodation (Jeremiah), alternative community (Qumran), divine intervention (Ben Sirach), eschatological judgment (1 Enoch) and Messianic intervention (2 Baruch, 4 Ezra). Jesus' proclamation is an enactment of creating an alternative community and establishment of new kingdom in the midst of Roman imperial power.

[39] Derek Tidball, *The Message of Leviticus*, The Bible Speaks Today, edited by Alec Motyer (Leicester, England: Inter Varsity press, 2005), 295.

[40] Daniel Jones Muthunayagam, "Globalisation, Debt burden, Debt Slavery: Response from a Biblical Perspective," *Bible Speaks Today: Essay in Honour of Gnana Robinson*, edited by Daniel Jones Muthunayagam (Delhi: ISPCK, 2000), 112.

[41] See, Herman C. Waetjen, "Intimations of the Year of Jubilee in the Parables of the Wicked Tenants and workers in the Vineyard," *The Christian Century* (May 20-27, 1998): 524-531.

[42] John Yoder, *The Politics of Jesus* (Michigan: W. B. Eerdmans, 1972), 36.

[43] J. Massynbaerde Ford, "Reconciliation and Forgiveness in Luke's Gospel," in *Political Issues in Luke-Acts*, Edited By Richard J. Cassidy and Philip J. Scharper (New York: Orbis books, 1983), 82.

[44] William J. Larkin Jr., "Mission in Luke", *Mission in the New Testament: An Evangelical Approach*, Edited By William J. Larkin Jr. Joel F. William (New York: Orbis Books, 1998), 160.

[45] In the words of M. Gnanavaram, Dalit theology is an expression of Christian faith and Christian responsibility for/ by the oppressed classes in their struggle for freedom from oppression by socio-economic and cultural forces in the Indian context. It is also a theology of the people from the margin. Cf. "Dalit Theology' and the Parable of the Good Samaritan," *JSNT* 50 (June, 1993): 63.

[46] Dhyanchand Carr, "Jesus' Identification with Galilee and Dalit Hermeneutic," *CTC Bulletin* 19/3 (Dec, 2003): 1-14.

[47] Sam P. Mathew, "The Poor and the Rich in Luke's Gospel" : 67.

[48] Gordon J. Wenham, *The Book of Leviticus*, New International Commentary on the Old Testament (Grand Rapids, Michigan: W. B. Eerdmans, 1979), 319.

[49] Christopher J. H. Wright, "Leviticus," *New Bible Commentary: 21st Century edition* (Secunderbad, India: OM Books, 2002), 153.

[50] K. C. Abraham, "The Struggle for Peace and Justice as Context for Biblical Interpretation," *Religion and Society* 21 (1974): 50.

[51] See, Herman C. Waetjen, "Intimations of the Year of Jubilee in the Parables of the Wicked Tenants and workers in the Vineyard," *The Christian Century* (May 20-27, 1998): 524-531.

[52] John Yoder, *The Politics of Jesus* (Michigan: W. B. Eerdmans, 1972), 36.

[53] Willard M. Swartley, *Israel's Scripture Traditions and the Synoptic Gospels: Story Shaping Story* (Peabody, MA: Hendrickson, 1994), 78.

Speech at Kannammoola Seminary, Thiruvananthapuram on 13.08.2019, inaugurating the 60th Anniversary commemoration of the visit of Martin Luther King Jr.

M.A. Baby

Respected President, Distinguished Guests, Sisters and Brothers,

I am extremely thankful to the organizers for having given me this opportunity to participate in the celebration of the sixtieth (60th) anniversary of the visit of the legendary leader of the Civil Rights Movement, Martin Luther King Junior to Kerala. I would also like to recall the visit of Martin Luther King III, ten years ago coinciding with the 50th anniversary of his father's visit to this state. I had the rare privilege of accompanying him then to a couple of programmes in VJT Hall and St. Mary's High School Pattom.

The time when we are assembled here to pay tribute to the legendary martyr MLK is very extra ordinary. In USA, the forces which worked behind the assassination of MLK are regrouping on a massive scale as part of the right reactionary and racist mobilization in different parts of the globe. It is well known that MLK was immensely inspired and influenced by Mahathama Gandhi. Strangely, like in MLK's USA, in Mahatmaji's India too, the forces of violence, sectarianism and racial and religious hatred are rearing their venomous hood. In other words, the forces which worked behind the dastardly assassination of these two great leaders of humanity, are trying to establish their hegemony in their respective countries, through unscrupulous means.

There are very important similarities between MLK and Gandhiji other than their commitment to non-violence and the fact that both of them met with violent martyrdom. Mahatmaji was initiated into popular struggle against injustice and racial discrimination, after he encountered an unruly uncivilized and illegal assault at the hands of a pro-apartheid racist ticket examiner while travelling in a train in South Africa near Peter Maris Burg railway station. MLK led Montgomery bus boycott struggle where an African American woman was illtreated on racial grounds while travelling in a bus. The form of nonviolent struggle followed by MLK was on the model of Mahathmaji. For Gandhiji, the inspiration came from Leo Tolstoy. Both MLK and Gandhiji were using their own interpretation of religion and God in their political movement. In their own way both of them believed and claimed that they were for creating a socialist society through nonviolent and democratic norm. Gandhiji supported national liberation struggles and the cause of Palestine. MLK extended his unequivocal solidarity with the liberation struggle of Vietnam and openly opposed US war against Vietnam.

Ideologically MLK was able to understand the exploitative working of the capitalist system better than Gandhiji. While propounding the 'Trusteeship' theory Gandhiji perhaps had an illusion. May be due to his 'innocence' and belief in a few relatively better and sympathetic capitalist supporters, Gandhiji might have had the pious hope that he would be able to persuade them as a class to part with a portion of the profit for the benefit of the whole society. Today in the times of crony capitalism, we are sure, that even Gandhiji would have realized the impracticality of his Trusteeship theory.

MLK said, "capitalism does not permit an even flow of economic resources. With this system, a small privileged few are immensely rich and almost all others are condemned to be poor at some level. That is the way the system works. And since we know that the system will not change the rules, we have to change the system". Here is the major difference between Mahathamaji and MLK.

In his autobiography MLK wrote, "I read Das Kapital and The Communist Manifesto years ago when I was a student in college. And many of the revolutionary movements in the world came into being as a result of what Marx talked about.

The great tragedy is that Christianity failed to see that it had the revolutionary edge. You don't have to go to Karl Marx to learn how to be a revolutionary. I did not get my inspiration from Karl Marx; I got it from a man named Jesus, a Galilean saint who said he was anointed to heal the broken-hearts. He was anointed to deal with the problems of the poor. And that is where we get our inspiration. And we go out in a day when we have a message for the world and we can change this world and we can change this nation". (Page 351, The Auto-Biography, Martin Luther King jr. edited by Clay Born Carson.)

I confess that I got inspiration from both Jesus and Karl Marx. Moreover we gain inspiration from legends of epics like Prometheus and Ekalavya. Budha and Spartacas too inspire us.

It is not just a coincidence that another great martyr of last century from the Western hemisphere, Che Guevara also visited India sixty years ago like MLK. He too was a great fighter against oppression, exploitation and racial discrimination. After having won his struggle in Cuba along with Fidel Castro he could have continued there as the leader of Socialist Cuba. But poverty, misery, destitution, and exploitation of the peoples of Latin American Nations called for his attention and assistance. While leading their liberation struggle in Bolivia, those who later murdered MLK assassinated him on 9th October 1967, almost six months ahead of the Lorraine Motel incident in which MLK was shot dead.

The role of CIA and the Mafia gangs entrusted by them in the assassination of MLK needs no specific elaboration. There were many attempts earlier on his life like that on Mahathmaji, before he was finally assassinated on 30th January 1948.

What is important today when we pay tribute to the memory of MLK is the need for all of us to explore the possibilities of closing the ranks of those who are opposed to the domination of certain neo colonial forces over former colonies of Asia, Africa and Latin America as well as over the dispossessed and marginalized sections of people in every corner of the world. This the exploiters do for maximization of their profits at the expenses of people and nature. How can we build a strong and broad platform of unity in defense of the weak, oppressed and exploited is the question of utmost importance. Those who believe in God or religion and those of us, who have our own world view, have something in common, as MLK had believed: Creating and egalitarian world free from oppression, exploitation and dominance of a few over many. Therefore, we must be able to evolve a strategy of co-operation even when we agree to disagree on a few ideological disputes, real or imaginary.

Today the importance of united or synchronized struggles for social justice quality freedom of expression and human rights are very essential. Fascist forces are gaining varying degrees of acceptability in different social strata. What MLK said once is very relevant today: "Never forget that everything Hitler did in Germany was legal". So, all of us are duty bound to be eternally vigilant as to how freedom and human dignity would be strangulated by the forces of darkness under one pretext or the other and how to resist such nefarious moves.

Mar Chrisostum Valiya Metropolitan and many other religious heads in India and Pope Francis uphold similar views. Absorbing inspiration from the teachings, struggles and sacrifice of MLK, Mahathmaji, Karl Marx and Che Guevara let us resolve to hold hand in hand in the common united movement for the creation of a world free from injustice, inequality and oppression. Let us be clear that our theoretical differences should not interfere with our united struggles and efforts for the toiling people, for their survival, sustenance and future emancipation.

Rich and Poor
in Pauline Understanding

NINAN JACOB

The rich and poor is an important subject in the Bible. Sociological study of the bible highlights the difference between human and his situation. When we read the letter of Paul the New Testament it can be seen that Paul was involved with his social environment, not just his theology. His letters being situational reflect his involvement with the people around him. The letters of Paul reflect the supportive interaction as well the conflicts. This article will look at the Pauline materials as they address wealth and poverty. This paper is trying to explain who are the rich and poor according to Paul in the light of conflicts in Corinth and in the light of collection for the Jerusalem church. This study also tries to find out how Paul handled the gap between rich and poor.

Rich and Poor in New Testament

The Bible has a large vocabulary for describing the poor man and his situation. The meaning of particular words does not always remain the same. It shifts as situation develops and changes. The

New Testament has different words for describing the poor but πoτωχς ισ the most common of them. The πoτωχς is the type of man who has to try to live completely without means and is therefore reduced to begging in order to live alive.[1] The other word for poor is πενες is the poor man who has to struggle hard to keep his head above water. The πoτωχς is the marginal man. It is his fate to have nothing, just as it is the fate of the "penes" πενες to have to live frugally. The πενες is respectable poor man, but the πoτωχς is not.[2] In addition to πoτωχς and πενες, biblical geek has a verity of words to describe the poor and poverty: the lowly, the needy, the insignificant, the weak, the simple, and the oppressed. For the rich, the most important word is πoτωχς which means something like full, much. To be rich is to have an existence which is full of good things where there are no shortages.

Defining the Rich and Poor

Defining who were the rich and poor in the first century is a vital issue. Many now agree that closely related to wealth and poverty in the New Testament period is the issue of social status. Bruce Malina, drawing on the field of cultural anthropology, sees economic distinctions embedded in kinship (family) and political ties. For Malina, the rich are those who can maintain their elite inherited status and honor (the aristocracy), and the poor are unable to maintain their status of any rank, subject to shame. The poor are those who have lost their honor and have fallen through the safety net. They are those also who suffer under the greed of the rich and powerful. Day laborers, the landless and street people are considered poor by the elites because of their precarious social position.[3] The rich are those who are greedy and avaricious and who wield power for their own aggrandizement.[4] According to Malina, in the social world of the New Testament period there existed not so much two classes of rich and poor as two separate societies, the aristocrats and the peasants. The contrast between rich and poor is one of access to and control of the necessities of life, and together they make up two minority poles of society. In Malina's model, the majorities of the population are neither rich nor poor, but are able to maintain their status according to lineage and sustain their lives in a "limited-goods" economy.[5]

Justin Meggitt suggested that the word 'poor' is redolent with a variety of possible meaning and many of these are not strictly 'economic' at all. He, taking the context of first century economy of the Roman Mediterranean put forwarded the definition of the 'poor' by P. Garnsey. Garnsey defines as "The poor are those living at or near subsistence level, whose prime concern is it to obtain the minimum food, shelter, and clothing necessary to sustain life, whose lives are dominated by the struggle for physical survival."[6]

Usage of Rich and Poor by Paul

Paul used the word of rich and poor in his letters in many times. According to Martin Hengel, at least in the genuine letters of Paul, the question of poverty and riches is left entirely on one side. The term 'rich' appears only once on Paul, transferred to the preexistence of Christ and therefore in a social context (2Cor. 8:9), where as in one passage he refers the word 'poor' to himself (2 Cor.6: 10).[7]

But it should agree that with Paul and the New Testament, wealth and poverty are best understood in close relationship to the social groups and social dynamics of the Greco-Roman world. Status distinctions in Paul's time and place were based primarily on family or kinship (birth), legal status, and political connections rather than on wealth.[8] "In terms of power, influence, money, and the perceptions of the time, we can divide the population of the Roman world into two main categories, those with influence and those without it, the 'honorable' and the 'humble,' those who governed and those who were governed, those who had property and those who did not. The upper category was very small, the lower one very large".[9] A general survey of urban social stratification in the Greco-Roman world finds a distinction between the upper and lower classes or strata being drawn, with a variety of dimensions being present in each.

The characteristic of Paul's usage is the theological significance of this word rich, in which it often functions to throw God's mercy into relief. Romans 2:4 speak of 'the rich of the God's kindness and forbearance and patience'. God makes known 'the riches of his glory' in 'the vessels of mercy' (Rom. 9:23). A variation of this usage appears Christologicaly motivated in Philippians 4:19. The idea is straight forwardly Christological in Romans 10:12.[10] . But the absolute use of 'Poor' in Galatians 2:10 does suggest that the term was a self designation of the primitive community in Jerusalem. It is a confession in view of Israel that with the events occurring in and around Jesus God's eschatological work with Israel has commenced.[11]

The Social Status of Paul

Paul was a citizen of Rome and Tarsus. Writing within a generation of Paul's time Dio Chrysostem (40-120 CE) encounters two clauses of citizen at Tarsus. In a broader circle including all those who were admitted to the public assembly of the people and narrow circle which included those who fulfilled at least one of the following two criteria either (1) they had to be enrolled in the register of citizenship by the responsible official or

(2) they had to pay a sum of 500 drachmas. The broader circle included rather poor people. The narrow circle were granted the privilege of full citizenship[12] . Paul was a tent maker and would have work with either leather or linen. In either case he would have belonged to the circle of privileged craftsmen because the processed linen worked with other materials such as leather.

Actually Paul himself had no possessions. During his missionary journey he earned his keep by hard manual labour as a tent maker and he did not ask the communities to look after him but accepted support offered freely with gratitude.[13] But as a Roman citizen, Paul had the privileges and status of the elite of his society. In addition, he was educated by Gamaliel (Acts 22:3). Evidence of his high social status is found in his access to the high priest (Acts 9:1-2) and his occasional exercise of the rights and privileges of his citizenship (Acts 16:37; 22:25)[14]. Yet Paul took on the occupation of an artisan working with his hands, an employment despised by the elite and affluent though not by the Jews. This in part explains why he spoke of having no status (1 Cor. 4:10, 12). As an urban missionary and church worker, Paul spent long hours supporting his unique apostolic vocation as an artisan, plying his trade in the workshop as a tent-maker (1 Thes. 2:9, 1 Cor. 4:12; 2 Cor. 11:27,7). On occasion, it is likely that this placed him near the central marketplace of the city, where he would have spoken of his faith.[15]

The life of an urban artisan was not easy one. Traveling and plying a trade were always exhausting and were frequently painful; consequently he could always summarize his experiences in catalogs of sufferings. Paul's travels, like those of other itinerant artisans and teachers, were often punctuated by delays, difficulties, and dangers. Making tents meant rising before dawn, toiling until sunset with leather, knives, and awls, and accepting the various social stigmas and humiliations that were part of the artisans' lot, not to mention the poverty-being cold, hungry, and poorly clothed.[16] Paul placed his apostolic identity not in the privileges of the powerful to which he was entitled, but in the sacrificial service of Christ. Through his example, Paul showed us the way to be cross-cultural and to build bridges across the economic gap. Given the integrity of his life, Paul was able to teach with authority about contentment (Phil. 4:4, 5, 11; 1 Tim. 6:6-9), stewardship (1 Cor. 10:31), simplicity (1 Cor. 7:30, 31), work (1 Thes. 4:11), costly urban discipleship (Phil. 2:4-8), and to warn against covetous-ness (Eph. 5:3; Col. 3:5) and greed (1 Tim. 6:7).

Wealth and Poverty and the Conflicts in Corinth

The city of Corinth provides a good example of the interrelationship between status, wealth, and poverty in the Christian community. Many in the Corinthian church were of low status, the throw away people of the Greco-Roman world (1:26-31). God chose the lowly as evidence of the treasure of his kingdom. But the social and theological newness of God's reign was not found in the homogeneity of the church, but in how it was composed of a cross-section of urban society.[17] Paul's statement in 1 Corinthians 1:26 is partly made for rhetorical effect but, even so it must have some basis in reality and there must have been many members of the Corinthian church who were slaves or belonged to the common people.[18] Yet it also knows that the church contained some wealthier people. But in the opinion of

Wayne Meeks, the church included not just only the lowly but those of comfortable means such as Crispus, a wealthy ruler of a synagogue (1:14; Acts 18:8), and Gaius, Paul's personal host and host of the whole church, which indicates he was of some financial means (1:14; Romans 16:23). Chloe (1:11), Stephanas (1:16), Fortunatus and Achaicus (16:15) were also likely to be people of financial means and status.[19] Gerd Theissen finds four criteria necessary for establishing who the people of high social status were (1) civil or religious office in the city of Corinth (2) to posees a house (3)to have been of material service to Paul or the church and (4)having the ability to make journey[20]. Given this background, "many of the problems at Corinth can be understood in the light of the fact that people from different social classes still found it difficult to relate to each other even after their conversion to Christianity.

Conflict and Controversies

In 1 Corinthians 1:26-29 Paul try to express the differences in the church. The popular image of Christianity of that time can be seen in this comment. This is a central text in the sociological interpretation of early Christianity.[21] Adolf Deisssmann argued that the adherents of early Christianity were very low social status. His justification for position lay in low level of literary culture which the New Testament displays judged in its contemporary Greek context.[22] The image of the early church as a movement of the poor and deprived has been well established and generally accepted. So even before Paul's ministry there are indications of wealthy and middle class people in the church. With Paul's conversion and ministry, the class basis of early church became even wider. Proponents of the 'New Consensus" have read the text more closely and drawn a radically different inference from it. For the scholars it is important to "distinguish between 'not many' and 'not any'", and consequently we should recognize that at least some amongst the earliest Pauline Christians came from more exalted circle.[23] Deissmann and Kautsky assume that the terms σοφὸς, δυνατὸς, ευγενης are indicative of high social rank. Indeed the terminology allows some of its advocates to locate the individuals amongst the upper class of the Corinthian society. For Andrew Clarke, Paul's use of these significant terms in 1Corinthians 1:26 clearly implies that there were in the congregation some from the ruling class of the society.[24] In the use of the term εὐγενης we can see this apparently the most socially precise of the three words. It was undoubtedly to signify noble birth by the elite of the Graeco Roman world. By itself Paul's word in 1Corinthians1:26 can tell nothing concrete about the social constituency of the congregation he addresses except that a small number were more fortunate than the others. These representatives of the upper classes were a minority within the congregation, but apparently a dominant minority. Paul does not wish to contest the significance of those congregational members from the upper classes but simply object to their consciousness of their own status

Strong and Weak

In 1 Corinthian 4:10 Paul again mentioned the divisions of the society. Here again it can find the same three categories- the wise, the powerful, the esteemed. For Theissen this verse is clear indication of the presence of the upper class and the lower class amongst the Corinthian congregation. According to Theissen these terms have a sociological significance, for Paul contrasts his circumstances with those of the Corinthians in terms bearing indisputable sociological implications. Paul puts himself at the bottom of the scale of social prestige but sees the Corinthians as occupying the top.[25] In 1 Corinthian 4.10 Paul is contrasting the unwelcoming nature of his daily life as an apostle with the Corinthians exalted, in order to highlight the illogicality of their claims, and bring them back to earthly reality.[26] But these representatives of the upper classes were minority and the common and poor people were the majority within the congregation but apparently a dominated majority.

Consumption of Meat Offered to Idols

In 1 Corinthians 8 and 10 Paul raises the issue of consumption of meat offered to idols. The quarrel between "the strong" and "the weak" in the Corinthian congregation is a matter of just such different customs. The weak avoid all meat scarifies to idols since it could never be known with certainly that ritual action had not accompanied the slaughter of the meat. The strong, on the other hand, appeal to their "knowledge": there is only one God; there are no idol and hence "no meat sacrificed to idols."[27]

Members of the lower classes seldom ate meat in their everyday lives. For that they were largely depended on public distribution of meat which was always organized around a ceremonial occasion. The community meals of the collegia were also religious feast. As a result those from the lower classes knew meat almost exclusively as an ingredient in pagan religious celebration and the act of eating meat and worshipping idols must have been much more closely connected for them than for members of the higher strata who were more familiar to consuming meat routinely. For the poor class, meat was something special. Theissen suggested that the conversion to Christianity brought similar difficulties to both Jewish Christian and gentile Christian of the lower classes.[28]

Gerd Theissen has argued that in 8:7-22, the weak are the poor, and the strong are the socially powerful and wealthier members of the Corinthian church. The strong would have been used to meals where meat was served. The poor on the other hand rarely ate meat, and associated its consumption with idolatry.[29] We must consider Paul's own position in this conflict between the strong and the weak. Paul does not consistently champion the enlightened position of the strong, even though he is in basic agreement with it. If we understand his argument it can be seen as a plea for consideration of the lower strata by the higher strata. Paul's recommendation based on love that the higher classes accommodate their behaviour to the lower classes, only mitigate the tension between the two but allows the different customs to continue to exist. Paul's solution to this problem is a compromise.

The "haves" and the "have-nots" in Lord supper

The dispute over the Eucharist in 1Corinthians 11 has belong been interpreted as a clash between poor and rich members of the society. The conflict at the Lord's Supper is revealed in the fact that "it is not the Lords supper that you eat for in eating, each one goes ahead with his own meal" (1Cor.11:20-21). The fact that one group involved in the dispute is referred to as τους μη ἔχοντας (11.22) which means "have notes" and the opponents are the "haves".[30] In 11:17-34, the hosts of the church invited their social equals to a meal, leaving the poor out (11:21). The basic division between the rich and the poor in 1 Corinthians 11:17-34 is between the economic "haves" and the "have-nots," with the rich adding humiliation to the lot of the poor.[31]

Recent socio- historical readings which have examined the incident in the light of Graeco-Roman dining conventions have made this interpretation appear all the more credible. Theissen argued that the dispute was caused by a particular habit of rich, that of serving different guest with different quantity and qualities of food in accordance with their social status. The conflict was a consequence of the divisive practice of a smaller number of wealthy members who followed the custom of their day by eating a private meal in a special group, at the same time as the poor were forced to eat rather less well and rather less comfortably, outside the gathering.

Rich and Poor in Litigation

In 1 Corinthians 6.1-11 Paul addresses the problem of the community's relationship to the outside world in terms of the way in which some Corinthian Christian exploited that to their advantages in the provincial court. It can be argued that the issue of court case should be seen as part of the larger problem of social division in the Corinthian community, i.e., upper status people were taking lower status people to court. The fact that at least some members of the Corinthian church were capable of taking civil action against one another has been interpreted by a number of commentators as incontrovertible evidence that a few Pauline Christians came from the social elite.[32] The language of 1 Cor. 6:1-11 indicates that the offenders were among the 'wise', those of high status. To identify the offenders as upper class rich individuals, special attention was given to: Paul's ironic question about whether anyone was σοφος enough to settle grievances, the meaning of that irony in light of the τοπος on whether the wise will litigate, the function of shame, a category of special interest to upper status people in antiquity and the confirmation of that from historical data on litigation in Graeco –Roman society, where higher status people had an advantage over lower status ones.[33] Reason for identifying the offended as lower as poor and lower status people were found in: the way Paul learned about the problem, showing that the complaint originated from below and Paul's preferred solution, private attribution, calling for upper status people to modify their behaviour when it offended lower status ones.[34]

Bruce J. Malina has shown how honour and shame were crucial values in the first century Mediterranean world. People of higher status postured for honour and avoided shame at all cost. They might have used the courts to defend their honour, but as Melina points out they would not likely attempt that against someone of equal status. [35] In 1 Corinthian 6:1ff it became clear that same members of the church had taken other members to the law courts. Paul criticizes the practice and insights and insists that any issue in dispute should be settled by the Christians internally.

Rich and Poor in Other Pauline Writing

The poor are not just those who have lost honor, but include those who are hungry as a result of famine (Rom. 15:26; Gal. 2:10). In other passages low status is linked with low economic conditions (2 Cor. 11:27; Phil. 2:8; 4:12). Redemption for Paul is holistic, so he sees God concerned for the person in her material need and social context (2 Cor. 8:4, 9:1, 12-13; Rom. 15:25). 1 Timothy 6:3-10, 17-19 summarizes many of Paul's points regarding wealth. It is clear from the way Paul relates the refutation of false doctrine with economic matters that wealth and poverty are not peripheral matters to the gospel.[36] Godliness is not a means to financial prosperity (6:5). Contentment is found in Christ, participation in God's kingdom, and basic provision

(6:6, 8). The Lord is to be glorified through the proper use of possessions (6:17).

Negatively, the pursuit of wealth can be a deadly distraction from (the) faith (6:9, 10), especially when it is at the expense of others (6:7; Eph. 5:3; Col. 3:5). Pride and self-security are two vital warnings. Rather than pursuing possessions through injustice (6:10), the wealthy are to be rich in good deeds and economic sharing toward the poor (6:18; cf. 2 Cor. 8:21). A proper view of wealth and poverty has a present and future dimension (6:19).A more in-depth study of Paul's theology regarding wealth would entail looking at the Pauline vocabulary and phrases of riches, wealth, treasure, possessions, abundance, power, nobility, and pre-eminence.[37]It would look more closely at the relationship between work, which produces wealth, and the accumulation of possessions (cf. Eph. 4:28; 2 Thes. 3:6-15).

Collection for the Poor in Jerusalem

The story of Paul's collection for the poor of Jerusalem is full of dramatic development. As the collection was a constant concern of Paul's from the days of the convention at Jerusalem until his last journey to that city, its story can be viewed truly as a mirror of the apostle's missionary effort as a whole. In the four of the major epistle[38] of the apostle Paul specific reference is made to a collection which he organized among his missionary churches for the relief of the Jerusalem Christian community. The significance of this collection for Paul was clearly more than that of a simple act of charity. These financial arrangements were made to meet a passing need in that the community had to provide relief for its large number of impoverished members and support its leaders.[39] Paul explains that his purpose in Jerusalem regarding funds for the poor is to meet the needs of his sisters and brothers (Acts 11:29-30). Whether the Jerusalem church was poor because of famine or difficulties in managing their resources, Paul took the poor to be those who in some serious manner lacked the basic necessities to sustain life (cf. 1 Tim. 6:8). Sometime the persecution by Jewish authorities may have added the poverty of the church.[40] "To remember" the poor for Paul was not a Thanksgiving food basket program or a general bid for cognitive remembrance, but rather a concrete and ongoing action.[41]

Collection in Galatians

In Galatians 2:10, Paul invites us to understand his apostolic ministry in terms of how he "remember the poor." Paul tells the Galatian readers that in response to the Jerusalem pillars' request to remember the poor, he is already fully engaged in this task, and that it is nothing additional to the exercise of his apostolic office. The offering Paul is collecting is not his attempt to buy neither Jerusalem's acceptance nor an act of subservience to their leadership. Paul explains that his purpose in Jerusalem regarding funds for the poor is to meet the needs of his sisters and brothers (Acts 11:29-30).[42] The importance of Galatians 2:10 for Paul's theology of wealth and poverty is twofold. First, Paul's relief work on behalf of the poor is integral to his apostolic vocation from its initiation, and therefore the formative role it takes in his theology and mission strategy is not surprising. Those most vulnerable to loss of social place and life are near to God's heart, and Paul organizes the church accordingly. Secondly, the collection of Galatians 2 can be understood as a "prototype" collection for the other Pauline collections, as mentioned in 1 Corinthians 16:1-4, 2 Corinthians 8-9, and Romans 15:27-29.[43] (Nickle, 1966).

The Collection in I Corinthians

The short passage in 1 Corinthians (16.1-4) indicates that the collection project had already been introduced to the Corinthians and that in their letter to Paul.[44] In this passage the terminology used here for the collection is interesting. In verse 1 the collection is called λογγια and in verse 3 as χάρις. Surely Paul was not thinking of a "tax" when employing the term λογεία. λογεία in this context means collection of funds.[45] The **No table of figures entries found.** Evidence by χάρις is contrary to λογεία. This meaning is reserved for thanks offering made to God. When Paul speaks of χάρις to bestowed on Jerusalem by Corinth, he does not consider either of the two parties concerned as superior to the others, but rather sees both are equal. The essential point being that the collection is described here as desire for true partnership.[46]

The Collection in II Corinthians

2 Corinthians, in the form which we know it, is probably a collection of parts of several Pauline letters to the Corinthians. Within this group of epistles are comments about the collection which originally belonged to two different letters written with in a short time of each other.[47] In 2 Corinthians Chapter 8 and 9, Paul does not use secular terminology for the fund such as λογγια, but always use χάρις (8:6,7,9) διακονια (9:1,12,13) ἁδροτης (8:20) ἐυλογια (9:5) λειτουργια (9:12) and κοινονια (9:13). These terms suggest two important things about Paul's understanding of the offering. One, that there was no fixed technical terminology for the money itself to the fund for the ecumenical church. Secondly Paul choose such terms not because he saw the fund as an occasion for the grace of God to do its work in particular acts. The offering was in effect, a χηαρισμα.[48]

The Collection in II Rome

In Romans 5:26 Paul raise the issue of poverty. In Romans, Paul wrote of the collection in connection with the intended extension of his missionary activity into Spain by way of the Christian congregation in Rome.[49] From this passage we learn that the collection was intended for the 'poor among the saints' at Jerusalem that the regions of Macedonia and Achaia participated in it. In 5:26 it has been demonstrated that there the economic side of poverty is more directly emphasized than Galatians 2:10. The collection is now meant "for the poor ones among the saints in Jerusalem."[50] In Romans 15:27f speaks of the fund as λετουργια while at the same time it speaks of it as an ὀφείλημα[51] Paul says that the Jerusalem church should share the spiritual goods with the Gentiles. He reveals the sharing as the duty of Christian believers.

Significance of the Collection for the Poor

The collection for the poor in Jerusalem is not only a charitable action. It has a far reaching significance for the relations between Jerusalem and Pauline churches. It is an undisputed fact that the poor, whom Paul undertakes to 'remember', are the poor of the church of Jerusalem. These poor were supported by the gentile churches. The gentile churches are to be brought to recognize their continuity with the church in Jerusalem and through it with Israel and to acknowledge their gratitude. The unifying purpose is inherent in the action as such and has been stressed and underlined by Paul himself.[52] It can see that the significance of the collection is connected with the conception of what the church is. The real significance of the collection is not the money as such for the amount, but the demonstration of unity between Jews and gentiles within the church. The delivery of the collection is no more fulfillment of an assignment but also a proof of value of Paul's work as apostle to the gentiles.

According to Dieter Georgi, as the collection evolved independently on Paul's own mission field it was transformed into a more general paradigm. Expressed in the traditional vocabulary of biblical scholarship and contemporary theology, Paul's concepts and terminology concerning the collection remains "eschatological."[53] Bengt Holmberg cited the words of Karl Holl that this collection is not only an expression of Christian love for needy brethren but also the expression of certain understanding of the church.[54] The "collection" is a demonstration of reconciliation with Jew and Greek in Christ, the same course of action as undertaken by the church of Antioch. A spiritual exchange is responded to by an economic exchange, all rooted in the riches of Christ. The multiple dimension of sharing is captured by some of the words and phrases Paul uses for the collection. It is a collection, a partnership, fellowship sharing. A service, relief work, service priestly religious service, a gift of grace, grace and a blessing. The supports for the Jerusalem church collected from other Christian churches were not primarily on moral grounds but also on theological ground. This reveals its unique salvation. The historical role which Paul gave it is more theological interpretation as an acknowledgement of Jerusalem's actual importance in God's election and salvation history.

Christology of Paul in Wealth and Poverty

Second Corinthians 8:9 brings together the themes of riches and poverty in the person and work of Jesus Christ. "For you know the grace of our Lord Jesus Christ, that though he was rich, yet for your sake he became poor, so that you through his poverty might become rich." Drawing on their personal and corporate experience of God's grace (2 Cor. 8:1), Paul stresses the incarnational aspect of God's mercy. Paul's need to speak to this topic suggests that the church had not implemented his earlier suggestions (e.g. 1 Cor. 11:22, 16:1-4) and that class divisions persisted within the congregation. What are the riches of Christ? John Murray takes them to be the riches of the fullness of divine being (Phil. 2:6,4:19; Rom. 9:23; Eph. 3:8, 16), the riches of divine intertrinitarian relations (1 Cor. 2:10), and the riches of divine possession.

Jesus abandoned his affluence in the incarnation. Christ's poverty in part consisted of his giving up for a time the riches of his heavenly existence. But we cannot miss seeing his poverty as that of being subject to disgrace and humiliation on the cross (Rom 15:3), and his subjection to exploitation. Jesus incarnated himself in a sin-cursed world (Rom 8:3-4; Gal.4.4) and lived among the poor (1 Cor. 1: 26f; 2 Cor. 8:2). It is poverty not unlike the marginalized experience of the Macedonian church (2 Cor. 8:1-2). It is Jesus in his identification with the poor, forming a church: "Not from the world's 'beautiful people' but from the lower classes, the nobodies, God chose those who for the most part would make up his people"[55]. Jesus is the poor one, the servant, the peacemaker who arrives in Jerusalem to bring forth salvation through his death. He is the suffering servant who gave up so much, oppressed and humiliated for his people (Phil. 2:8). Through Christ's poverty, the church receives in exchange abundant and lavish riches of grace (2 Cor. 2:14, 5:18, 9:15), which become the foundational resource for mutual sharing. The church of the cross, the suffering church of the marginalized, becomes rich through the incarnation and its ecclesiastical implications.

The contrast between rich and poor is one of the main features of Pauline letters. Paul mentioned these differences using the terms strong and weak, upper class and lower class and haves and have-nots. The Epistle to the Romans and Corinthians demonstrate the existence of rich and poor in Pauline context. For Paul haves and have-nots constituted together what is called the church. By raising the collection for poor in Jerusalem, it reveals the mutuality of the sharing of gifts and resources which the kingdom demands will move them towards equality. Here for Paul equality is not rigid uniformity—but rather closing the gap between rich and poor in the body of Christ. Through this action Paul tries to tell that the church must show the tremendous sensitivity to how the issues of status, wealth and poverty influenced the way it functions and the people it serves. The community of sharing was part of what it meant to be the servant people of God. Servant hood was to touch both interpersonal relationships and the communal situation, breaking down barriers of status. Unlike the widespread Greco-Roman professional and religious clubs, the church existed not for itself, but for the service of others.

Bibliography

Boerma, Conrad. *The Rich, the Poor and the Bible*. Philadelphia: The Westminster Press, 1979.

Georgi, Dieter. *Remembering the Poor: The History of Paul's Collection for Jerusalem*. Nashville: Abingdon Press, 1992.

Gornik, Mark R. "The Rich and Poor in Pauline Theology." *Urban Mission* Vol. 9, no. 01 (Sep 1991): 15-26.

Hengel, Martin. *Property and Riches in the Early Church*. Philadelphia: Fortress Press, 1974.

Holmberg, Bengt. *Paul and Power-the Structure of Authority in the Primitive Church as Reflected in the Pauline Epistles*. Philadelphia: Fortress Press, 1980.

Keek, Leander E. "The Poor among the Saints in the New Testament." *ZNW* Vol.56 (1965): 100-129.

Malina, Bruce J. *The New Testament World: Insights from Cultural Anthropology.* Louiseville: John Knox Press, 1981.

__________. "Wealth and Poverty in the New Testament and Its World." *Interpretation* XLI, no. 3 (July 1987): 355-368.

Meeks, Wayne A. *The First Urban Christians: The Social World of the Apostle Paul.* New Haven: Yale University Press, 1983.

Meggitt, Justin J. *Paul, Poverty and Survival.* Edinburgh: T & T Clark, 1998.

Merkiein, H. "Πτωχος." In *T D N T*, ed. Horst Balz and Gerhard Schneider, 3. Michigan: William B. Eerdmans, 1994.

__________. Πλουσιος. Edited by Host Balz and Gerhard Schneider. Vol. 3, T D N T. Michigan: William B. Eerdmans, 1994.

Mitchell, Alan C. "Rich and Poor in the Courts of Corinth : Litigiousness and Status in 1corinthians 6:1-11." *New Testament Studies* 39 (1993): 562-586.

Nickle, Keith F. *The Collection: A Study in Paul's Strategy.* London: S C M Press LTD, 1966.

Stambaugh, John and David Balch. *The Social World of the First Christians.* London: SPCK, 1986.

Theissen, Gerd. *The Social Setting of Pauline Christianity.* Philadelphia: Fortress Press, 1982.

__________. "The Strong and Weak in Corinth: A Sociological Analysis of a Theological Quarrel." In *Understanding Paul's Ethics- Twenteth Century Approaches*, ed. Brian S. Rosner. Michigan: William B. Eerdmans Publishing Company, 1995.

__________. "Social Conflict in the Corinthian Community: Further Remarks of J.J. Meggitt,Paul, Poverty and Survival." *J S N T* Vol. 25, no. 3 (March 2003).

Tidball, Derek. *An Introduction to the Sociology of the New Testament.* Exeter: The Paternoster Press, 1983.

Endnotes

[1] Conrad Boerma, *The Rich, the Poor and the Bible* (Philadelphia: The Westminster Press, 1979), 7.

[2] Boerma, *The Rich, the Poor and the Bible*, 8.

[3] Bruce J. Malina, "Wealth and Poverty in the New Testament and Its World," *Interpretation* XLI, no. 3 (July 1987): 354-358.

[4] Malina, "Wealth and Poverty in the New Testament and Its World," 357.

[5] Mark R. Gornik, "The Rich and Poor in Pauline Theology," *Urban Mission* Vol. 9, no. 01 (Sep 1991): 16.

[6] Justin J. Meggitt, *Paul, Poverty and Survival* (Edinburgh: T & T Clark, 1998), 5.

[7] Martin Hengel, *Property and Riches in the Early Church* (Philadelphia: Fortress Press, 1974), 36.

[8] Gornik, "The Rich and Poor in Pauline Theology," 17.

[9] John Stambaugh and David Balch, *The Social World of the First Christians* (London: SPCK, 1986), 110.

[10] H. Merklein, ed., Πλουσιοσ, ed. Host Balz and Gerhard Schneider, T D N T, vol. 3 (Michigan: William B. Eerdmans, 1994), 116.

[11] H. Merkiein, "Πτωχοσ," in *T D N T*, ed. Horst Balz and Gerhard Schneider (Michigan: William B. Eerdmans, 1994).

[12] Gerd Theissen, "Social Conflict in the Corinthian Community: Further Remarks of J.J. Meggitt,Paul, Poverty and Survival," *J S N T* Vol. 25, no. 3 (March 2003): 373.

[13] Hengel, *Property and Riches in the Early Church*, 36.

[14] Derek Tidball, *An Introduction to the Sociology of the New Testament* (Exeter: The Paternoster Press, 1983), 91.

[15] Gornik, "The Rich and Poor in Pauline Theology," 18.

[16] Gornik, "The Rich and Poor in Pauline Theology," 19.

[17] Gornik, "The Rich and Poor in Pauline Theology," 19.

[18] Tidball, *An Introduction to the Sociology of the New Testament*, 98.

[19] Wayne A. Meeks, *The First Urban Christians: The Social World of the Apostle Paul* (New Haven: Yale University Press, 1983), 57-58.

[20] Gerd Theissen, *The Social Setting of Pauline Christianity* (Philadelphia: Fortress Press, 1982), 73-96.

[21] Meggitt, *Paul, Poverty and Survival*, 102.

[22] Tidball, *An Introduction to the Sociology of the New Testament*, 92.

23 Meggitt, *Paul, Poverty and Survival*, 102.

24 Meggitt, *Paul, Poverty and Survival*, 103.

25 Theissen, *The Social Setting of Pauline Christianity*, 72-73.

26 Meggitt, *Paul, Poverty and Survival*, 107.

27 Gerd Theissen, "The Strong and Weak in Corinth: A Sociological Analysis of a Theological Quarrel," in *Understanding Paul's Ethics-Twentieth Century Approaches*, ed. Brian S. Rosner (Michigan: William B. Eerdmans Publishing Company, 1995), 108.

28 Theissen, *The Social Setting of Pauline Christianity*, 128.

29 Theissen, *The Social Setting of Pauline Christianity*, 121-143.

30 Meggitt, *Paul, Poverty and Survival*, 118.

31 Meeks, *The First Urban Christians: The Social World of the Apostle Paul*, 68.

32 Meggitt, *Paul, Poverty and Survival*, 122.

33 Alan C. Mitchell, "Rich and Poor in the Courts of Corinth: Litigiousness and Status in 1 Corinthians 6:1-11," *New Testament Studies* 39 (1993): 572-580.

34 Mitchell, "Rich and Poor in the Courts of Corinth: Litigiousness and Status in 1 Corinthians 6:1-11," 581-584.

35 Bruce J. Malina, *The New Testament World: Insights from Cultural Anthropology* (Louiseville: John Knox Press, 1981), 39.

36 Gornik, "The Rich and Poor in Pauline Theology," 20.

37 Boerma, *The Rich, the Poor and the Bible*, 7.

38 In Romans, 1 and 2 Corinthians, and Galatians.

39 Keith F. Nickle, *The Collection: A Study in Paul's Strategy* (London: S C M Press LTD, 1966), 24.

40 Bengt Holmberg, *Paul and Power-the Structure of Authority in the Primitive Church as Reflected in the Pauline Epistles* (Philadelphia: Fortress Press, 1980), 36.

41 Gornik, "The Rich and Poor in Pauline Theology," 19.

42 Gornik, "The Rich and Poor in Pauline Theology," 21.

43 Nickle, *The Collection: A Study in Paul's Strategy*, 60.

44 Nickle, *The Collection: A Study in Paul's Strategy*, 15.

[45] Dieter Georgi, *Remembering the Poor: The History of Paul's Collection for Jerusalem* (Nashville: Abingdon Press, 1992), 53.

[46] Georgi, *Remembering the Poor: The History of Paul's Collection for Jerusalem*, 54.

[47] Nickle, *The Collection: A Study in Paul's Strategy*, 17.

[48] Leander E. Keek, "The Poor among the Saints in the New Testament," *ZNW* Vol.56 (1965): 128.

[49] Nickle, *The Collection: A Study in Paul's Strategy*, 14.

[50] Georgi, *Remembering the Poor: The History of Paul's Collection from Jerusalem*, 163.

[51] Keek, "The poor among the saints in New Testament," 129.

[52] Holm Berg, "*Paul and power – the structure of authority in the primitive church as reflected in the Pauline epistles*, 37.

[53] Georgi, *Remembering the poor: The history of Paul's collection from Jerusalem*, 158.

[54] Holm Berg, "*Paul and power – the structure of authority in the primitive church as reflected in the Pauline epistles*, 36.

[55] Gornik,   "the rich and poor in Pauline Theology," 22.

The Interfaith Understanding and Subaltern Historiography

M. STEPHEN

This article deals with interfaith understanding in the light of subaltern historiography. Our faith has to be understood and interpreted in the light of the new understanding of history. Our faith has to be expressed in the context of other faiths and in the context of the new awareness of History. Today history, as in the old times, is not a descriptive discipline, but it is a dynamic discipline as we take seriously the history and struggles of the subaltern or the marginated people. As theology has become the people's theology, history has become the people's history.

History and historiography

The attempt here is to explain history and Historiography

a.   Defining History

How we understand history is a serious question. In Marxian analysis, history is the history of struggles. It portrays the struggles of the proletariat or the labour class. In Hegelian dialectics, in history there is conflict of the opposites and that's how development takes place. In Marxian dialectics, in history there is conflict of the labour class and the bourgeoisie class. So, history is an arena of struggles. History is the arena of struggle of have's and have nots.

The social movements are also playing a vital role in history for the emergence of the subaltern. The Dalits, Tribes, the blacks, women, fisher folk, slum-dwellers, transgenders and the poor are struggling in the history to emerge in order to affirm their identity, dignity and rights. We have to read or interpret history from the experience of the people in the grass roots. It is so happened that history is written by the dominant to affirm their dominance and to subjugate the marginalized. The Brahmanical dominance and the class- caste superiority is asserted in the Indian history and it dehumanized the subaltern people. The westerners and colonizers underestimated the life, race and culture of the blacks and the colonized countries and people. History is highly prejudiced as it ignored the contributions of the victimized and subaltern people.

History is written to justify the cruel activities and the victimization by the powerful rather than the concern of empowering the powerless. In the post-modern and post-colonial understanding of history, the 'other' or marginated are significant than the powerful. The prejudiced past histories have legitimized the cruelties against blacks, the Red Indians, Maoris, Amerindians. It also justified the Jewish holocaust in Germany and rest of the Europe.

According to E.H. Carr, "History consists of a corpus of ascertained facts. The facts are available to the historian in documents, inscriptions and so on, like fish on the fish monger's slab. The historian collects them, takes them home, and cooks and serves them in whatever style appeals to him."[1]

In his words, history is concerned of the happening in the past and present. Historical accuracy is very important.[2] The past is also living in the present, says Carr.[3] He continues of state, "the function of the historian is neither to love the past nor to emancipate himself from the past, but to master and understand it as the key to the understanding of the present."[4]

The history is to disclose the meaning of the happenings in objective way without prejudices. According to Romila Thapar, "It is a strange paradox that the historian, who is concerned professionally with the past, plays a crucial role in the future of the society which he studying."[5] In her words, the historians interest lies in trying to understand the emergence and evolution of a society in a historical perspective, where the term society includes every aspect of people's life.'[6]

b.   Historiography

The science of writing history is also very important subject that is discussed today. Writing history from the prospective of the powerless and marginated is very much suggested. According to Romila Thapar," the time has come for us to free ourselves from the necessary polemics of the history writing of the colonial period"[7]. There is a shift in writing history today, from the traditional writings of history. Romila Thapar states, "there is a qualitative change between the traditional writings of history and history as we know it today."[8]It is observed that only from 19th century a scientific, or ordered and systematic study of history began.[9] Majumdar and Srivastav continued to say that "The subject that makes an imaginative reconstruction of the past from the data derived by historical methods is known as historiography."[10]

Historically speaking, the history recorded till the 19th century suffer from certain defects, states Majumdar and Srivastav. They are as follows:

1. Non-critical approach: The authors adopted a non-critical approach and accepted the materials from the available resources without bothering to examine their authenticity. They did not make an effort to separate legends from historical facts.

2. Study of limited area- they covered a very limited area and mainly confined themselves to this study of the Christian church or confined themselves to political history.

3. Religious and moral interpretations – the causes of historical events were interpreted in the light of the religious and moral principles and no effort was made to find out the natural causes.[11]Now there is a critical study of documents which is an influence of renaissance. The source materials are being examined and the forged materials are rejected. Beside the study of political events, religious events, social, economic and literary life of the people are studied.[12]According to Sheik Ali, "history which is a record of unique events in the life of mankind in the stir and vibration of life. It is not only the conserving and understanding of what has happened, but also the completion of what has been going on at present. History in this sense is philosophy in motion. To exist is to change, to change is to mature and to mature is to advance and make progress. History is the barometer to record this progress of mankind."[13]

Sheik Ali, continues, "History is a Greek word which means inquiry, research, exploration, or information. The Greeks were the earliest to define history. It was Dionysius of Halicarnassus, who gave us the idea that history is philosophical teaching by examples. What he meant by this was that history offers us the quintessence of human experience whose study has universal value."[14]According to Sheik Ali, the theory and the methodology of history would be understood better, if we survey how history has been written through the ages.[15] In his words, "historiography is nothing but the history of history. We may say, it is the history of historical thought. It is an independent branch of history in its own rights, although the latest to make its appearance on the scene. It is neither solely political nor social, cultural, moral or literal history, but it is a way of combination of all these into one. It comes under the history of ideas, where the job is not the examination of any particular object but study of the ideas which prompted a historian to adopt a particular line of thought.[16]According to Sheik Ali, historiography is the product of the Greek mind, who made it as powerful a branch of knowledge as literature and philosophy.[17] The Greeks have little interest in their origin, as they concentrated more on their contemporary history than their past. Herodotus, states Sheik Ali, the father of history who gave it narrative form, put it in simple prose, liberated it from the clutches of poetry and made it interesting as romance[18]. There is an interesting comparison between Herodotus and Thucydides. Herodotus was interested in the past. Thucydides is known as checking the sources and analytical in his approach. Herodotus had confined to the question 'what' but Thucydides was interested in 'How' and 'why.'[19]In the words of Sheik Ali, "From rational approach of the Greek and the political treatment of the Romans in the ancient period, we have to pass on to the church and the Arab historiography of the medieval period, which is characterized by the hold of religion on the mind of man. History liberated itself from the hands of Romans; who has reduced it to a descriptive category of political events and personalities; but it is slipped again into a philosophical trend which attempted to explain historical change in terms of transcendental forces"[20]. The Arabs also had a strong sense of history as they offered a new dimension, under the inspiration of religion, in terms of range, interpretation and technique of writing history.[21] Sheik Ali states, "church historiography is entirely different from that of the Greco-Roman period. The Christians, like the Arabs and Jews, had a very strong historical sense which was oriented to the religious needs. It was far from rational and cultural history and its main purpose was to build faith in transcendental forces.[22]

Describing the Roman historiography Rev. K. A Ipe states, "the prestige of Greek as a language of art and learning was so great that the first Roman historiography, even by Romans, was written in Greek, Cato the elder was the first to write Roman history in Latin, and his example inspired others."[23] He continued to say that Sallust developed a brilliant Latin style that combined intellectual reflections with psychological insights. Cicero tried to apply the traditional and moral standards to the events of public life.[24]The Hebrew historiography according to K.A. Ipe, has a comprehensive and accurate historical narrative. It reveals and describes the divine plan. The Christian historiography traces the growth of the churches. Eusebius of Caesarea (C.E 324), the historian of the church included the documentary evidences and combined secular and religious history with moral interpretations[25].

According to Sheik Ali, "Renaissance and reformation inaugurated the era of modern historiography which took the stand that it should be different from medieval historiography which was the product of a lively interest in events and desire to relate them to divine providence. The modern age bought new ideals. History should be secular, non-Partisan, instructive and philosophical"[26]. According to Majumdar and Srivastav, "The renaissance marked a new stage in the development of historiography. The historians in the post-renaissance period emancipated the history and thought from the "other-worldliness" which was a pre-dominant feature of the middle ages."[27]

There are now new trends in historiography. 'New history' is a trend which aims at reconstruction of the history of civilisation in its totality, states Majumdar and Srivastav[28]. They stated that it implies that a writer who intend to work in the field of new history must have basic knowledge of history, anthropogeography, psychology and sociology"[29].

India has its own way and notion of writing history. According to Majumdar and Srivastav, "It is commonly held that before the dawn of the modern age in India did not possess any historiography of any value and the study of Indian history was introduced by the foreigners. This impression seems to be ill founded"[30]. Indians have the consciousness of history and they have their history, biographical notes, chronicles, edicts and religious epics. There are also so much of history and other philosophical elements are found in manuscript form[31]. The Tripitakas of Buddhism provide light on the important emphasises in the life of Buddha. It provides information about India during the time of Buddha, States Majumdar and Srivasta.[32]

Historiography from Subaltern Perspective

History today in written form the perspective from the subaltern people. Their history struggles, aspiration and experiences are considered very much. It so happened that there is prejudice, silence and neglect in writings of history in relation to the subaltern. History was used to be the history of the powerful. The role and contributions of powerless are ignored by the dominant historians.

The post-modernism and post-colonial have given outmost importance to the victimized, powerless, marginated and the other. They gave importance to the contextual realities. The indigeneity, alternate reading and experiential dimensions of people are considered. The orient and their contributions are central to post-colonialism. It also challenges the colonial power and their cruelties against the colonized. The colonizers took pride in their brutality against natives and rejected the values of their identity, culture and nationhood. Sri kumara Guru, the founder of 'Prathyaksha Daivasabha' once lamented that their history is not found in any history books and no one was there to write the history of their race.[33]This is true with several subaltern groups in India and abroad. The western historians and the historians from Indian dominant groups have a dehumanizing attitude towards the subaltern groups. In the social, economic, cultural, religious and political development of a nation, subaltern groups play very vital roles. The deconstruction of history is taking place today as we understand the reality in a new way. History has to be inclusive rather than exclusive as it has to integrate the history and struggles of the subaltern.

India has also pioneered the subaltern historical studies through the volumes 'subaltern studies' (in volumes). The first one was 'subaltern studies I: writing on South Asian History and Society' (1982). Ranajit Guha also had a work 'Elementary aspects of peasant Insurgency in colonial India' (1983). These are well recognised in the east and west.[34] The subaltern historiography has now impacted on theological researches, states George Oommen.[35] The subaltern school starts with criticism of the historiography of Indian nationalism, which according to them has been dominated by colonialist elitism and bourgeois-nationalist elitism', states George Oommen.[36] Both of these are understood and as the products of British rule.

According to George Oommen, "so subalterns historiography also can be perceived as a clear oppositional movement and as a post-colonial research to find the real locatedness of agencies of the change and transformation in the Indian society and to identify politics of the people that are left out in the 'un-historical historiography."[37]The subaltern school in concerned of marginalized masses. They tried to deconstruct history from the subaltern people. According to George Oommen, "So subaltern studies is a kind of an effort to hear people and their voices which were silenced by the dominant discourses, making them to speak in their own language, language of protest, resistance and negation."[38] The subaltern movements are very strong in history which is a sign of their consciousness, identity, rights and protest. It creates a new awareness in the writings of history, giving due importance to their significant contributions.

According to Gayatri Chakravarthy Spivak, "The word of Subaltern studies groups offers a theory of change."[39] According to her, there is a radical confrontation is taking place in relation to histories of domination and exploitation. "The revision or shift" in perspectives in that the agency of change is located in the insurgent or the subaltern, states Spivak.[40] It is important to deconstruct the elite and Bourgeoisie historiographies. The subaltern collective consciousness has to be recognised in writings of history and even in sociology.

According to Ranajit Guha, "Feudal historiography, too, was identified with the ruling culture and situated snugly with in the relations of dominance and sub-ordination specific to feudal society. Dominance without Hegemony and its Historiography."[41] The Hegemony or Dominance are to be questioned in the light of Subaltern Consciousness in the writing of history. History should be written from the perspective and life experience of the silenced and suffering ones.

According to Jose John, "subaltern methodology is the child of Marxist historiography. Marxist historiography has always tried to study history from the bottom. It began to pay attention to the ethnic, religious and cultural factors as Karl Marx believed that the real history was the record of all social life" (Methodological issues of history of Christianity in India with special reference to the historiography of the St. Thomas Christians in the Malabar Coast."[42]He continued to say that 'the subaltern historians tried to produce history from below of a history that is people oriented.'[43] The main task of Subaltern historians, according to him, is as follows:

- To give emphasis on people's movement and their struggles.

- To give meaning and relevance to local histories like oral tradition, myth, legends, etc.,

- To find a central palace to the consciousness and subjectivity of the marginalized ones.

- To recover and restore the history of the subalterns.

- To deconstruct and re-read written history by using new methodology;

- To be the voice of the voiceless; and to make history from history-less people.[44]Subaltern history is the history of the oppressed, neglected and exploited class, caste and gender. As post-colonial history is de-constructive which challenges the dominant and dehumanizing interpretation of the west and east, it is important to deconstruct history from subaltern perspective.

The western historians have created a negative attitude towards the culture of the Indian people, especially the Dalits, the Tribals and the Adivasis without realizing the intrinsic value of them. They are critical without having a creative evaluation. This has been challenged by a post-colonial history. The Brahminic and the other dominant history writings have also de-valued the history, culture and religion of the subaltern people. The culture and religiosity are under-estimated as demonic and uncivilized. Radical responses are formed to these perspectives also.

The historical texts are also reconstructed in the light of subaltern histography. According to V.V Thomas "in order for us to give subjectivity to the subaltern, we must re-read the text and reconstruct history from the perspective of the subaltern. The assumption here is that the historical texts are the products of an agenda, and they're in nothing like a neutral or objective text. Every text therefore in a product of a given time, and as an agenda, it involves in the context of politics and affiliation to circumstance. The subaltern school has produced tools for critical reading of the text in favour of the subaltern even if the sources of the information are almost entirely the creation of the elite."[45]

Reading history from the perspective of the natives or the indigenous people is an important task as the real history lies in the life of experience of the subaltern. The real history lies with the Dalits, Tribes, Adivasis, victimised women the Blacks, the Maoris, Red Indians and Amerindians. It also lies in the poor working class or the proletariat / subaltern. It is important to identify and to recognize the history of the oppressed and the subjugated people.

Subaltern Historiography and Inter-Faith Perspective

The postmodern and the post-colonial theories have influenced the subaltern historiography. The concerns for the 'other' or the marginated (Postmodernism) and the challenge of the imperial attitudes and the perspective and the emphasis on the natives and indigenous and the oppressed people (post-colonialism) are having the serious impact on the subaltern historiography. In both these theories the deconstruction of history, culture and religiosity are found. According to Jose John, "subaltern history is the history of oppressed, the marginalized children of the soil, the working class and the less fortunate who had been silenced by rulers and past historians."[46] He continued to say that contemporary subaltern historians are trying to rewrite and re-read history written in the past because most of them were written for and by the upper caste / class in the society. Their main task is to dismantle elitistic historiography by decoding biases and value judgment in records, testimonies and narratives of the ruling classes.[47]The inter faith perspective in the context of subaltern historiography is a very important issue. In the context of Martin Luther king Jr., he was leading civil right movement based on the Christian principle. At the same time Marcolin X had led the movement from the perspective of Islam. Though there were ideological conflicts on the basis of integration and disintegration, the movements were not in conflict. They worked together for the right of the black people from an inter-religious understanding. Both of them were conscious of their black religiosity and black consciousness. They had an inclusive approach and following parallelism and inclusivism in order to confront the reality and to achieve their goal.

It is very important to note that the exclusivistic attitudes will never do good in order to have a harmonious existence. We are to appreciate what is valuable in other faiths and also respect the people of other faiths, as we live with people of other faiths. Raymond Panikkar has suggested different attitudes like inclusivism, interpretation, parallelism and pluralism in order to enhance the inter-faith understanding.[48]It is quite significant to re-understand religion and religiosity also from the context of subaltern historiography. It is happened that the value of folk religions and traditions which are integral to the Dalits, Tribes, Adivasis and other subaltern groups are not valued, instead they are misconceived. The western and elitistic historiography always underestimate the value of the folk religions. They had a confrontational approach to the subaltern religious traditions. These superior and inferior notions will not uphold an inter-faith understanding. The reference like 'primitive', 'pagan' and 'heathen' to subscribe the subaltern religiosity have to be questioned. There is also an underestimation in referring subaltern religions as 'folk' religions and to overate the value of dominant religions like Hinduism. According to V.V Thomas in India subaltern religion is the religion of the majority of this country although it may not have the so called 'great' tradition that philosophical Hinduism talks about.[49]It is very clear that religion and history are also related and not isolated. History also deals with culture, religion and sociology of the people. History is also religious and cultural history and subaltern historiography cannot exclude the religious traditions and religiosity of the subaltern people. It is very crucial to have an inclusive approach to subaltern religious traditions, which will also facilitate our relationship with them and also to have a harmonious co-existence or pro-existence.

Subaltern historiography may enable us to have inter-faith understanding in the following directions.

- Subaltern historiography is an eye-opener to see the existence and value of different faiths.

- Subaltern historiography provokes us to relate us with even the popular and folk religious traditions without grading small or great.

- Subaltern historiography challenges us to have dialogue with subaltern religious traditions for a meaningful and harmonious existence.

- Life is dialogical is the lesson that subaltern historiography teaches us that we may consider seriously the culture, social setting, religion and history of the marginalized.

- Is also teaches us that it is important to re-read the culture and religious history and text in order to relate with the subaltern people.

- Subaltern historiography tells us that any kind of neglect to the religious traditions of the subalterns should not be promoted that it might negatively affect the inter-faith perspectives.

- It also points that any kinds of arrogance and exclusive views by the dominant religious traditions and cultures can bring harm to dialogical existence.

The Observations in the Light of Martin Luther king's Visit to India

So many books on Martin Luther king Jr., is written but his India visit is missing. It is nothing but a gross neglect from the side of historians. There is observation that Gandhiji Satyagraha or non-resistance has influenced Martin Luther king Jr., but we never know about his visit to India. This year is the 60th year of his visit to India. It is also important to note that he visited a Dalit school in Trivandrum (E.M.S. Nambuthiripad was the chief minister of Kerala at that time) on 22nd February 1959. He was introduced by the headmaster of the school in the following way: "young people I would like to present to you a fellow untouchable from the United State of America." He was shocked by the word 'untouchable' as he realized the fact of discrimination[50]. No historian had seriously looked into the visit of Martin Luther King Jr. The dominant history writers must have deliberately silenced the fact.

King's Indian visit was a response to Nehru's invitation. They started their journey to India on 3rd February 1959 from New York. They reached New Delhi on February 10th 1959 as there was some disturbances on their onward journey. They spent one month in India (till 10th of march 1959, king, his wife and biographer were here in India). He had meeting with Dr. S. Radhakrishnan. He was very much conscious of the Dalit experience in India. The school where he was introduced as an 'untouchable' is Thampanoor (Trivandrum) upper primary school. The record of his Kerala visit is very brief and scanty even in Newspapers.[51] It is interesting to note the Indian historians had not given deserving importance to the visit and speeches of Martin Luther King Jr. There might be some deliberate effort of dominant historians to suppress this significant event.King's wife Coretta Scott king has recorded in her book 'My Life with Martin Luther king Jr.' that 'early in march 1959, Martin and I accompanied by professor Lawrence D. Reddick, flew to India. Our plane was supposed to land in New Delhi, but due to some difficulty we were diverted to Bombay, where we arrived the night of March 9th.[52] *(The dates and place of landing of Martin Luther King Jr and the team are found different in the description in Bhashaposhini by E.K Premkumar and in the autobiography of Corretta king).* They had seen the poverty and homeless situation of the poor in India. In Coretta king's description, it is found that king had discussions with Nehru. When he flew from Bombay to Delhi, in the New Delhi airport he stated that 'to other countries I may go as a tourist, but to India I came as a pilgrim'[53]. The history was sometimes reduced to the history of the dominant that is why the history and struggles and events of the subaltern people are ignored. The records about their life are not projected. Deconstruction of history and writing of history is essential tackle this kind of discrimination.

Inter- faith, Subalterns and Historiography: Implications for a Deconstructive History

The subaltern people and their experiences and struggles are accounted very much in present history. The post-modernism and post-colonialism have given clues to deconstruct the history and historiography. The mass movements have a subaltern emergence as people are coming out from different religious traditions. Talking about indigenous origins of churches in India, quoting David B. Barrett, Thomas Kadankavil has stated that from 1858 to 1975 India had more than 150 Hindu-Christian movements or churches as well as modern Neo-Hindu groups of devotees of Jesus who explicitly acknowledge Jesus and number of more Christian movements.[54] The Pentecostal movement is also indigenous and subaltern in nature. People from different faith come to Pentecostalism seeking for an authentic hope, faith and existence.

In the Dalit mass movements to Christianity, there is break away from Casteism of Hinduism. Their aspirations have found fulfilment in Christianity[55]. The tribes and Adivasis also from different parts of our country had their mass movements to Christianity leaving their own ancestral faith and beliefs. But here in India, in the religiously plural context everyone will have harmonious existence. According to V.V. Thomas, "It is as Indians that Hindus, Muslims, and others participate in the common historical destiny of the land. A deep sense of being participants in a common community that enables men and women of different faith to contribute towards the development of composite culture and a common social ethos. From this understanding, the history of Christianity needs to be interpreted as participatory history of the people of this land and not as an exclusive history of a section of the people of the country."[56]The subaltern historiography has understood faith in wider ecumenical sense as it is important for the dominant religious faiths to recognise the faith of the subaltern people. It is also faiths and inter-faith perspectives that we relate each other without a discriminatory attitude. The subaltern historiography has to integrate the struggles of the subaltern people and their religious consciousness. The historiography today has undergone changes and it has to be continued as it integrates the subaltern people's struggles and it should promote the inter-faith understanding to co-operate and to have peaceful co-existence accepting the identity, dignity and the rights of the subaltern people.

The historiography has to be developed from the subaltern perspective by considering the different faiths in an objective and un-prejudiced manner. It is also important to value the religiosity and religious traditions of the subaltern groups in a positive manner. It is so that the Dalit religion and beliefs are considered as inferior by caste Hindus. This is also true with religion of the tribes and other subaltern people. Abraham Ayrookuzhiel has stated "Dalits Gods, rituals and occupation are considered "low" "inferior" and "unclean" by caste Hindus[57] .There are critical approaches to evaluate a religion of subaltern group but it is also significant to look at their religion in an objective and creative way. Their religious traditions are very tolerant dialogical and very inclusive in nature than confrontational. The subaltern historiography considers their religious history and inter-faith understanding very seriously. Their history cannot isolate their religion and culture from social life. Their religiosity promotes harmony, unity, community and fraternity which are very crucial for inter- faith perspectives.

The Dalits and other subaltern groups are interested in sramanic tradition rather than the Brahminic tradition. The protest against anti-dalit, anti-woman and anti adhivasi stance of the Brahminic religious traditions are found in lokayata, Buddhist and jainist tradition. They are counter cultural in nature.

The subaltern religiosity and values have de-legitimised the oppressive elements in Vedas and epics of Hinduism. The interfaith understanding is critical and creative and not accepting every oppressive element. The subaltern historiography has to have new dimensions in the understanding of history and religious consciousness of subaltern people who are culturally, religiously and socially alienated. This should be found in all historiographical endeavours.

The inter disciplinary aspects are now considered in history writing as every phenomenon in the context are interrelated including culture, religion, economics, social life and politics. Historiography is now becoming inclusive by integrating the caste, class, gender questions. The cultural aspects are also included. In a dynamic and in-depth way life cultural and religious aspects are also to be integrated. The cultural and religious consciousness of people especially the subaltern people is integrated to their life and relationship. Subaltern people have an all-inclusive attitude to other religions which are to be explored to have tolerant attitude to people of other faiths and have a more holistic and liberative subaltern historiography. It will certainly facilitate a harmonious existence in the culturally and religiously plural world.

Endnotes

1 *What is history?* (Harmond's worth: Penguin books, 1983),9.

2 Ibid., 10-11.

3 Ibid., 22.

4 Ibid., 26.

5 *The Past and Prejudice,* (New Delhi: National Book Trust of India, 1975), 1.

6 Ibid., 1.

[7] Ibid., 2

[8] Ibid., 3.

[9] R. K. Majumdar and A. N. Srivastav, *Historiography,* (Delhi: SBD publishers, 2009), 1.

[10] Ibid., 1.

[11] Ibid., 2.

[12] Ibid., 2.

[13] *History its theory and method,* second edition, (Madras: Macmillan India Limited,1996), 3.

[14] Ibid., 3.

[15] Ibid., 179.

[16] Ibid., 179.

[17] Ibid., 181.

[18] Ibid.

[19] Ibid., 185.

[20] Ibid., 198.

[21] Ibid., 198.

[22] Ibid., 200.

[23] *Christian presence from its beginning with the present,* (Kottayam: FIC Publishers, 2009), 11.

[24] Ibid., 11-12.

[25] Ibid., 13.

[26] *History: Its Theory and methods,* 220.

[27] *Historiography,* 107.

[28] Ibid., 120.

[29] Ibid., 120.

[30] Ibid., 293.

[31] Ibid., 290.

[32] Ibid., 295.

[33] P.E Joseph. *Poikail Sree Kumara Guru: Jeevithavum Darasanavum,* (English translation of title is the Life and Vision of Poikail Sree Kumara Guru) Thiruvalla, CSS, 1984 53ff.

[34] George Oommen, "A commentary on Subaltern studies collective: methodological implications for theological research" in *Interweaving methodology and praxis-Exploring disciplinary options in today's world,* (Bangalore: BTESSC/ SATHRI, 2007), 130.

[35] Ibid., 131.

[36] Ibid., 131.

[37] Ibid., 132.

[38] Ibid., 134.

[39] "Subaltern Studies: Deconstructing Historiography" in *Subaltern Studies IV writings on South Asian history and society,* edited by Ranajit Guha, (New Delhi: Ovp, 1994), 330.

[40] Ibid., 330.

[41] *Subaltern Studies IV writings on South Asian history and society,* edited by Ranajit Guha, (New Delhi: Oup, 1994),217.

[42] *Methodological issues in the Theological Research: An Exploration Vol-3.* Edited by P.G George, (Serampore: SATHRI/SSC, n.d.), 125.

[43] Ibid.,126.

[44] Ibid.,126.

[45] Understanding subaltern history: Theoretical tools, (Bangalore: SATHRI/BTESSC, 2006), XV-XVI.

[46] Op.cit., 126.

[47] Op.cit., 126.

[48] The Intra-religious dialogue, (Bangalore: ATC, 1984),20-21.

[49] *Understanding Subaltern history: theoretical tools,* xv.

[50] Bhashaposhini (Malayalam magazine) April 2019, 4.

[51] Ibid., 22-29.

[52] Ibid., 187.

[53] Ibid., 188.

[54] Thomas Kadankavil, *Religion and politics from subaltern perspective,* (Bangalore: Dharmaram publications, 1999), 37. Quoting David B. Barrett, world Christian encyclopaedia, Nairobi, Oxford, 1982.

[55] John C.B. Webster, *The Dalit Christians: A History*, (Delhi: ISPCK, 1992),5.

[56] V.V. Thomas, *Dalit and Tribals Christians of India: issues and challenges,* (Malappuram; Focus India Trust, 2014),67.

[57] "Dalit Theology: A Movement of Counter Culture" in *Indigenous people: Dalits* edited by James Massey, (Delhi: ISPCK, 1994), 254.

The Oral Lore in Luke and in the North East Indian Tribal Context:

An Interpretation through Tribal Biblical 'Reoralizing' Hermeneutics

SUPONGMAYANG LONGKUMER

As a little boy growing up in the small tribal land of Mokokchung in Nagaland, North East India, my understanding of the native land that surrounded me, its history, heritage, and people, were direct products of the oral lore[1] I received from tribal elders. The folktales, songs, fables, myths, and legends that held me in awe as a child, still fascinate me today. However, it is only now I am an adult that I have realized I have never fully grasped the entirety of their meanings. This realization has since developed into a passion for wanting to study in as much depth as possible the tales that held me in awe and wonder as a child. This paper is therefore a product of that passion. However, even after more than two decades of study, I am still finding new questions to ask about the oral lore of my native land. And one question in particular fascinates me: what role does oral lore play when applied to biblical texts and what implications could such a meeting of text and orality have upon the tribal context wherein the oral lore originates? And it is upon this question that this article focuses.

The connection between oral lore and biblical interpretation in tribal settings has therefore provided me with an opportunity to propose a new form of contextual hermeneutics, a 'tribal biblical hermeneutics.' It is the assertion of this paper that this new form of hermeneutics can be used in the place of, or alongside, established hermeneutical tools when seeking to interpret biblical texts in a tribal setting. In addition to this, a 'tribal biblical hermeneutic' not only allows for biblical texts to be read from the perspective, and in light of the context of, tribal peoples (and thus create fresh insights into such texts), but it also allows for the oral lore of the tribal peoples performing the reading to be *reoralized*,[2] as both the biblical text and oral lore are being spoken aloud.

Since it is widely accepted that a vast majority of biblical texts have oral origins,[3] it is both pertinent and relevant to re-read such texts from the perspective of contemporary socio-cultural settings that are also oral in nature. The prominence of oral lore in Indian tribal communities therefore make such settings ideal environments in which to both begin this process of re-reading biblical texts and to establish a new form biblical interpretation. The contextual focus of this paper will therefore be on the tribal setting of Nagaland, and more specifically on the Ao Naga folktale "The Two Orphan Girls and Lijaba." This folktale, along with the contemporary contextual concerns of the tribal peoples, will be used as the contextual lens through the Lucan parable of the rich man and Lazarus (Luke 16:19-31) will be re-read. In order to achieve this, this article will discuss three areas in particular. 1. An explanation of how 'oral lore' has been used and understood within this paper, as well as a detailed examination of why there is a need for tribal biblical hermeneutics; 2. An introduction to the basic principles of using reoralizing tribal lore as a tool for tribal biblical hermeneutics; and finally 3. An interpretation of the Lucan parable of the rich man and Lazarus utilizing a tribal lens to illustrate the approach.

And finally, through the tribal interpretation of Luke 16:19-31, I seek to demonstrate how re-reading biblical texts in this manner can lead to a better understanding of Indian tribal contexts and their historical and contemporary concerns. However, before I move onto the areas outlined above, I would first like to clarify three key terms that have come to play significant roles in this paper, namely 'tribal' and 'reoralizing.' And, in the following section 'oral lore.'

Key Terms

Tribal: I am using the term 'tribal' to refer to the multiple communities that are recognized as 'Scheduled Tribes' by the Constitution of the Indian Republic. Whilst it is widely accepted that India has two tribal belts (the North West belt and the Central Eastern belt), this article does not focus on one specific belt (primarily owing to the vast difference that exists between tribal communities across each belt), but rather it concentrates more specifically on the tribal communities of the most North Eastern region of the Central Eastern belt, namely the region of Nagaland.

I acknowledge that the term 'tribe' or 'tribal' is often problematic and contested (primarily owing to its colonial heritage), it is however a widely accepted and openly used term within contemporary Indian society. In addition to this, it is also the term that tribal peoples use to describe their community, context, history, and heritage. Therefore, as tribal peoples readily and proudly identify as tribal, I will use this term throughout.

Reoralizing: This study seeks to coin the term 'reoralizing' to refer to a process of biblical interpretation that 'revives oral lore.' However, to understand this process in its entirety, it should be seen as both a theoretical process and a pragmatic process, as it is both a concept and a means of developing interpretation. The way in which one understands the term matters just as much as how the process the term represents is utilized, namely how one understands and relates contemporary oral lore to biblical texts.

The Concept and Prospect of Oral Lore

Before I begin describing how oral lore exists, is understood, and functions within Indian tribal communities, I would like to first clarify how I am using the term in this article. Whilst 'oral lore' will be the main term used within this article, I will however use it interchangeably with 'oral tradition,' 'folklore,' and 'oral history.' Whilst I am using these terms interchangeably, I still wish to acknowledge however that I am aware that each term can be used to refer to something specific. For example, 'folklore' is often used to refer to both verbal and non-verbal forms of communication and 'oral history' may be used to refer to a specific qualitative research methodology.

In addition to this, I would also like to emphasize that whilst each different North East Indian tribal community possess its own unique oral lore (as well as its own distinct traditions and customs), Indian tribal oral lore on the whole also consists of a number of shared features and can be considered to have a common purpose. Therefore, whilst oral lore may vary from one tribe to another, tribes share the same core concepts and central meanings, which originate from the wider notion of the nature of tribal communities. Therefore, my focus is on the tribal communities of Nagaland, much of what I write may also be applicable to other Indian tribal communities.

In his volume *The Voice of the Past: Oral History*, Paul Thompson emphasizes that "[a]ll history depends ultimately upon its social purpose . . . Oral history is not necessarily an instrument for change; it depends upon the spirit in which it is used."[4] An understanding of history that emphasizes its social purpose and ability to bring about change given the right set of socio-political circumstances, is particularly pertinent for the tribal regions of North East India, and in particular, the way in which oral lore is understood by these communities. For example, oral lore is understood by these communities as "the sole link between the past and the present"[5] and that the continued oral transmission of a tribe's particular folktales and oral lore is needed to not only ensure that a tribe's values, customs, and traditions are successfully transmitted from one generation to the next, but also that the community's tribal heritage still plays a significant role in determining its future. However, oral lore is more than just a means of recording and retelling history for tribal peoples, it also carries sacred status. Because of this, oral lore is only taught in a 'Morung' – a sacred location within each tribal community reserved solely for the teaching of traditional knowledge. Understanding the sacredness of oral lore is essential in grasping just how important oral lore is to tribal communities. If one fails to appreciate the sacred nature of oral lore, then one cannot hope to ever understand how deeply significant oral lore is to tribal communities.[6] Oral lore should therefore be considered the most important knowledge system of a tribal community as it is the sole means through which a community's history and culture is communicated to each new generation.

Suresh Awasthi describes the nature of oral lore in the following manner:

> Oral narratives being a part of the memory heritage of the community, the audiences also cultivate the same sense of absorption of structures and patterns, and become familiar with the conversations and devices of performance. With such inheritance and sharing of performance culture between the performers and the audience, oral narratives smoothly float as cultural texts and continue to generate a sense of social value and celebration at the time when mass media are manipulating a remote control of our cultural longings and turning us into consumers of entertainment products.[7]

Oral lore can therefore be considered a performance, as there is always a storyteller and listeners. We must always remember that oral lore is not narrated in a vacuum, but that it exists in a physical presence.[8] Hence, Chitrasen Pasayat observes, "[i]t has been found that the most common way of defining folk culture is its mode of communication, i.e., oral tradition."[9]

In the tribal context, oral lore functions as the 'chronicles of human history' as it incorporates a vast array of folktales from different peoples.[10] Oral history is passed on from one generation to another so as to recall previous events and preserve practices in the tribal context. It is more or less a means to connect with the past for the benefit of both the present and the future. Scholars like Temsula Ao and Werner H. Kelber[11] agree that ". . . the oral can never be fully expressed in the written, experience cannot be duplicated into text"[12]; in another sense, "The written version of an oral tale always freezes the message, the form, the style and the language-format."[13] For instance, each tribe and community has its own creation myth, yet each one is equally sacred and is the fundamental part of each tribe's identity.[14]

In recent times however, the importance and value of oral lore (particularly in relation the role oral lore plays in charting the origins and history of a tribe), has been challenged. However, Antony J. Frendo believes that "[h]istorical evidence does not necessarily have to stem from a context where eye-witnesses immediately write down their memoirs or impressions of events; that would be the ideal situation for history writing. But this is not the only possible scenario."[15] There is also the possibility that oral lore that keeps alive historical traditions, religious practices, and cultures of a particular group or community. Therefore, even though there are limitations in dating the origin of ideas or their transformation in the course of time, in deciphering the characters in the stories and understanding the nomenclature utilized or the places mentioned, the underlying values that are carried in the oral lore are not affected or weakened by these doubts and difficulties, and these provide significant meanings to a tribal community.

Oral Lore and Bible

When reading biblical texts in light of and alongside tribal oral lore, it is vital that we consider why we are endeavouring to bring the two into conversation. There must therefore be a purpose to the development of a tribal reoralizing hermeneutic in relation to the Bible. This purpose can therefore act as a directive to the process. There are in fact two purposes that underpin developing a tribal hermeneutic and these are as follows: 1. A tribal reoralizing hermeneutic must have the goal of bringing about social justice; and 2. A tribal reoralizing hermeneutic must value both tribal oral lore and the biblical text equally. These two purposes however require further unpacking.

When locating and applying an oral lore paradigm to biblical texts, Felix Wilfred states that the purpose of such an endeavour should be:

> [to explore] how an encounter of theology with the world for folklore can help to fulfill its (theology's) task. The quest for justice is placed within the overall approach. Interpreting the theological task in relation to the marginalized of our Indian society . . . the change folklore can affect in theological methodology, in the understanding of the Bible, in hermeneutics, in the critical function of theology and in the development of contextual categories.[16]

Secondly, when seeking to bring oral lore and biblical texts into conversation, one must at all times remember that oral lore is a valid and legitimate activity in its own right, with its own autonomy and authority. Therefore, just as it is not the purpose of a reoralizing tribal hermeneutic to distort or undermine the biblical text, it is similarly not the purpose to use the biblical text to distort or undermine oral lore. The intention of bringing the tribal oral lore and the biblical texts into dialogue is therefore to discover more about each. In particular, it is my hope that through this dialogue a greater understanding can not only be gained of both contemporary tribal settings and tribal peoples, but also that we can "learn from the world of experience . . . to meet the challenges in the present"[17] when re-reading biblical texts through a tribal lens. Since religion, theology, biblical studies, and oral lore all function according to experience and within relational frameworks, a tribal reoralizing hermeneutic requires respect for both text and context in all settings since both rely on experience and dialogue. For example, whilst this hermeneutic seeks to place at the fore of the interpretative process the experiences and struggles of contemporary communities (in particular, tribal communities), it does not seek to use the contemporary context of oral lore to undermine by replacement the context in which the biblical traditions arose, nor to undermine the biblical texts themselves, or the contemporary non-tribal and tribal context of Indian Christians. It therefore seeks to be a holistic process that draws upon all aspects of experience.

The Synoptic Gospels in the New Testament (NT), draw on oral traditions, and traces of the oral origin of the narratives, or the transmission of those incidents and interpretations, can be felt through the genres of proverbs, riddles, aphorisms and parables now found in the texts which are common in oral traditions. The oral traditions and genres however are now found fully absorbed in the biblical texts themselves and need to be reconstructed if they are to be recognised and recovered. This is not to gainsay that written texts can 'copy' oral genres in their attempts to give 'invented' sayings an oral authenticity. If the biblical texts themselves have an oral background and the synoptic tradition was transmitted in oral forms this demonstrates the possible folkloric nature of the tradition and its transmission. If the biblical tradition combined oral and written forms, or translated oral forms into written ones, and in the process forged folklore genres with emerging 'gospel' genres, tribal readers are thereby provided with something of a platform to incorporate their own folklore with biblical texts. Indeed, the Synoptic tradition might be seen as emerging from an oral-tribal context itself and may show the reasoning and understanding of 'tribal' communities. Even though there has been enormous interest in the reconstruction of Q ('sayings source') for example in NT scholarship, the majority emphasis of classical hermeneutics has been with exegesis of the transmitted text- a literary rather than oral preoccupation and way of thinking. If our concern is with the oral folklore traditions of tribal groups in North East India, for example, the concerns of classical hermeneutics with the written text become less interesting than a focus on the oral dimensions of those written texts, which might take the tribal reader back to an oral lore phase. It is in the oral lore that contextual interrelationships between cultural, political, economic, psychological, and spiritual interpretations of life and society are worked out.

The process of bringing oral tribal lore into dialogue with biblical texts and traditions, does not depend on only working with texts or experiences that are, so to speak, 'real' in the sense of historical and subject to empirical verification. It is instead the constructive function of such experiences of oral lore and biblical texts that this process seeks to emphasize and the meanings to which such experiences lead. For example, if we consider the fact that the creation accounts in Genesis are widely accepted to be mythological in nature rather than factual, the importance and significance of such texts for many Christians is not thereby undermined. Therefore, just because these accounts are understood and experienced as myths does not mean that they play any less an important role in constructing meaning (as these accounts function for many Christians as the explanation of the origin of life). Similarly, if we consider the Ao Nagas' creation account, we find that it too is considered a myth and consists of an equally allegorical tale (as the Ao Nagas believe that their ancestors emerged out of *Long Terok* (or six stones) in a place called *Chungliyimti*.[18] Just as the Genesis account is a myth (for many Christians and non-Christians) afforded with sacred status by the Christian community, so too is the Ao Nagas' myth also afforded sacred status. Whether both 'events' actually took place as narrated does not matter, since it is the ideology that underlies each myth that concerns each community the most. Both myths can lead to the formation, legitimization, and preservation of identity.

My development of a tribal reoralizing hermeneutic does not seek to negate the importance of more Western hermeneutical tools (such as the various forms of higher criticism), but rather I am arguing that since the world is comprised of innumerably diverse contexts, it may be more appropriate to develop and utilize a more (local) contextual tool for the interpretation of biblical texts (since Western hermeneutical tools are designed for Western contexts), suited to the situation of specific users of scripture: in this case the Ao Nagas. I propose that both Biblical Studies and theology should make greater use of more contextual methods of interpretation. When it comes to interpretation, we should not fall into the trap of believing that it's a 'one size fits all' process. My development of a tribal reoralizing hermeneutic situates itself alongside other already established methods of contextual biblical interpretation, such as contextual exegesis/hermeneutics, Contextual Bible Study, vernacular hermeneutics, and lay person's interpretation. My focus on re-reading biblical texts through the lens of Indian tribal communities' oral lore therefore is a new addition to this rapidly growing field of study.

The Need for a Tribal Biblical Reoralizing Hermeneutic

As I have already noted, each Indian tribal community has its own unique customs and traditions, all of which combine to provide each tribe with its specific identity. This identity is carried in the oral lore and is preserved for each generation as a cultural treasure. However, the relentless march of modernization, globalization, and advances in communication and technology have had a considerable, and widely negative, impact on tribal communities. For example, Luis Macas Ambuludi has observed that whilst "native cultures have endured for millennia and have diverse identities; [and] are different ways of life . . . these cultures are changed into something superficial, simple *folklore*, a tourist attraction . . . they disappear into a homogenized world."[19] Two examples that demonstrate how Indian tribal communities have been affected by the modern world are the changes to the Hornbill Festival[20] and tribal traditional dress. If we first consider the Hornbill Festival, Wati Longchar has observed that:

> Local and indigenous customs, rituals, sacred shrines, places of worship, sacred music, ceremonial dress, traditions, and handiwork are commercialized to take advantage of tourists. Musicians, dancers and other artists perform, exhibit and sell their creativity to earn some income, at the cost of their self-respect.[21]

Similarly, Visakhonu Hibo also remarks that "[t]he annual state hornbill festival is seen by the younger generation as a time when evil manifests its ugly head more prominently as compared to other cultural festivals. The objective of the Government of

Nagaland is to showcase 'Naga' and their culture but that is often abused by many people for momentary gains and also just for the sheer pleasure of enjoyment with evil intentions."[22]

If we then consider traditional tribal dress, we similarly find that the meaning and significance of traditional costumes is being lost, particularly because such items have now become highly commercial. For example, Sangtinuk has observed that:

> Traditional shawls are transformed into neckties, coats, waistcoats and the like. This does not mean that the tribal traditional shawls are no longer existent in their original forms. The Tribal people continue to use their own traditional costumes and ornaments. Rather, it adds beauty to the traditional costumes of the tribals. In this way, the tribal people, rather than being swept away completely by the current trends of modernization/westernization, are coping with it. This is an evidence of a response to cultural erosion from the point of view of culture being dynamic.[23]

Furthermore, Pursowa has observed that "during the olden days, strangers never used traditional dresses and ornaments which did not belong to them. But today, many people (can) use others' traditional dresses comfortably without paying much attention to the original values."[24]

Whilst the advancements of the modern world have led to many individuals having multiple or hybrid identities, for tribal communities this could lead to the loss or suppression of the more traditional tribal identity. If the traditional oral lore of tribal communities is not embraced as a valid part of contemporary tribal peoples' identity and taught to each new generation, then what was once considered sacred could soon be forgotten and lost forever. Whilst there are multiple factors and events that have led to this progressive loss of traditional tribal identity, one event in particular that has had (and continues to have) a considerable impact on tribal identity was the arrival of Western missionaries in tribal regions. For example, Sangtinuk argues:

> Having embraced the gospel preached to them by the western missionaries, the tribal Christians (have) developed negative attitude(s) towards their traditional beliefs, practices, cultural values, stories, dances, folk songs, etc. They consider them evil, or at least a preparation for (the) Gospel. So, (today) they stop telling their own stories. Instead they read (the) Bible, organize family prayer, attend worship service, conduct revival camps, and tell Bible stories.[25]

Such attitudes and activities have led to oral lore being forgotten, suppressed, and in many cases, replaced with the Bible. I do not seek to negate the importance of the Bible for tribal Christian peoples, but I do emphasize that the one sacred textual tradition should not negate the other, and that actually traditional practices can be compatible with the Christian faith. This paper therefore argues that tribal and Christian are not mutually exclusive identities, and that tribal peoples can be both tribal and Christian. In fact, if Christianity in tribal settings seeks to suppress tribal traditions then it may in fact become culturally poorer since native folklore consists of a multitude of deep and meaningful values, customs, and experiences (that agree with, reinforce or constructively challenge the values and worldviews of the Bible and Christianity). For example, C.S. Song claims that the "[s]tories of [tribal] people are rich in meaning, going beyond their simple language, their moving scenario, their obvious moral."[26] However, M.M. Thomas has argued that modernization might have had a positive impact on tribal societies, as a reaction to it, since tribal identity has "in part [been] enforced by the dynamic of modernity from the outside ever since the opening of tribal peoples by the British power and Christianity during the last century, and in part it is the result of the tribal leader's own decision to enter modern history and its development process without losing their tribal self-identity." [27]

In addition to the impact that modernization and Christianity have had upon tribal identities, the Indian educational system has also had a devastating impact on the perseveration of tribal oral lore. For example, tribal history and heritage does not feature on any of the curricula in tribal regions. As a result of this, not only are the younger generation denied access to tribal knowledge, but those that wish to educate the next generation in the ways of traditional oral lore are finding themselves pushed to the margins as they are no longer being afforded any space within their community.

In such a context, there is therefore a vital need for a revival of oral lore and for all generations to re-embrace their tribal history, heritage, culture, and identity if tribal traditions and ways of life are to be maintained. Biblical interpretation and theology can play a vital role in this process of revival so long as both the Bible and oral lore are treated with equal respect and afforded equal significance, validity, and authority. Bringing oral lore and biblical texts together as conversation partners would therefore help in Christian tribal peoples negotiate their hybrid identities.

Principles of a Tribal Biblical Reoralizing Hermeneutic

K. Thunzauva and R.L. Hnuni in their joint article "Ethnicity, Identity and Hermeneutics: An Indian Tribal Perspective" assert that "biblical hermeneutics no longer remains the monopoly of

Western scholars; it has local dimensions as well."[28] Similarly, Razouselie Lasetso has argued that "[h]ermeneutical principles need to be developed to enter the scriptures to find ourselves in the various pages of the Bible as we take the Bible as the Word of God and not simply a book to be read."[29] I will now therefore turn to three dimensions that are essential to the development of a tribal biblical reoralizing hermeneutic. These dimensions have both internal (originating from the mind) and external (originating from nature and the rest of humanity) elements. The three dimensions I will now explore are: 1. The thought patterns of tribal peoples; 2. The connection between land and identity for tribal peoples; and 3. The role of collectivity in tribal communities.

The Thought Patterns of Tribal Peoples

Immanuel Kant claimed that "[a]ll our cognition starts with the sense, goes from there to the understanding, and ends with reason."[30] In a tribal setting, a person's senses, understanding, and reasoning are all driven by their belonging to a tribal community. For example, first a person uses their senses to detect that s/he belongs to a tribal community, then s/he begins to understand their positionality as a tribal person by learning about and participating in community activities, and finally, s/he uses reason to explain her/his experiences of belonging. This steady process of cognitive development is how tribal individuals come to recognize their positionality and context as tribal and thus come to have both a collective and individual tribal identity. Identifying as tribal, and the unique way in which tribal individuals and communities think and act therefore plays a distinct role in the way in which tribal peoples read, interpret, and understand biblical texts.

The way in which tribal individuals think and act is first and foremost influenced by their experience of the tribal environment, namely the tribal community in which they were born and raised. One highly influential aspect of community life is the ideology that resides behind (and thus drives) the community's oral lore. This plays a vital role in determining how a person understands and interprets reality, in particular the origins of the earth and humanity and humanity's relationship with both nature and the divine. Abstract concepts, for which an individual may not be able to readily understand, are explained by the shared ideology of the whole community. An individual does not therefore need to seek out knowledge of the universe, but it is instead provided for them by their surrounding community. One such ideology is the way in which tribal peoples perceive the world around them. For example, "the whole cosmos is the sacred space in which the Supreme Being is manifested through natural process and regular intervals. For them [tribals], all of space and all of time could be regarded as the exegesis of the supernatural powers."[31]

As this knowledge is then passed from one generation to the next, a sense of identity then develops and the knowledge develops into tradition. However, active oral repetition and transmission is required in keeping oral lore alive. Therefore, the regular performance of oral lore is needed. Active performance of oral lore therefore provides tribal peoples with a space in which they can live, experience, and enact their tribal identity, ideology, and mind-set. It is within this space, and during this performance that we can also approach biblical texts, so as to ensure that the thought patterns of tribal peoples are drawn upon to interpret meaning.

Land and Identity

First and foremost, oral lore functions as the primary means, the lives of tribal peoples are connected to the divine, nature, and the rest of humanity. Tribal communities therefore have their own ways of relating to the world, including supernatural relations. In a tribal setting, oral lore therefore carries the purpose and meaning of all aspects of one's life. For example, it contains information regarding the origins of one's culture, one's belief system and set of cultural practices, the way in which one should act socially, maintain kinship connections, how individual social status is recognised, and how a community can live in harmony.

Shanbha Hayong asserts that "[t]ribal people have a close attachment with the natural environment around them and that their whole life system and thought pattern is embedded in, and influenced by, nature."[32] Thereby, the mountains and plains, hills and valleys, rivers and lakes, trees and rocks, birds and animals, fish and insects, and earth and air, are all understood by tribal communities to be connected to both the divine and humanity. Yangkahao Vashum similarly asserts that,

> A human being, according to the Tangkhul worldview, is never in isolation. He or she is always part of a community. A human being is always part of the universal community which includes all of creation, the earth itself and also the spirit world. At the same time, the individual belongs to the larger human community. A human being is thus essentially a relational being. A human being is inseparably related to nature and the whole of creation and to his or her fellow beings at the same time.[33]

What Hayong and Vashum so eloquently articulate is the way in which the realities of the environment that surround a tribe become an integral part of the tribal mindset. From my own personal observations I can say that such descriptions of tribal attitudes are highly accurate, as it is a sense of living in community and harmony with the surrounding world that is the nucleus of tribal oral lore, and it is enacted in everyday life. To accurately understand the relationship between land and oral lore in providing an identity for tribals, it is important to note that "[f]or the tribal, the land is not just a source of life, but it is also a symbol of identity and unity."[34] The land is therefore a temple for tribal peoples and is seen as sacred. It functions as the center of their religion. For example, K. Thanzauva states that "[a]ccording to the tribal myths as well as the biblical narrative, the earth is a mother from which human beings came forth. Most of the tribes have myths which say that they were born out of earth."[35] Above all, "land is viewed as a gift from God and therefore it is sacred."[36] This tradition of considering land as sacred has practical implications for tribal communities as it means that land is seen as shared property and belongs to the community as a whole. This therefore strengthens kinship and collective identity. Each member of a tribal community therefore has ownership of the land, which provides them with identity as both an individual and as part of a collective. The tribal connection to land therefore leads to a sense of belongingness. Land is thus life in a tribal context.

However, the deep connection that tribal people have with the land, nature, and the universe does have problematic repercussions for those struggling to negotiate hybrid identities since these latter values are often not understood as the core values of the Abrahamic faiths. For example, Vashum states that when we ask the question "who am I?" those tribal individuals that identify as Christian feel as though they need to choose between their tribal identity and their Christian identity. However, as this paper has already claimed, this need not be the case, as such people can identify as "tribal Christians."[37] Vashum argues that this is not contradictory and that the two identities can live in harmony with one another as the "[t]ribal worldview affirms the integrity of all creation and sacredness of life . . . the inter-relatedness of all creation",[38] thus a tribal worldview can accept the Christian faith.

Collectivity

Tribal societies believe in the existence and practice of a connected community in all aspects of life. Sashikaba Kechutzar explains this connectedness in the following manner: for Naga communities,

> [k]inship is not confined to humans alone but it is also extended to animals, plants and non-living objects through the 'totemic' beliefs or totemism. As it is commonly understood, a totem is an animal, plant, or natural object from which a clan's name is derived, and with which the clan members feel related, and towards which they display religious attitudes. Different families, which need not be related to each other, may share the same clan symbol. The totem unites them in an all-embracing community. People who possess the same totem have responsibility to look after each other as if they were related.[39]

The imparting and practicing of oral lore ensures that the culture of belongingness is well formed in each and every member of a tribal community. Just as A.W. Davis[40] noted ". . . it would be hard to find anywhere else more thoroughly democratic"[41] than in a tribal society (Davis was in fact basing his comments on his observations of Ao-Naga society). Such observations therefore highlight that tribal societies are unique in the way that they function and that they are distinct from all other forms of society. One particularly demonstrative example of the uniquely democratic way in which tribal societies function can be seen in the way in which one Ao-Naga village collectively determines the administration of the 'Putu Menden'[42] (or 'generation seat'), which is a particular important seat of authority. 'Putu Menden' is the system of government used within Ao-Naga villages. It is a divided into five groups that rotate one after the other in every generation (circa every 25-30 years). Senior representative members of each clan are elected as members of this overall governing body and collectively they govern the village. However, it is not just the senior clan members that are responsible for upholding tribal values and traditions. All members of the community in fact share the same responsibility for the application, practice, and preservation of oral lore. Whilst it is the duty of each tribal member to preserve the oral lore, it also widely recognized that oral lore needs to be changed and updated so that it is relevant for each new generation.

As the above example highlights, collectivity, unity, and the notion of a collective consciousness is a central part of tribal society.

Biblical Texts through a Tribal Lens

Michael Frisch emphasizes that "[o]ral history enables us to see history, according to this view, as more or less direct and unmediated experience, rather than as the abstracted and ordered rendering of objective historical intelligence."[43] This unique nature of oral lore therefore allows contemporary communities to connect the past to the present and to derive relevant meaning from ancient events or stories. For example, when a folktale is narrated to a contemporary audience, the listeners will try to connect their present reality rather with the oral lore or history being narrated. It is therefore important that the story being narrated contains some relevance for the contemporary setting, as otherwise those listening will find the process of connecting to and thus interpreting the story difficult. If this is the case, then the meaning of the story is lost. However, as we have already seen, the encroachment of modernization on tribal communities has resulted in a contemporary tribal people becoming detached from their traditional culture, folklores, religious rites and festivals, and social practices. Much of these once deeply prominent aspects of tribal society are therefore being abandoned as they are now unintelligent to many members of tribal communities.[44]

With this in mind, this article therefore modestly attempts to develop a tribal hermeneutic that is not only based upon the tribal worldview, but also seeks to provide a framework for how contemporary tribal peoples can re-engage with their traditional culture without bringing their tribal identity into conflict with either their modern or Christian identity. The development of a tribal biblical reoralizing hermeneutic is therefore of benefit to both the academy and tribal peoples. What follows is therefore a demonstration of how to make use of and apply the tribal context in dialogue with the biblical text through the process of reoralizing. In this instance, the possible oral origins or tendencies in the NT passage are not concentrated upon; rather, an oral folk tale (now accessible in written versions) is brought into dialogue with the NT text, and in the process the oral lore is reoralized and shared meanings between the oral lore and the NT text are brought out.

The Orphan Girls and *Lijaba*: A Tribal Oral Lore

The folktale that I have chosen to use to demonstrate the process of a reoralizing hermeneutic is the Ao-Naga folktale 'The Two Orphan Girls and *Lijaba*.' A version of this folktale can be found in Appendix I. This version has been put together from two sources which re-tell the tale: *The Religion of the Ao Nagas* (1990) and *The Ao-Nagas Oral Tradition* (1999). The nucleus of this story can be summarized as follows:

> There once lived two orphaned sisters that one day met *Lijaba* (who in Ao tradition is the Supreme Being and creator of the universe). *Lijaba* was visiting the village in which the girls lived disguised as an old man, who had sores all over his body and was wearing dirty and torn clothes. *Lijaba* proceeded to visit each door in the village, however he was not welcomed by any of the villagers, with each one giving him a different excuse as to why he could not enter their home. However, the two orphan girls, who lived in the corner of the village, did welcome him. The girls had no food but offered to share their shelter with *Lijaba*. The hospitality offered by the two orphan girls towards the old man led to the two orphans receiving both material blessings and recognition by the rest of the villagers. Following the girls' example, the rest of the villagers endeavoured to be more hospitable.

I will now use this folktale to read the Lucan parable of the Rich man and Lazarus so as to produce a tribal reoralizing reading as an example of the hermeneutic. The parable is found in Luke 16:19-31. I focus in particular on the opening verses, namely, 19-21. An attempt will therefore be made to connect this tribal folktale with the biblical text so as to communicate the significance of oral lore.

Interpreting the Rich Man and Lazarus Parable through a Tribal Biblical Reoralizing Hermeneutic

I will divide my reading into three section: identity, hospitality, and hope. The first section seeks to understand how the issue of identity is negotiated in both the biblical text and folktale. The second section seeks to interrogate the concepts of hospitality and acceptance. And the third and final section will investigate the presence of hope in both stories.

Struggle for an Identity

In both the biblical parable and the tribal folktale an unequal socially divided social setting is depicted. However, in each tale the response the characters have to their society's stratification is different. For example, in the Lucan account, the rich man displays a negative (and according to interpretation, undesirable) attitude towards Lazarus. Since the rich man's name or background is not given in the parable, we can assume that the character functions as a metaphor for any individual who may have more wealth and/or power/authority in comparison to those they interact with in wider society. It could therefore be suggested that it was the intention of the parable's author to prioritize the metaphor, rather than just the issue of wealth or the specifics of the rich man's character.[45] The term '*plousios*' (often translated to mean 'rich'), can also be interpreted to mean 'well to do' or 'wealthy', therefore we could argue that Lazarus may not just have longed for food from the rich man, but also desired the means to live an alternate, and better, life (as anyone belonging to the margins[46] might similarly wish for).

The Lucan parable vividly depicts the earthly struggles that those on the margins regularly suffer. In doing so, the parable challenges the reader to think more deeply and critically about society and the injustices that happen within it every day. The rich man's encounter with Lazarus is therefore a parable that is meant to provoke the moral reasoning of its readers/listeners.

When analyzing the 'poor'[47] characters in Luke-Acts, Patrick E. Spencer asserts the following: "These individuals and groups range from those in need of material benefaction . . . spiritual benefaction . . . who are ethnically unclean . . . [need] physical healing . . . [or who are] social and/or religious deviants."[48] When we consider Lazarus in light of Spencer's analysis, it is immediately clear that Lazarus' poor status functions in accordance with the society in which he lived. Lazarus is placed on the margins of society (something that is demonstrated by the use of the adjective '*ptōchos*', which is used in Lucan narrative to draw attention to the fact that he is more metaphorically poor rather than literally poor). Thus, we can infer than whilst Lazarus is literally poor, he is also culturally poor as those that exist on the margins are culturally isolated and are no longer considered to belong to the same ethnic community of wider society. The parable therefore becomes one of "ethnic culture and minority discourse."[49]

In terms of the tribal setting, the tale of the two orphans also encourages us to consider how society treats diversity. Joseph S. Thong and Phanenmo Kath describe Naga culture as consisting of:

> . . . the inherited behaviours and thoughts of their fore-parents, passed on to the new generation, through oral traditions, and day to day practices and conservative life styles – in the form of customs, traditions, norms, values, beliefs and conventions; acquired through the process of time, change, innovation,

evolution and growth; contact, diffusions, integration, imitation and acculturation.[50]

All of the above also include culturally specific understandings of respect, understanding, recognition, tolerance, and acceptance, which all enhance the unique identity of tribal society. The folktale of the two orphan girls therefore causes the reader/listener to question why the characters are not hospitable when hospitality is such a central part of tribal oral lore. The tale is able to challenge the listener/reader to consider the notion of hospitality through the use of *Lijaba* as a metaphorical representation of the margins of society. *Lijaba* roams in the village requesting hospitality and kindness yet is denied at every turn. This is a reality that those on the margins experience daily. Just as *Lijaba* is rejected and forced to corner of the village (where the orphan girls who have also been rejected reside), so too are contemporary marginalized individuals cast aside and forgotten. They are afforded no space within society and left to scratch a meagre existence on the margins. The power of the hospitality offered by the two orphan girls (and thus the strength of the implication that those reading/listening to the tale should also act hospitality) is emphasized when we find that nature itself has rewarded the two girls (as their harvest was bountiful). It is through hospitality that a bridge is built between each member of society, a bridge that enables a collective identity where all are accepted as valid members of society, rather than forcing those deemed undesirable to the outskirts of community identity.

Whilst it is easy to think of this folktale as little more than a story, it must be remembered that it is much more than this as it is part of tribal oral lore. For example, Birendranath Dutta remarks that,

> [t]he Ao-Naga oral tradition is not a mere form of 'story telling' as opposed to written, recorded version. It is indeed in many ways the source of the people's literature, social customs, religion and history. But at the same time, it is much more than that. It has evolved into a comprehensive and integrated network of indigenous knowledge systems, incorporating art with reality, history with imagination, and the ideal with the practical. In this sense the tradition constitutes for Ao the world of his (*sic*) origin as well as the idiom of his (*sic*) continuance within the world.[51]

When interpreting Luke 16:19-31 through the lens of this tribal folktale we are reminded of the many different marginalized groups and individuals that have existed throughout history and how each group has had to fight to live in harmony with wider society and to share in the established collective identity. Both the biblical text and the tribal oral lore are products of specific societies, each of which comprised of members of different social statuses and different identities. However, whilst both narratives draw upon a similar theme, the fact that each tale originates from a specific culture and has a specific intended reader/listener, reminds us that in order to draw a deep understanding and connection with a narrative it is necessary for the reader/listener to come from the same cultural setting of the narrative itself. For example, if one did not identify as Christian, then it is more difficult to connect with the notion of hospitality that NT texts encourage its readers to adopt. When we read biblical texts through the lens of tribal oral lore, the issues at hand are therefore experienced double, as the reader/listener is both tribal and Christian. In terms of this reading, the tribal Christian reader is therefore doubly encouraged to consider how they practice hospitality. The meaning and relevance of such texts are therefore greatly enhanced the more one connects to them.

Hospitality without Boundaries

The Rich Man and Lazarus parable, in its narrative does not depict a culture where humanity as a whole willingly accepts one another, overlooking social status. The narrative instead depicts a clear boundary between two socio-economic contexts - rich and poor. So as to better understand this narrative, these boundaries require further consideration and unpacking. Within this parable there is the suggestion that such boundaries should be transgressed so that friendship can develop between all peoples, regardless of the diversity of their social status.[52] Verse 20 is particularly important here as '*pulōna*' (used to denote a 'porch' or 'vestibule') is used rather than '*pulē*' (which is used to literally denote a 'larger sort of gate' of a city, palace, or temple' or metaphorically denote power and authority).[53] By using the former instead of the latter, the narrative locates the reader in a smaller, more personal setting and prepares them to read the passage in light of intimate social relations. This more intimate setting is enhanced in verse 21 where the phrase "what fell from the table" is used. Therefore, whilst the wider concern of the passage is about large-scale social-cultural boundaries, we are being led by the author to directly consider the encounter that takes place in the narrative and thus judge the actions of each party. Again, the closeness of the social world we are reading is brought to the fore in verse 23 as we are informed that the rich man recognizes Lazarus, which calls to our attention the fact that they must have already met. By forcing us to pay close attention to the specifics of Lazarus' encounter with the rich man (for example, the fact that they had already met before) we are then invited to not only critique how hospitality has been practiced in this specific encounter, but to critique how hospitality is practiced by the whole of society. We therefore move from the clear and specific boundaries that exist between Lazarus and the rich man, to the larger and more ambiguous boundaries that exist in society as a whole.

Just as "[k]nowledge of the culture that informs the text of Gospel parables is crucial to a full understanding of them",[54] we also need knowledge of tribal cultures so as to understand oral lore. In tribal communities, their culture is defined by its emphasis on sharing and hospitality when the need arises. For example, no individual or family should be made to feel out of place in a tribal society, even in the case of sickness or misfortune. It is the responsibility of every villager to show their concern by offering physical resources, either in the form of helping cultivate food or even providing food. Therefore, when any village member or stranger experiences the need for hospitality or help, the whole village is expected to accept the person in need and offer them whatever assistance they require. For example, when undertaking my own ethnographic research, the following hospitality story was narrated to me by a tribal elder in Ungma (a Naga village): when E.W. Clark (one of first Christian missionaries in India) came to Nagaland, he was invited to stay in the house of one of the village elders (Senayangba Jamir). What makes this significant, is that during this time the Naga people had a great fear of outsiders as a series of raids had recently been conducted on the villages of this region. In addition to this, Clark had also come to the village during *anempong* (a Naga holy day), and during this time it is forbidden for villagers to host strangers in their home. Regardless of this, the villager opened their door for Clark and showed him hospitality. In the case of the folktale, the villagers did not fulfil their duty to be hospitable. They only realized that they should have been hospitable once they saw the orphan girls' harvest – much like the rich man in Lucan narration, who realized he should have been hospitable much later in verse 27.

Hospitality for tribal societies transcends borders as it should be offered both community members and strangers. The presence of *Lijaba* "earth walker"[55] emphasizes this as he appears as a stranger in the village yet seeks out the same degree of hospitality that would be afforded to a village member. By reading the Lucan narrative in light of a tribal oral lore understanding of borderless hospitality, we are encouraged to seek out and practice borderless hospitality in all societies.

Struggle Now, Hope for Tomorrow

The contrasting lives of the rich man and Lazarus as depicted in the Lucan parable could be interpreted as a mirror image of modern life. The details of Lazarus' struggle for survival only form a small part of the narrative as the focus soon shifts to the afterlife. In both the biblical and tribal accounts, both Lazarus and *Lijaba* (dressed as the old man) tackle their struggle for survival one day at a time. For example, both seek the bare essentials of life, such as food and shelter. However, this does not mean that they do not hope for a better life where they no longer have to face this daily struggle.

Both tales therefore remind us that to exist is a continuous struggle, and for those on the margins this struggle is even more difficult. However, this dark cloud contains a silver lining – hope. If we struggle but have hope, our struggles are lessened. If we do not have hope, then we become fixed by our struggles and pushed further to the margins. By reading the Lucan narrative through the lens of this particular tribal folktale, we are reminded that if we maintain a hopeful attitude and inspire hope in others, we will be rewarded both in this world and the next.

This article has been an attempt to demonstrate how a biblical text can be read through the lens of Indian tribal oral lore. The purpose however of reading this particular text through the lens of an Ao-Naga folktale is to highlight how by drawing upon the multiple cultural resources that surround those with hybrid identities, we can better work towards a just society (as demonstrated in this case by a call for hospitality). In addition to this, it has also demonstrated how a tribal biblical reoralizing hermeneutic can not only provide us with a new interpretation of a biblical text, but that it can also revive ailing traditions and customs.

And finally, the tribal reading of Luke 16:19-31 identifies three further issues for consideration: Firstly, that the margins of any given society are continually struggling to attain acceptance as belonging to the same identity as those in the centre; secondly, that hospitality (particularly the form found in the tribal folktale) is the key to the development of a just society that respects, recognizes, and accepts diversity. Being hospitable to both people and nature should therefore become a mutual aspiration of all of humanity; and thirdly, making even the smallest gesture or hospitality provides those in need of it with hope.

Appendix One: The Two Orphan Girls and *Lijaba*
One day *Lijaba*, the spirit whom the Aos believe to be the creator of the earth and also the god of prosperity, came to the village where the two orphans lived. But he was in disguise. He came in the form of an old man, wearing rags, was dirty and had many soars over his body. He went from house to house asking for

food and shelter,[56] but everyone gave their own excuses saying, "Behold we wait for the coming of *Lijaba*," some would say "we are observing *anempong* because a child is born to us today and so we cannot have you here." Again, another person said, "We have genna because of the delivery of a calf by our cow today and we cannot allow you to be our guest." None welcomed him. At the end of the village there were two orphan sisters living in a small hut. They were Yarla and Asatula, daughters of Nokdensanger. *Lijaba* asked Yarla and Asatula for shelter.[57] The girls told him [*Lijaba*] that though they are willing to have him as the guest, they had no food in the house to offer him. But *Lijaba* gladly accepted their hospitality.[58]

After a while, he asked them to heat some water for cooking rice. The elder girl replied, "But we have indeed no rice to cook." *Lijaba* nevertheless told her to boil some water. When the water was being heated, *Lijaba* began to scratch his knee, murmuring something to himself. Eventually a grain of rice was seen in his palm which he put it in the boiling water. The single grain of rice began to expand and eventually became the entire potful, more than enough for the three of them. In the meantime, *Lijaba* produced a small piece of meat by simply scratching his head. When cooked, this also became a potful of delicious meat curry. This was the only full meal for the two sisters in many days, as the harvest of their tiny patch of field was still not ready and they had already exhausted their stock of rice many days ago. They also realized that their guest was no ordinary human being but was surely powerful god.[59]

The following morning, the old man casually looked towards the village fields and asked the two sisters to identify the owners of the fields. They named the owners of each field except theirs because their field was too small to be disclosed to others. But the younger sister disclosed it while the elder sister went to get the comb that had fallen. However, her embarrassment was turned into a great blessing. The old man cursed all the fields that belonged to the villagers and blessed the field of the two orphan girls. He said, "let there be a good harvest". The old man instructed them to cut strings or rope out of their basket when they have enough harvest. Having blessed them, *Lijaba* left them and disappeared out of their sight. The two girls kept the old man's word in their heart. The harvest time came. The field belonging to the harvest time came. The field belonging to the two girls had a good harvest whereas others did not. Yarla and Asatula had rich and abundant harvest that they had no place to store their grains. Then, as instructed by the old man, they cut their basket-strings and to their surprise the harvest was complete. When the villagers came to know what had happened to their harvest, they realized that the old man who visited them was none other than *Lijaba* and wished they had accepted him at first.[60]

Bibliography

Aier, Anungla and Tiatoshi Jamir. "Re-interpreting the Myth of Longterok." *Indian Folklife* 33 (July 2009): 5-9.

Alem, O. *Tsüngremology: Ao Naga Christian Theology.* Aolijen, Mokokchung: Clark Theological College, 1994.

Ambuludi, Luis Macas. "Abya Yala and the Decolonization of Democracy, Knowledge, Education, and the State." In *New World of Indigenous Resistance: Noam Chomsky and Voices from North, South, and Central America.* Edited by Lois Meyer and Benjamin Maldonado Alvarado. New Delhi: Orient BlackSwan Private Limited, 2011. 239-250.

Ao, Tajen. *Christianity versus Ao Nagas.* Mokokchung: Tribal Gospel Mission Publishers, 1984.

Ao, Temsula. "From Antiquity to Modern." *Indian Folklife* 33 (July 2009): 3-10.

Ao, Temsula. *The Ao-Naga Oral Tradition*. Baroda: Bhasha Publications, 1999.

Armstrong, Chloe. *Oral Interpretation of Biblical Literature*. Minneapolis: Burgess Publishing Company, 1968.

Atsongchanger, Mar. *The Historical Memoranda of the Nagas and their Neighbours*. Mokokchung: Tribal Communication and Research Centre, 1995.

Awasthi, Suresh. "Oral Narratives: The Strategies and Structures of Performance." In *Narrative: A Seminar*. Edited by Amiya Das. New Delhi: Sahitya Akademi, 1994. 153-165.

Bailey, Kenneth E. *Poet and Peasant and Through Peasants Eyes: A Literary-Cultural Approach to the Parables of Luke*. Michigan: William B. Eerdmans Publishing Company, 1983.

Baral, Sarangadhar. "Selected Oral Poetry of Northeast India and the Ecological Space." In *Emerging Literatures from Northeast India: The Dynamics of Culture, Society and Identity*. Edited by Margaret Ch. Zama. New Delhi: SAGE Publications India Pvt. Ltd., 2013. 76-89.

Bendangangshi and I. T. Apok Aier. *The Religion of the Ao Nagas*. Mokokchung: By the Authors, 1990.

Datta, Birendranath. *Cultural Contours of North-east India*. New Delhi: Oxford University Press, 2012.

Förster, Eckart. *Kant's Final Synthesis: An Essay on the Opus postumum*. Cambridge: Harvard University Press, 2000.

Frendo, Anthony J. *Pre-exilic Israel, the Hebrew Bible, and Archaeology: Integrating Text and Artefact*. New York: T & T Clark International, 2011.

Frisch, Michael. "Oral History and *Hard Times*: A Review Essay." In *The Oral History Reader*. Edited by Robert Perks and Alistair Thomson. London: Routledge, 1998. 29-37.

Grele, Ronald J. "Movement without aim: Methodological and Theoretical Problems in Oral History." In *The Oral History Reader*. Edited by Robert Perks and Alistair Thomson. London: Routledge, 1998. 38-39.

Hayong, Shanbha. "Revisiting the Eco-Spirituality of the Tribal in the Era of Globalization." *Mar Thoma Seminary Journal of Theology* II/2 (December 2013): 79-96.

Hibo, Visakhonu. "Good and Evil: Naga Society." In *Construction of Evil in North East India: Myth, Narrative and Discourse*. Prasenjit Biswas and C. Joshua Thomas. Edited by New Delhi: SAGE Publications India Pvt Ltd, 2012. 114-127.

Hultgren, Arland J. *The Parables of Jesus: A Commentary*. Michigan: William B. Eerdmans Publishing Company, 2000.

John, V.J. "Teaching the Bible from the Margins: Rediscovering the Biblical Message for Today." In *Borders and Margins: Re-visioning Ministry and Mission*. Edited by Dexter S. Maben. Tiruvalla: Christave Sahitya Samithi; Bangalore: United Theological College, 2015. 298-317.

Kant, Immanuel. *Critique of Pure Reason*. Translated and edited Paul Guyer and Allen W. Wood. Cambridge: Cambridge University Press, 1997.

Kechutzar, Sashikaba. "Ecological Values from Ao Naga Tradition and Culture." In *Tribal Ecology: A Search for Ecological Values from the Cultures and Practices of the Tribes of North East India*. TTS 20. Edited by Razouselie Lasetso, Marlene Ch. Marak, and Yangkahao Vashum. Jorhat: ETC Programme Coordination, 2012. 215-229.

Kelber, Werner H. *The Oral and the Written Gospel: The Hermeneutics of Speaking and Writing in the Synoptic Tradition, Mark, Paul, and Q*. Philadelphia: Fortress Press, 1983.

Kothari, Komal. "Tales: Oral and Written." In *Narrative: A Seminar*. Edited by Amiya Das. New Delhi: Sahitya Akademi, 1994. 1186-195.

Kumar, B.B. *Naga Identity*. New Delhi: Concept Publishing Company, 2005.

Lasetso, Razouselie. "Tribal Theology and the Bible: A Contextual Reading of the Bible." In *Tribal Theology: A Search for Quality Theological Education and Relevant Ministry*. TSS 17. Edited by Yangkahao Vashum; Jorhat: Tribal Study Centre, 2009. 31-44.

Lee, Charlotte I. *Oral Interpretation*. Boston: Houghton Mifflin Company, 1952.

Lloyd, David. "Ethnic Cultures, Minority Discourse and the State." In *Colonial Discourse/Postcolonial Theory*. Edited by Francis Barker,

Peter Hulme and Margaret Iversen. New Delhi: Viva Books, 2012. 221-238.

Longchar, A. Wati. *The Tribal Religious Traditions in North East India: An Introduction*. Revised edition. Jorhat: Eastern Theological College, 2000.

Longchar, Wati. *Returning to Mother Earth: Theology, Christian Witness and Theological Education: An Indigenous Perspective*. PTCA 4. Tainan: PTCA, 2012.

Longkumer, Lanusashi. "Oral Tradition in contemporary conflict resolution: A Naga Perspective." *Indian Folklife* 33 (July 2009): 11-13.

Longkumer, Supongmayang. "The Ao Nagas: Clanic System." *Journal of Tribal Studies* IX/1 (January-June 2005): 81-99.

Neal, Jerusha Matsen. "The Spoken Word: Implications of Oral Culture for Christian Doctrine and Practice." In *Encounter Between Gospel and Tribal Culture*. Edited by A. Wati Longchar; Jorhat: Tribal Study Centre, 1999. 74-91.

Pangernungba. "Land Being and *Ali-Rongsen* (Cultural-political-Economy): An Ao-Naga Perspective." In *Tribal Ecology: A Search for Ecological Values from the Cultures and Practices of the Tribes of North East India*. TTS 20. Edited by Razouselie Lasetso, Marlene Ch. Marak, and Yangkahao Vashum. Jorhat: ETC Programme Coordination, 2012. 157-195.

Pasayat, Chitrasen. *Tribe, Caste and Folk Culture*. Jaipur: Rawat Publications, 1998.

Pulloppillil, Thomas. "Ethics from the Perspective of Tribals." *Jeevadhara* xxxviii/168 (November 1998): 465-470.

Pursowa. *The Ao-Naga Traditional Dress as a Medium of Communication in the Society*. Changtongya Town, Mokokchung: Longchara, 2011.

Ritchie, Donald A. "Introduction: The Evolution of Oral History." In *The Oxford Handbook of Oral History*. Edited by Donald A. Ritchie. Oxford: Oxford University Press, 2011. 2-19.

Sangtinuk. "Story-Telling: A Means to Conserve Culture." *Journal of Tribal Studies* XIV/2 (July-Dec. 2009): 54-68.

Shishak, T.A. "Higher Education for Nagaland." In Unpublished Ph.D. Thesis, University of New York (1973).

Song, C.S. *Tell Us Our Names: Story Theology from an Asian Perspective*. Indore: Satprakashan Sanchar Kendra, 1985.

Spencer, Patrick E. *Rhetorical Texture and Narrative Trajectories of the Lukan Galilean Ministry Speeches: Hermeneutical Appropriation by Authorial Readers of Luke-Acts.* New York: T & T Clark, 2007.

Takatemjen. *Studies on Theology and Naga Culture.* Mokokchung: Clark Theological College, 1997.

Tannehill, Robert C. *Luke.* Nashville: Abingdon Press, 1996.

Thanzauva, K. "Community Ownership and Management of Land and Forest: The Mizo Perspective." In *Tribal Ecology: A Search for Ecological Values from the Cultures and Practices of the Tribes of North East India.* TTS 20. Edited by Razouselie Lasetso, Marlene Ch. Marak, and Yangkahao Vashum. Jorhat: ETC Programme Coordination, 2012. 125-138.

Thanzauva, K and R. L. Hnuni. "Ethnicity, Identity and Hermeneutics: An Indian Tribal Perspective." In *Ethnicity and the Bible.* Edited by Mark G. Brett; Boston: Brill Academic Publishers, Inc., 2002. 343-357.

Thomas, M.M. Inaugural Address, "Dr. M.M. Thomas, Governor of Nagaland in the Social Scientists Meet," on December 6, 1990, in MMT 61. Source from UTC Library Archive.

Thompson, Paul. *The Voice of the Past Oral History.* Oxford: Oxford University Press, 1978.

Vashum, Yangkahao. "Tribal Theology: A Search for Relevant Theology and Ministry in Tribal Context." In *Tribal Theology: A Search for Quality Theological Education and Relevant Ministry.* TSS 17. Edited by Yangkahao Vashum. Jorhat: Tribal Study Centre, 2009. 16-30.

Vashum, Yangkahao. "Towards A Tribal Theology of Eco-Human Rights: Resources from the Tangkhul Tradition." *Journal of Tribal Studies* III/1 (January-June, 2009): 47-68.

Venuh, Neivetso. *British Colonization and Restructuring of Naga Polity.* New Delhi: Mittal Publications, 2005.

Vine, W.E. "Gate." In *An Expository Dictionary of New Testament Words with their Precise Meanings for English Readers.* London: Oliphants, 1969. 141-142.

Wilfred, Felix. "The Challenges of Folklore to Indian Theologizing: Some Preliminary Reflections." *Jeevadhara* xxiv/139 (January 1994): 60-80.

Walotemjen. "Recovery and Significance of Oral History: A North East India Tribal Reading." *Journal of Tribal Studies* xviii/1 (January – June 2013): 44-60.

Endnotes

[1] An explanation of how this paper seeks to utilize the term 'oral lore' will feature immanently.

[2] A discussion of my development of the term 'reoralizing' will be presented shortly.

[3] For example, in the late seventeenth century Richard Simon asserted that "unwritten tradition lay back of written texts." Walter J. Ong, "Foreword," in *The Oral and the Written Gospel: The Hermeneutics of Speaking and Writing in the Synoptic Tradition, Mark, Paul, and Q* (Philadelphia: Fortress Press, 1983), xiii. Furthermore, Werner H. Kelber argues that, "[t]he oral medium, in which words are managed from mouth to ear, handles information differently from the written medium, which links the eye to visible but silent letters on the page." Hence for Kelber there are oral origins of the Synoptic texts, often focused in the reconstruction of Q, and Paul can be shown to be repeatedly favoring oral speech. See: Werner H. Kelber, *The Oral and the Written Gospel: The Hermeneutics of Speaking and Writing in the Synoptic Tradition, Mark, Paul, and Q* (Philadelphia: Fortress Press, 1983), xiii-xv.

[4] Paul Thompson, *The Voice of the Past: Oral History* (Oxford: Oxford University Press, 1978), 1-2.

[5] A. Shishak, "Higher Education for Nagaland," Unpublished Ph.D. Thesis, University of New York (1973), 21.

[6] Charlotte I. Lee, *Oral Interpretation* (Boston: Houghton Mifflin Company, 1952), v.

[7] Suresh Awasthi, "Oral Narratives: The Strategies and Structures of Performance," in *Narrative: A Seminar*, ed. Amiya Das (New Delhi: Sahitya Akademi, 1994), 159.

[8] Komal Kothari, "Tales: Oral and Written," in *Narrative: A Seminar*, ed. Amiya Das (New Delhi: Sahitya Akademi, 1994), 186.

[9] Chitrasen Pasayat, *Tribe, Caste and Folk Culture* (Jaipur: Rawat Publications, 1998), 15.

[10] See: Temsula Ao, "From Antiquity to Modern," *Indian Folklife* 33 (July 2009): 3; and, Lanusashi Longkumer, "Oral Tradition in Contemporary Conflict Resolution: A Naga perspective," *Indian Folklife* 33 (July 2009): 11.

[11] Kelber, *The Oral and the Written Gospel*, xv.

[12] Ao, "From Antiquity to Modern," *Indian Folklife*, 3.

[13] Kothari, "Tales: Oral and Written," in *Narrative: A Seminar*, 187.

[14] Anungla Aier and Tiatoshi Jamir, "Re-interpreting the Myth of *Longterok*," *Indian Folklife* 33 (July 2009): 8. Whilst the value of written records is rarely disputed, little attention is given to the value and importance of the oral communication of such texts and their traditions. To understand the meaning of a particular group of people from their worldview and consider the usage of words, phrases, and idioms on their myth, see, O. Alem, *Tsüngremology: Ao Naga Christian Theology* (Aolijen, Mokokchung: Clark Theological College, 1994), 4. Moreover, oral lore is not only about origin and migration, but it also includes social life, religious practices, polity, culture, economic concerns, ideology, and communitarian life of people. Such oral lore has the capacity to transform or destroy a community when misinterpreted. Therefore, oral lore remains a sacred element and can be considered to be the primary chronicle of how a tribe charts its origins and its history.

[15] Anthony J. Frendo, *Pre-exilic Israel, the Hebrew Bible, and Archaeology: Integrating Text and Artefact* (New York: T & T Clark International, 2011), 18.

[16] Felix Wilfred, 'The Challenges of Folklore to Indian Theologizing: Some Preliminary Reflections', *Jeevadhara* xxiv/139 (January 1994): 60.

[17] Wilfred, "The Challenges of Folklore to Indian Theologizing: Some Preliminary Reflections," 60-61.

[18] Temsula Ao, *The Ao-Naga Oral Tradition* (Baroda: Bhasha Publications, 1999), 7-8.

[19] Luis Macas Ambuludi, "Abya Yala and the Decolonization of Democracy, Knowledge, Education, and the State," in *New World of Indigenous Resistance: Noam Chomsky and Voices from North, South, and Central America*, eds. Lois Meyer and Benjamin Maldonado Alvarado (New Delhi: Orient BlackSwan Private Limited, 2011), 242.

[20] The Hornbill Festival's official website describes the festival in the following manner: "the Hornbill Festival held in the first week of December shows that with its stunning natural beauty and great cultural traditions, Nagaland can offer a rich fare to tourist." See: http://www.hornbillfestival.com/ (accessed on 7/8/2015).

[21] Wati Longchar, "Hornbill Festival: Who is benefited – Rich or Poor?," *Nagaland Post* (December 2, 2013), 2.

[22] Visakhonu Hibo, "Good and Evil: Naga Society," in *Construction of Evil in North East India: Myth, Narrative and Discourse*, eds. Prasenjit Biswas and C. Joshua Thomas (New Delhi: SAGE Publications India Pvt Ltd, 2012), 125.

[23] Sangtinuk, "Story-Telling: A Means to Conserve Culture," *Journal of Tribal Studies* XIV/2 (July-Dec. 2009): 57-58.

[24] Pursowa, *The Ao-Naga Traditional Dress as a Medium of Communication in the Society* (Changtongya Town, Mokokchung: Longchara, 2011), 58.

[25] Sangtinuk, "Story-Telling: A Means to Conserve Culture," 61.

[26] C.S. Song, *Tell Us Our Names: Story Theology from an Asian Perspective* (Indore: Satprakashan Sanchar Kendra, 1985), x.

[27] M.M. Thomas, Inaugural Address, "Dr. M.M. Thomas, Governor of Nagaland in the Social Scientists Meet," on December 6, 1990, in MMT 61. Source from UTC Library Archive.

[28] Thanzauva and R.L. Hnuni, "Ethnicity, Identity and Hermeneutics: An Indian Tribal Perspective," in *Ethnicity and the Bible*, ed. Mark G. Brett (Boston: Brill Academic Publishers, Inc., 2002), 343.

[29] Razouselie Lasetso, "Tribal Theology and the Bible: A Contextual Reading of the Bible," in *Tribal Theology: A Search for Quality Theological Education and Relevant Ministry*, TSS 17, ed. Yangkahao Vashum (Jorhat: Tribal Study Centre, 2009), 34.

[30] Immanuel Kant, *Critique of Pure Reason*, trans. and eds. Paul Guyer and Allen W. Wood (Cambridge: Cambridge University Press, 1997), 387.

[31] Sashikaba Kechutzar, "Ecological Values from Ao Naga Tradition and Culture," in *Tribal Ecology: A Search for Ecological Values from the Cultures and Practices of the Tribes of North East India*, TTS 20, eds. Razouselie Lasetso, Marlene Ch. Marak, and Yangkahao Vashum (Jorhat: ETC Programme Coordination, 2012), 221.

[32] Shanbha Hayong, "Revisiting the Eco-Spirituality of the Tribal in the Era of Globalization," *Mar Thoma Seminary Journal of Theology* II/2 (December 2013): 82.

[33] Yangkahao Vashum, "Towards A Tribal Theology of Eco-Human Rights: Resources from the Tangkhul Tradition," *Journal of Tribal Studies* III/1 (January-June, 2009), 67.

[34] A. Wati Longchar, *The Tribal Religious Traditions in North East India: An Introduction*, rev. ed. (Jorhat: Eastern Theological College, 2000), 118; cf. Wati Longchar, *Returning to Mother Earth: Theology, Christian Witness and Theological Education: An Indigenous Perspective*, PTCA 4 (Tainan: PTCA, 2012), 7.

[35] K. Thanzauva, "Community Ownership and Management of Land and Forest: The Mizo Perspective," in *Tribal Ecology: A Search for Ecological Values from the Cultures and Practices of the Tribes of North East India*, TTS 20, eds. Razouselie Lasetso, Marlene Ch. Marak, and Yangkahao Vashum (Jorhat: ETC Programme Coordination, 2012), 126-127.

[36] Pangernungba, "Land Being and *Ali-Rongsen* (Cultural-political-Economy): An Ao-Naga Perspective," in *Tribal Ecology: A Search for Ecological Values from the Cultures and Practices of the Tribes of North East India*, TTS 20, eds. Razouselie Lasetso, Marlene Ch. Marak, and Yangkahao Vashum (Jorhat: ETC Programme Coordination, 2012), 161.

[37] Yangkahao Vashum, "Tribal Theology: A Search for Relevant Theology and Ministry in Tribal Context," in *Tribal Theology: A Search for Quality Theological Education and Relevant Ministry*, TSS 17, ed. Yangkahao Vashum (Jorhat: Tribal Study Centre, 2009), 24.

[38] Vashum, "Tribal Theology: A Search for Relevant Theology and Ministry in Tribal Context," in *Tribal Theology: A Search for Quality Theological Education and Relevant Ministry*, p. 25.

[39] Sashikaba Kechutzar, "Ecological Values from Ao Naga Tradition and Culture," in *Tribal Ecology: A Search for Ecological Values from the Cultures and Practices of the Tribes of North East India*, 221.

[40] A. W. Davis was the Deputy Commissioner of Naga Hills from 1907 to 1908. For more information about A W. Davis, see: B.B. Kumar, *Naga Identity* (New Delhi: Concept Publishing Company, 2005), 124; Neivetso Venuh, *British Colonization and Restructuring of Naga Polity* (New Delhi: Mittal Publications, 2005), 46.

⁴¹ Mar Atsongchanger, *The Historical Memoranda of the Nagas and their Neighbours* (Mokokchung: Tribal Communication and Research Centre, 1995), xiii.

⁴² See: Supongmayang Longkumer, "The Ao Nagas: Clanic System." *Journal of Tribal Studies* IX/1 (January-June 2005): 87.

⁴³ Michael Frisch, "Oral History and *Hard Times*: A Review Essay," in *The Oral History Reader*, eds. Robert Perks and Alistair Thomson (London: Routledge, 1998), 31.

⁴⁴ Takatemjen, *Studies on Theology and Naga Culture* (Mokokchung: Clark Theological College, 1997), 14; Tajen Ao, *Christianity versus Ao Nagas* (Mokokchung: Tribal Gospel Mission Publishers, 1984), 43.

⁴⁵ For example, Arland J. Hultgren reports that there have been a multitude of names that have been attributed to the rich man. For more, see: Arland J. Hultgren, *The Parables of Jesus: A Commentary* (Michigan: William B. Eerdmans Publishing Company, 2000), 111.

⁴⁶ When defining the margins, V.J. John asserts that "[m]arginalized persons are those who are not part of the mainstream of social set-up and hence found within the periphery of society. They are the people whose experience is that of hunger, sickness, exploitation and rejection." See: V.J. John, "Teaching the Bible from the Margins: Rediscovering the Biblical Message for Today," in *Borders and Margins: Re-visioning Ministry and Mission*, ed. Dexter S. Maben (Tiruvalla: Christava Sahitya Samithi; Bangalore: United Theological College, 2015), 306.

⁴⁷ When seeking to re-read this text through a tribal lens, it is essential that one first understands how the term 'poor' is used and understood in both the biblical text and tribal societies. This is necessary to make sense of the many different concepts that are at play when using this term in a contextual interpretation. Firstly, we must consider how the term is being and understood in the biblical text. There are in fact four different words used for 'poor' in this passage, these are: the adjective *'ptōchos'*, which carries with it both literal and metaphorical connotations (owing to the way it is used in Matthew 5:3, Luke 6:20, and Revelation 3:17); the adjective *'penichpos'*, which translates as 'needy' and is used mostly often in relation to the widow of the passage (Luke 21:2); the noun form *'penēs'*, which means 'a labourer' (just as in 2 Corinthians 9:9); and finally, the verb *'ptōcheuō'*, which evokes the idea of 'to be a poor as a beggar' or 'to be destitute' (again as in 2 Corinthians 8:9).

For more, see: W.E. Vine, "Poor," in *An Expository Dictionary of New Testament Words with their Precise Meanings for English Readers* (London: Oliphants, 1969), 192. In addition to understanding the different words used for 'poor' within the biblical text and what meanings each of these convey, we must also consider how 'poor' is understood in a tribal context. It is widely accepted that the term 'poor' is understood in a tribal setting as more of a metaphorical denotation rather than literal reality. This is because in a tribal setting a person who has shelter and land to cultivate cannot be considered poor. As I have already noted, land is life for tribal peoples. Therefore, so long as a person has access to land, such a person cannot be poor. In relation to the folktale under discussion, because the two orphan girls possess land then they cannot be considered poor. However, because the girls were not recognized as community members or as individuals belonging to the same village then they can be considered poor as they are lacking in terms of identity. 'Poor' is therefore understood in a metaphorical manner in tribal communities and relates to identity, rather than literal belongings.

[48] Patrick E. Spencer, *Rhetorical Texture and Narrative Trajectories of the Lukan Galilean Ministry Speeches: Hermeneutical Appropriation by Authorial Readers of Luke-Acts* (New York: T & T Clark, 2007), 188. Cf. Luke 4:1-10; 5:17-26; 7:36-50; 19:1-10.

[49] David Lloyd, "Ethnic Cultures, Minority Discourse and the State," in *Colonial Discourse/Postcolonial Theory*, eds. Francis Barker, Peter Hulme and Margaret Iversen (New Delhi: Viva Books, 2012), 222.

[50] Joseph S. Thong and Phanenmo Kath, *Glimpses of Naga Legacy and Culture* (Kottayam, Kerala: Society for Naga Students' Welfare, 2011), 57.

[51] Ao, *The Ao-Naga Oral Tradition*, vii.

[52] Tannehill, *Luke*, 251.

[53] E. Vine, "Gate," in *An Expository Dictionary of New Testament Words with their Precise Meanings for English Readers* (London: Oliphants, 1969), 141-142.

[54] Kenneth E. Bailey, *Poet & Peasant and Through Peasants Eyes: A Literary-Cultural Approach to the Parables of Luke* (Michigan: William B. Eerdmans Publishing Company, 1983), 43.

[55] Takatemjen, *Studies on Theology and Naga Culture*, 39.

[56] Ao, *The Ao-Naga Oral Tradition*, 126.

[57] Bendangangshi and I. T. Apok Aier, *The Religion of the Ao Nagas* (Mokokchung: Self-published, 1990), 15.

[58] Ao, *The Ao-Naga Oral Tradition*, 126.

[59] Ao, *The Ao-Naga Oral Tradition*, 126-127.

[60] Bendangangshi and I. T. Apok Aier, *The Religion of the Ao Nagas*, 15-16.

Women Property Owners
in the Book of Acts

SAJITHA VARGHESE

Luke's second volume - the book of Acts - talks about Peter, Paul, and other disciples and their society of Jerusalem, Antioch, Asia minor, Greece, and Rome.[1] It is a biblical document written in the first century Mediterranean context. The characters in this work are mainly from Jewish and Greco-Roman cultures. There was a fusion of cultures because Hellenism still continued its influence, imperial Rome, the ruling power, enforced their legislations and the Jews were trying to recapture their sovereignty. Although Rabbinic Judaism prescribed racial purity and religious monotheism, interactions with great cultures resulted in many alterations in their thinking patterns and social dynamics. Women also experienced great emancipation in almost all areas of their lives. A growing proportion of women sought expression in cultural pursuits: they learned Greek, studied philosophy, wrote poetry, gave public lectures, played, sang, and danced, and opened literary *salons*; some engaged in business; a few practiced medicine or law.[2] Sociologically Mediterranean societies in the first century were marked by the values of honour-shame, status and patronage system. Patronage was open to all and many women also made use of this opportunity because it was a means to boost their social status and manifest their economic power and affluence. To get an idea about the background of women property-owners in the book of Acts, a brief discussion of the economic position of Greco -Roman and Jewish women is essential and the same is done below.

Economic Background of Women in Greece

Ancient Greece was divided into city-states and Athens and Sparta were the most important among them. Athens, the largest and most prosperous of the Greek city-states, had produced greatest philosophers and they were the forerunners of democracy. But women in archaic and classical Athens were of inferior status and they suffered more restriction than the women in other city states. A daughter was an economic liability, because dowry had to be supplied at her marriage and seldom did families raise more than one daughter.[3] Responsible fathers in Classical Athens did not raise female babies unless they foresaw a proper marriage for them at maturity.[4] However, Athenians were protective of their women economically because dowry was compulsory in marriage and   it was the   asset of a woman throughout her life.

Sarah B. Pomeroy observes:

A woman's dowry was to remain intact throughout her lifetime and to be used for her support; neither her father, nor her guardian, nor her husband, nor the woman herself could legally dispose of it…. The groom could use the principal but was required to maintain his wife from the income of her dowry, computed at eighteen percent annually. Upon divorce, the husband was required to return the dowry to his ex-wife's guardian or pay interest at 18 per cent.[5]

The children were to remain with the father in the case of divorce and the divorced woman was free for remarriage with the full amount of dowry added most probably with compensation.

Contrary to Athenian women Spartan women were economically independent. They controlled property and spent the money according to their wishes. E.g. Spartan women were the first to join men in owning racehorses by hiring charioteers to run in the Olympic Games.[6] The freedom, the Spartan women enjoyed, was unheard of in the rest of the Greek world. They had education, physical training and economic freedom because their men were away, sacrificing their life for the protection of their state. Thus, ancient Sparta became a model and inspiration for women emancipation and empowerment.

Hellenistic Empire was very different from classical Greece. Cosmopolitan culture brought many changes in the attitudes of people. Both men and women migrated into colonies seeking good prospects in life. One of the most effective favourable factor concerning women during this period was economic power. Through their personal wealth women were able to gain legal rights and a voice in public affairs. Women were honoured because of their contributions to the state. In the fourth century BCE and the Hellenistic period some Spartan women were extremely wealthy and were conspicuous consumers.[7] They owned forty percent of the land and exercised great political and economic power.[8]

Economic Background of Roman Women

Ancient Rome was male-oriented than ancient Greece. The daughters were considered a cause of anxiety because a good match required a commendable dowry to satisfy groom's family and the social standing of bride's family. Over the centuries, families gave houses, land, and slaves to their daughter. In the event of divorce, a settlement was made in favour of the one who was not initiating the divorce. If the husband had initiated the divorce, he was to refund the dowry unless he could prove that she had been guilty of misconduct.[9] The divorced wife could use her personal wealth and dowry independently and it is the fathers' duty to take care of the children.

During the Republic, the law code called Twelve Tables (451-450 BCE)[10] restricted the freedom of women considerably. According to this law a woman had to be under the control of a male figure throughout her life. The system of *tutelage*,[11] that is, a relative from the father's side had to control the daughter as her tutor with the authority of the father over his daughter, compensated for the death of the father. This system was prevalent because women were considered to be incapable to manage their affairs. But by the late republic, women started to cross boundaries of restriction in choice of partners, control of wealth, selection of job and so on. Later consolidation of Roman Empire and the inter-mixture of cultures brought about great changes in the role and position of women.

There were different types of marriages in Rome: *Manus* (with hand) marriage was the marriage pattern in the 5th century BCE. *Manus* marriage meant that the wife joined the family circle of her husband and conferred all her property on to the groom and his family. Thus, women were passed from the sovereignty of their fathers to that of their husbands. This ancient form of Roman marriage held women in total subjection to their husbands as they had been in total subjection to their fathers. But by the 2nd century BCE women became discontent at this bondage and they abandoned *manus* marriage. A new system emerged called free marriages or *sine manu*[12] (without hand) marriages which became a significant milestone in the emancipation of women. A woman married *sine manu* inherited an equal share of the family estate with her brothers and she was free or independent of paternal authority like her brothers after the death of her father. Traditionally, these women had been obliged to keep a guardian, or *tutela*, until they died.[13] He would supervise the sale of certain types of property or slaves and approved her will.[14] But by this time this system became very weak.

Augustus Caesar also relaxed the rule of *tutela* in order to increase the birth rate and that provided freedom for married women to do their economic transactions without external control. Citizen women with three children (and freedwomen with four) became legally independent from the tutor, a status known as *sui iuris*.[15] Later Claudius in the first century CE abolished altogether agnastic *tutela*, that is, in the male familial line, thus doing away with male control of the property of citizen women.[16] Therefore, as citizens of Rome by birth or marriage, women acquired the right to own and dispose their property and became in control of their persons.[17] Freedom from guardian helped Greco-Roman women cross over traditional boundaries.

In the matter of inheritance daughters inherited equally with their brothers though with some legal restrictions on how to use their wealth. Though many girl children were exposed, if the father agreed to raise his daughter, she had a position almost equal with her brothers. After marriage they inherited at least ten percentage from the husband's property also. Women with estates and in business of all sorts were attested in Pompeii.[18] Shipping business was flourishing from the Principate to the imperial period and in order to keep the benefits for the future generations, shippers passed the trade on to their daughters and sons. Thus during the Principate, women of Rome and the East owned ships.[19] There are many examples of women who owned businesses and were influential members of their communities.[20] Suppression or domestication were not mandatory or imposed and because of a woman's earning capacity she could freely walk out of oppressive situations and establish herself.[21] It is understood that the greater the relative contribution of females to subsistence tasks, the higher their status tends to be.[22] The most important criterion for social stratification in the Roman empire was ownership of property , which defined one's legal status.[23] In the Empire money could buy legal privileges, and women's wealth performed the same function. More money meant more freedom, which resulted in social boundaries becoming a little more porous and through money women could purchase access into the outside world.[24] Roman citizens set their slaves free in remarkably large numbers, and each manumitted slave became not only a *libertus* or *liberta* (freedman or freedwoman) but also a Roman citizen.[25] Thus even slave women had opportunities to come out of their oppressive situations. The next major people group we have to discuss to assess the economic position of women in book of Acts is Israelite or Jewish women.

Economic background of Israelite/Jewish Women

To understand the role and economic position of women in Israelite/Jewish families, the pre-exilic, post-exilic and women under Rabbinic Judaism must be taken into consideration. The Torah is the major source of information for the task of investigating the lives of Israelite women during this pre-exilic period. God had given rules and regulations through Moses concerning various stages of woman's life such as daughter, wife, mother, widow and so on.

Perpetuation of family and protection of property were the most important concerns of an Israelite family and sons were honoured more than the daughters. The disparity was clear in the purity laws after the birth of male and female children (Lev.12). The father had authority even to sell his daughter as a slave (Lev. 21: 7-11; Neh. 5:5). But the girls were not seen as an economic burden because there was no dowry system; the bridegroom had to give bride- price to the bride's father. The term *Mohar* (bride price or marriage present[26]) occurs three times in the OT (Gen. 34:12; Ex. 22:17; 1Sam. 18:25). The groom's family pays a price to the head of the *paterfamilias*[27] to acquire the woman for him. As a result the groom becomes the *ba'al* (owner) and the woman is the *b'ulat ba'al* (Deut. 22:22, translated as wife).[28] Gifts, ornaments, crops, wine, labour for certain years, deeds of valour and so on were considered as *mohar* (Gen 24: 22, 30, 53; 29:18, 30; Judg.1:12-13; 1Sam. 18:21; Hos. 3:2). This was given probably as the compensation for the work which otherwise the daughter would have continued to contribute to her parent's household.[29] And *mohar* was an indication that girl children were not unwanted but they were duly compensated because they contributed much to the workforce in an agricultural household. Bride price also specified the status of an unmarried daughter as a valuable part of the household's economic assets.[30]

Though, giving of dowry by the bride's father was not commonly practiced in Israel we see some references to the same. E.g. when Solomon married Pharaoh's daughter, the latter gave him dowry because Egyptians practiced this (1Kgs 9:16). There are scanty references to dowry in our Scripture but the Hebrew terms *zebed* (Gen. 30:20) and *Silluhim* (literarily 'those which are sent' or 'gifts'[31][1Kgs. 9:16; Mic. 1:14]) may refer to property ceded to the woman at marriage and therefore to the household of destination (Gen. 31:14-16). The bridal gift could include land (Josh. 15: 18-19; 1Kgs. 9:6), and the value of the dowry was an index of the wealth, status and honour of the bride's household. This feature is better attested elsewhere in the ancient West Asia than in Israel. [32]

Apart from their household chores, Israelite women were working along with their husband or other members of the family. Carol Meyers observes that, men, women and children carried out the multifarious activities such as producing and maintaining most tools and implements, garments and other textiles, and built structures (dwellings, pens, terraces, and sheds). Agricultural tasks such as harvesting, tending of orchards, and vineyards and regular need to milk animals were tasks performed by both men and women. They were interdependent and acted as farm-partners. The boundaries of a woman's world were virtually the same as those of a man's in the highland hamlets and villages of early Israel. But normally sheep-shearing and tanning might have been done by men and spinning, weaving (Ex. 35:22), sewing, basketry and ceramic production were probably female jobs which need planning, skill, experience, and technological knowledge.[33] They did skilled jobs such as weaving and spinning and the produce of their hands and the income earned from these were also at their disposal. They used to spin blue and purple, scarlet stuff, fine twined linen and goat's hair and earned income (Exo. 35:22-29). The sheets and sashes produced by Israelite housewives appealed foreign customers.[34]

In ancient Israel, a woman could not inherit property normally. A daughter could inherit from her father if there were no sons, though with the provision that she marries within the tribe (Num. 27: 1-11; 36:1-12; Josh. 17:3-6). Widows also occasionally inherited their husband's possessions (2Kgs. 8:1-6; Ruth 4:3, 9) but normally they could not dispose it as they wish; they had to submit to the will of near male relative. But the existence of names of women on Hebrew seals shows that women were in fact 'persons from a judicial point of view.' These seals inscribed with their names also attest that upper or middle-class women might dispose of their property.[35]

Both sexes wore such jewellery as they could afford –finger rings, bracelets, armlets necklaces, anklets, nose-rings were especially feminine adornments.[36] Parents gave daughters gold and silver ornaments and when they got married the bridegroom and their relatives (Gen. 35:4; Ex. 3:22; 32:2) also used to give ornaments as gifts. Women considered these ornaments as their special asset and they were free to handle it according to their wishes (Ex. 32:2-3; 35:22).

Post-Exilic Jewish Women

After the division of Israelite nation, the history of Jewish nation is important for our study because the Northern kingdom or nation Israel lost its identity because of its mixing with Assyrians.

Jewish people interacted with different empires and cultures beginning from their Babylonian exile. To get an idea about the social position and economic status of women in the NT period, it is important to understand the customs and mores the Jewish people imbibed and absorbed from different world cultures. During the Babylonian exile Jewish people started synagogues in which interpretation and exposition of Torah started formally. The Rabbis started interpreting the Torah considering the positive side of the culture they were exposed and brought about new regulations especially concerning the economic protection of women and *ketubah* was a consequence of this development.

Dowry/ Ketuhah/Mohar

During the post-exilic period, formal marriage contracts are seen and it might have been started by the contact with the Babylonian customs by the returnees. The contractual character of marriage in the second temple period   might have worked well for the protection of women in situations of divorce and widowhood.[37] Dowry became a compulsory item for marriage during the second temple period and the fathers had to provide dowries for their daughters but the *mohar*[38] was routinely included with the wife's dowry, and the formal recipients, the bride's father, received no benefit from it. Besides, if the woman was divorced the father had to accept her. Eventually, the Rabbis limited the size of a dowry to ten percent of the father's possessions. Dowry was a kind of inheritance given to the daughters at the time of marriage from the family's goods, money, and property. The *Mishna* stipulated that a poor orphan should be given a minimum dowry of fifty zuz (twenty-five shekels) from the community's poor-fund.[39]

The custom of paying the mohar was also changed by the rabbinic times that the groom did not actually have to provide the *mohar* but only to promise it. It became payable in the event of divorce, and it came to be known as *ketubah* or 'written document.'[40] This reform was credited to Rabbi Simeon ben Shetach in the first century BCE.[41] He decreed that the husband must write for the wife in her *ketubah* that all his possessions are security for her *ketubah*. [42] Normally a virgin's *ketubba* was two hundred denars and a widow's one hundred denars.[43]

Economic Sources of Jewish Women

Jewish women also were not confined in the kitchen but they were doing different kinds of income earning jobs. Wives and mothers who were able to provide clothing for their families were successfully performing their proper role in society and this earned them respect.[44] Excavations from Masada included large amounts of loom weights that can be dated to the mid-to late first century.[45] Jewish women were also found doing farm work.[46]There were business women who sold their families' produce or artefacts in the market.[47] Both sexes involved in field work and vending, in the production   of goods for use and sale.[48] There were even fisher women and women tax collectors.[49] Women were imagined as moving freely through the thoroughfares and market places of village and city-and beyond. The papyri from Egypt make it clear that Jewish women engaged in commercial transactions of various sorts.[50] Mishna reveals that women were entrusted with maintaining their husband's shops or being guardians, or even creditors.[51] The common practice among Rabbis was, wives maintained the family and business while husbands and possibly elder sons studied the

Law. Another development of post-exilic Jewish people was the deeds of gift.

Deeds of Gift: Usually women could not inherit property but *Mishna* imagines the practice of deeds of gift, including those in contemplation of death.[52] The rabbis would not give legal sanction to give inheritance to people other than sons, the legal heirs, because it is disobedience to Torah. Richard Baucham also gives information about the deeds of gift.[53] Property could be conferred on a woman by a deed of gift. She had full ownership and disposal of such property even after marriage.[54] Deeds of gift seem to have been used to circumvent the laws of inheritance that otherwise prevented daughters and wives from inheriting in most circumstances. .[55] In the second Temple period illustrations for Jewish women's inheritance were discovered in legal archives. [56] Jewish people adopted Egyptian and Greek practices of using deeds of gift to confer property on persons other than the heirs.

Jewish women were freer than Gentile women in economic matters because they had no rule of *tutela*. Their income and emancipation were utilized to the full and many did start and flourish in different kinds of businesses ranging from the produce of the fields to even construction companies. Non elite women could more easily make a career of their own, through various crafts or as vendors and merchants.[57]Inscriptions from Asia Minor suggest that Jewish women had considerable financial independence and were publicly active.[58] Therefore it is evident that Jewish women also got opportunities to get rid of oppressive situations as their Greeco-Roman counterparts. Establishment of empires, exile and consequent exposure to different cultures made tremendous improvement in the economic position of women during the NT period. Patronage was an important means to attain status through economic resources even for the women of servile origin during this period.

Patronage

Patronage was a sign of economic independence and a channel for replacing lower status and attaining commendable social prestige. There were many examples of professionally active women who established an autonomous economic basis through their own business activity. A number of inscriptions dating from first to third centuries CE attest to the fact that Greek women especially in Macedonia and Asia Minor played a prominent role in the life of the cities and a number of them held the Roman citizenship also. [59] These inscriptions reveal women as benefactors, holding office, and receiving public honours. [60] They held distinguished civic and federal magistracies and priesthoods, discharged liturgies which required lavish expenditure on various ceremonies, games, banquets, and on civic buildings such as baths and colonnades. [61] Jewish women also were donours as evidenced by inscriptions and received the title patrons and mothers of synagogues.[62] A patron might provide her home for meetings, construct a separate building, or pay the expenses for sacrifices, festivals and the like.[63]Likewise Christian women-women converts from Greco-Roman and Jewish cultures- too contributed from their own means, independent of their husbands, to Jesus movement and later to apostles/missionaries, fulfilling the role of patrons. The attempt in this chapter is to discuss the economic position and resources of certain women property owners in the book of Acts.

Women Property Owners in the Book of Acts

There are so many women characters in the book of Acts who fulfils different roles such as waiting for the Holy Spirit (1:14), witnessing (21:6), suffering persecution (9:2), teaching(18:26), prophesying (21:9), and so on. But here we are examining the cases of only Sapphira, Tabitha, Mary and Lydia because it is evident that they possess some property or economic resources. The first person we discuss is Sapphira because she has voice in the economic transaction of her family.

Sapphira, the Property Owner (Acts 5:1-2)

After the outpouring of the Holy Spirit and birth of the Christian church in Jerusalem the community was in one accord and they led a communal life, sharing their possessions with one another. As Robert W. Wall commented, the church's internal witness was centred by the sharing of goods, even as its external witness was centred by the proclamation of the gospel.[64] Those who possessed lands or houses sold them and brought the proceeds to the apostles and they redistributed it according to the financial needs of the members.(Acts 4:34-35). Barnabas was an illustrious example of this practice and Ananias and Sapphira were trying to follow his model.

Ananias was a familiar Hebrew name (Dan. 1:6; 3:13)[65] and Sapphira was the feminine of a Hebrew adjective meaning beautiful. Inscriptions demonstrate the use of the name in Jerusalem at about the relevant time.[66] Ananias together with his wife Sapphira sold a piece of property (κτῆμα). In older Greek this noun seems to have been used more frequently of personal than of real, landed, property, but later to have come into use in the singular for an estate, farm or field.[67] In the OT period also married women had economic influence in the family. They handled money independently or with the knowledge of their husbands. The Shunemite lady received Elisha on her own but when she wished to build a separate chamber for him, she consulted her husband (2 Kgs. 4:8-10). The prudent lady (Prov. 31:10-11) also handled money independently without any hindrance from her husband.

Luke calls those who give the property here "owners," and as Peter makes clear with Ananias and Sapphira, the giving and the amount given were voluntary.[68] But, while Barnabas gave the whole portion, this couple kept aside some of the proceeds and brought only a part of it and laid it at the apostles' feet. ἐνοσφίσατο (kept back/appropriated) frequently refers to misappropriation of funds belonging to others, even to theft.[69] This same word is seen in Josh. 7:1 in the LXX[70] when he held back a portion of the loot that had been dedicated to God and the sin of Ananias and Sapphira conform to an OT archetype of the bad Israelite- namely Achan (Josh. 7:1-26).[71] As John Gillman observes, they kept back some of the money for security, as if God's providence were not enough.[72]

Sapphira shared in her husband's plan is evident from the term Συνειδυίης καί τῆς γυναικός (share the knowledge of, to be implicated in or privy to it). Gail R. O' Day says Ananias does not make unilateral decisions for the household but instead consults with his wife about the sale and disposition of the property. The focus of this passage is the true partnership of Sapphira in the economic dealings of her husband. Acts 5:1-2 shows Sapphira as having an equal voice in the economic management of her marriage.[73] She is an active partner in this business deal because the land may be either her parental share/dowry or part of *ketubah*. In 1952 many duplicate documents were discovered in Wadi Murabba'at.[74] Three duplicate documents[75] Mur. 26 (first century CE), 29 (134 CE), and 30(135 CE) are important here. These are contracts for sale of land, all of them signed by women as co-sellers. This is a documentary evidence to prove that a wife had rights over her husband's property. The signature of the wife appears to have been necessary, for the sale, even though she was not a contradicting party or seller. Since a married man's property was guarantee for the debt he owed his wife, he could not sell any of it without his wife's consent. Papyrus Murabba'at 30(134CE) is a bill of sale of a house and land, and includes the seller's wife's renunciation of her claims on the property sold on condition of remaining in her husband's house after his death and receiving 30 denarii every year from the estate. [76]

In Acts 5:1 Ananias sold a piece of land with his wife which means that Ananias required Sapphira's consent for the sale, because the land apparently served as security for her *ketubah*. It is part of the Jewish law of private property, and especially the marital property, that every woman, when she enters into the marriage, is to be assured a *ketubah* from her husband in the marriage contract. That means he promises her a specific sum of money, to be given in case the marriage is dissolved. The husband is responsible with his entire property, whether it be great or small, for his wife's *ketubah*. Therefore, the wife must consent to the sale of real property. [77] Therefore, it can be assumed from this passage that either the piece of property is Sapphira's dowry or part of her *ketubah*. And this rabbinic reformation secured protection for women from exploitation and provided economic security to them.

Prema Vakayil thinks that as in the case of Greco-Roman

world there are only scanty references to women landowners in Judaism. Perhaps one such person in the Hebrew world would be Judith.[78] This is a very peripheral observation because from the OT period itself there were women property owners such as Achsah, the Shunemite lady, Naomi, Ruth and so on. In the NT also Mary, mother of John Mark, Martha and Mary, Lydia and many others possessed property and economic stability even to support Christian mission.

Implications

The first detailed characterization of a woman in Acts occurs with Sapphira. She was a well-to-do woman like Lydia or Priscilla but was condemned along with her husband for lying about their donation because she was a privy to her husband's act.[79] She had an equal role in decision making along with her husband. She was depicted neither as a subordinate nor as a passive observer   but a participatory agent in the sale of the land and the distribution of the funds.[80] That she was named alongside her husband probably indicates that she was a woman of influence.[81] Sapphira was economically independent and she had power and authority over her family's property. The story of Sapphira and Ananias is a frightening incident for the believers even today because of the severity of punishment they faced but the story gives some evidences to the economic independence of married women of that time.

Tabitha, the Charity Worker (Acts 9:36,39)

Tabitha was a woman disciple in Joppa renowned for almsgiving and acts of charity. The word 'tabitha' means gazelle, for which Dorcas is the Greek.[82] She was a Jewish woman of independent means, a seamstress living in the Jewish city of Joppa.[83] V. 36

is a biographical introduction to Tabitha. The location of the narrative is Joppa (modern Jaffa), a port city near Lydda and presently a part of Tel Aviv-Jaffa, and it was a profitable port city. Since the conquest of Joppa, by Simon Maccabeus in 145 BCE (1 Macc.12:33;13:11), it had been a Jewish city.

Tabitha was a female disciple (μαθήτρια) but this term appears only here in the NT.[84] The feminine form is not common, but occurs in a few pagan authors and in the *Gos. of Pet.*12:50(with reference to Mary Magdalene).[85] Tabitha was a real Christian and her faith was manifested through praxis which included good works and charity. She made clothes and tunics for others, especially for widows and when she died after an illness, her friends became very sad. They washed the body[86] and placed it in the upstairs room and sent for Apostle Peter from Lydda. They asked him to help them, showing the lovely garments and other dresses that Tabitha had made for them, with great sorrow. Peter came immediately, having excluded the mourners, knelt down and prayed and fulfilled the divine commission of raising Tabitha. The healing of Tabitha took place in the first years of expansion of the Christian faith in Palestine: roughly 30-40CE.[87] But Luke may be writing this account after the Jewish war and destruction of Jerusalem.

In Greco-Roman culture women could be patrons and Tabitha may have been a patron or benefactor of widows.[88] The term 'doing good' (ἀγαθῶν ἐργῶν) may include or even be equivalent to, early Christian benefaction – as a replacement for the standard Greco-Roman patron-client relationships requiring reciprocity.[89] Evidences prove that Jewish women also were active in charity projects. There are typical Lucan style evident in the episode: the metaphorical use of πλήρης (Acts 6:3,5;7:55;

11:24), and the translation of the name Tabitha for his Greek readers. These elements show that Luke has not borrowed a source completely.[90] The words μαθήεητρια, διερμηνευομένη (woman disciple, being translated: these words are seen only in Luke and Acts) demonstrate that Luke has not invented the episode and this passage (Acts 9:36-42) is within the historically reliable source.[91] But the language and style of the narrative is predominantly Lucan.[92] The historical basis of the episode is a stay of Peter in Lydda and Joppa and the raising of a benefactress of the widows of Joppa.[93]

Ἀγαθῶν ἔργων καὶ ἐλεημοσυνῶν (the acts of charity and almsgiving) anticipates the parallel description of the generosity of powerful Cornelius in 10:2. The Greek word ἐλεημοσυνῶν is same in both texts. In addition, this description of her conforms to Luke's implicit association of faithful believers with the responsible use of possessions (4:36-37;16:15; 20: 33-35).[94] Both these descriptions suggest that she was a woman of means, with the leisure and freedom to do good deeds for others.[95]

V. 39. proves her contributions to the community.[96] It is possible, of course, that she was commissioned to do this by the church at Joppa and that this explains the unusual concern of the church at her death.[97]

Luke gives a detailed   presentation of Tabitha and this indicates that women believers were not neglected in the early church. Her reputation was so revered, and her ministry so valued within the larger community of saints and widows. By the raising of Tabitha a beloved and respected religious leader, activist, and philanthropist was restored to the community.[98] F. D. Bacon observes that the name of Dorcas has entered into history as synonymous with a high standard of charity and benevolence. She was full of good works and alms deeds, being especially charitable to the sick and poor, whom she was diligent in visiting and relieving. Upon her death all her neighbours held up her name to praise, bringing forth practical evidence of her good works; and so much was Peter impressed with her Christian character and example that he prayed she might be raised up again, which prayer God answered.[99] She was felt so valuable to the Christian community that many widows wept at her death and Peter rushed to her side from a neighbouring town to raise her from the dead- the first such miracle done by an apostle.

Implications

There is no mention of Tabitha's husband's name and it can be assumed that she was a single or widowed. She was a woman of means, for she had enough to share with others. There were a number of widows present at her home, who received help from her. And most probably Tabitha had a spacious house. Jane D. Schaberg and Sharon H. Ringe observe that most members of the earliest Jesus movement were from the ranks of the poor and these women could not be wealthy philanthropists or benefactors.[100] But Mary mother of John Mark, Lydia and Phoebe were wealthy benefactors of many missionaries and travelling apostles. The women were so associated with Jesus and when they enter his life, they enter into a life of sharing in the performance of good deeds.[101] Luke's attitude to wealth was that it must be shared among the poor (4:32-5:11; 12:15-21; 16:19-31; 19:1-10). These women put into practice the commands of Jesus and throughout the spread of Christianity both in Jewish and Gentile mission women played a tremendous role in spreading the Gospel, exercising spiritual gifts, and supporting financially.

Mary, the Hostess of Jerusalem Church (Acts 12:12)

Mary the mother of John Mark had a house in Jerusalem and the primitive church in Jerusalem used to gather there for prayer and worship. Political authorities started persecuting the church, but Mary gave leadership to the church by opening her house to daily prayer of early Christians even among the mounting opposition. There were no church buildings at that time and believers gathered in houses.

The conflicts between the Christians and the ruler Herod Agrippa I in Acts ch.12 is the immediate context of the passage. James, the brother of John was killed with the sword and Peter was arrested. Peter was to be killed the next day, but the believers gathered together in Mary's house and prayed earnestly. God delivered Peter from the prison and he went to Mary's house. Traditionally it was believed that this was the house in which Jesus and the disciples ate the Last Supper and where the disciples were praying when the Pentecost arrived. This house was at the disposal of the Christian community (Acts 12:12-13; cf 2:46) and it may even be that they had gathered in the place where they assembled after the ascension of Jesus (1:14-2:4) and this is the reason why Peter went to that house.[102] Another tradition says John Mark was Peter's interpreter in Rome. If this is so, a Jew residing in Jerusalem and learning Latin means Mary could afford a good education for her son, either by hiring a tutor or sending him to Rome for studies.[103] Their relative Barnabas was also a landowner and it is possible that this was a wealthy landowning family in the Jerusalem community.

From this reference, it is evident that, Mary, the mother of John Mark is a woman of considerable means, having a house to entertain many Christians who frequently assembled for prayer. It is possible that this house may be a part of her dowry, deed of gift, *ketubah* or her husband's share if widowed, as in the case of Judith. If the house was Mary's husband's share, John Mark would have been the owner of the house. Therefore, it is likely that the house is Mary's dowry or the deed of gift by her parents. Throughout the ancient Mediterranean, dowries varied but, over the centuries, included houses, lands, slaves (Gen. 24:59-61).[104] Dowry is according to the wealth of the bride's family and status of bride groom's family. And thus, it was a display of honour and prestige for both families.

A home with an outer gate, a servant girl who could serve as a porter and a gathering much farther back in the house would suggest the home of a fairly wealthy resident of Jerusalem's Upper City.[105] As Levites[106] they may have had ties with the priestly aristocracy; many well to-do priests lived in the Upper City.[107] Thus the home is not far from the temple mount hence not far from the fortress Antonia, where Peter may have been held.[108] And it is remarkable that Mary sheltered an escaped prisoner without any fear of authorities.

Mary is mentioned only once but John Mark is mentioned more than once (Acts 12:25; 13:5; 15:37; Col. 4:10; 2Tim. 4:11; Phlm. 24; and 1Pet. 5:13). This indicates John Mark had a reputation as a Christian missionary but the house where the primitive church met was owned by Mary. Thus in the church as well as in urban society in general, certain women of wealth and influence could play prominent roles.[109] It was not impossible that some women who owned property and joined Jesus' band of travelling followers retained the property and put the income from it into the common fund.[110]

Implications

Mary's house must have been of some size, with a vestibule opening onto the street, an intervening court , and a rear living quarters.[111]The fact that she had at least one servant, Rhoda, in her employ, also suggests that she may have been a woman of some financial means.[112] Mary is named and it is striking that no man is mentioned as husband of Mary and father of John Mark; somewhere behind Luke's narrative lies a tradition of a Christian family in Jerusalem where the father either was already dead or had not become a Christian.[113] The house is most probably Mary's parental property through deed of gift or dowry and thus the house owner is Mary not John Mark. Mary was apparently the head of the house; the identification of the head of a household as a woman is striking but not unparalleled (cf. Lk. 10:38-42; Acts 16:14-15). Besides, in that atmosphere of persecution and arrest Mary fearlessly opened her house for this 'illegal religion', indicates her decision making capacity attained through economic independence.

Lydia, the Hostess of Philippian Church (Acts 16: 14,15,40)

During the second missionary journey of Paul, he travelled to Philippi, a Roman colony and the leading city of that district of Macedonia which was founded by Alexander the great. On the Sabbath day Paul and Silas began to share the Gospel and Lydia responded to their message positively. Her entire household got baptized following her conversion and they were the first fruits in Philippi. The first church in Philippi was also the first in Europe and hence Lydia, a rich businesswoman was the first Christian believer in Europe.

Lydia was a Thyatiran dealer in purple fabrics. Thyatira was known for its dyers' guilds and textiles, and inscriptions show that other Thyatiran business agents also sold purple dye in Macedonia, becoming prosperous.[114] Purple dye was a murex secretion from mollusks used for colouring materials, much in demand in the Roman era and earlier. West Asian people prized this rich red-blue colour, using it for royal robes. Purple clothes were a luxury item and used by the wealthy (Lk. 16:19) and the royal people.[115]

It was used for the Tabernacle curtains, priest's ephods, and finally for the robe placed on Christ when he was ironically crowned 'King of the Jews.'[116] A fragmentary Latin inscription from Philippi (CIL 3.664.1) appears to refer to dealers in purple. Several local inscriptions refer to guilds of dyers.[117] In Rome, the emperor and no other enjoyed the privilege of wearing a robe entirely of "royal purple." Lower nobility, freeborn boys, and certain priests could sport at most a purple stripe, and others no purple at all.[118]Lydia's profession indicates that she probably possessed a fair amount of wealth and had relatively high economic status.[119] Her name, occupation and place of origin show that she belongs to the Greek-speaking merchants who have settled in Philippi. It is evident from the inscriptions that dyeing was a trade practiced by slaves, and selling purple goods was an occupation of former slaves. [120] In that case she may have been a freed slave. The city Thyatira lay in Lydia and Kingdom Lydia was one of the ancient kingdoms[121] subsumed by the Roman province of Asia, and among its industries was the production of textiles and dyes. [122] The people of that area were famed for their skill in the manufacture of purple dye, extracted from the juice of the madder root and the purple-fish (Porphyra). This was continued for the dyeing of carpets till the end of the nineteenth century, before it was superseded by chemical dyes.[123] Various forms of purple dye were used, ranging significantly in price. Lydia was a worshipper of God (σεβομένη τόν θέον): Lydia was not a Jewish by birth. Like Cornelius she was a devout Gentile worshipper of God. According to general concensus in the NT research, the god-fearers were gentiles attracted to Judaism, but unconverted, not having been circumcised.[124] They believed in Jewish monotheism but were not the full converts. It may have been that she was a Gentile adherent of the synagogue, a Jewish sympathizer.[125] She had large household (ὁ οἶκος) which included relatives and slaves[126] and when she received gospel all of them followed her new-found faith.

Another remarkable thing we see in this narrative is that she invites Apostle Paul and Silas to her house to stay there (Εἰσελθόντες εἰς Τὸν οἶκον μου μείνατε). This imperative sentence reveals the authority and influence of Lydia. Like Martha (Lk. 10:38), She herself is inviting the guests earnestly. And this indicates that she was the owner and the leader of the household and her opinion was respected and obeyed by other members. Concerning Lydia's invitation to Paul and Silas to her house to use her house as a centre of their ministry, Richard R. Losch opines that 'Jewish law would not have allowed a woman to make such an offer, but Macedonian women were unusually independent for those times.[127] But Losch is saying this without considering the openness of Mary, the mother of Mark in Jerusalem and Martha in Bethany.

After the conversion of Lydia, Paul and Silas healed a demon-possessed slave girl who brought much gain to her owners through divination. This incident led the missionaries' arrest and persecution. After their release they went to Lydia's house, because Philippian church was in Lydia's house. There they met the brethren, encouraged them and departed to next destination. It is remarkable that Lydia had the determination to opt for a new religion, not respected and approved by authorities, and even to lodge 'the convicts,' the main advocates of this faith, in her house. She was an alien businesswoman but she started a new church in her house even in the midst of political opposition. This shows her influence and authority that when she found a new faith she and her household got baptized together and she hosted the Philippian church in her house.

By this period, some women were engaged in business; even slave women could become managers, just like slave men.[128] The Diana cult in Philippi may have made women more prominent than in other Greek centres. Moreover, Macedonian women traditionally exercised more freedom than Greek women.[129] They had greater independence and importance in public affairs.[130] In Asia Minor and Macedonia women engaged in private businesses, served in public offices, and had prominent roles in various religious cults.[131] During this period, it was not unusual for a woman to develop a business of her own or through inheritance from her husband. [132] And well-to-do women became patrons of pagan religious associations or Judaism also.

Implications

Lydia, an economically independent non-elite woman[133]was attracted to Christianity, propagated by Paul and his team. She was a single woman either divorced or widowed. Her husband is not mentioned, and she might have advanced from the inheritance of her father or she might herself earned and started business. She was a dealer of purple, a luxury good that has been associated with wealth throughout the Mediterranean culture for over a thousand years.[134]

Lydia is said to have a household, an expression not normally attached to a married woman's name.[135] This financially independent lady was the ruler of her household [136] because her household followed her when she was baptized and joined a new community.[137]

This rich merchant woman had a house in which several guests could be accommodated and her prosperity put her in a position to invite Paul and Silas to accept hospitality in her home.[138] Her sizable home as well as a hospitable disposition[139]helped her to host Philippian church in her house and thus upon conversion she made her home and resources available for the life and work of the church.[140] And the Scriptures suggest that she was the leader of this house church.[141] Receiving her invitation, Paul and Silas returned to this house-church after the release from jail and before their forced departure.

Lydia is portrayed as a benefactor who provided resources to the missionaries who depended upon local patrons. Literary and inscriptional evidence indicates that from Hellenistic times women in Macedonia, as well as in Asia minor and Egypt, enjoyed more personal freedom and participation in social and economic life than women in most of the eastern Mediterranean lands. It is therefore not surprising that women played a significant role in the early years of the Philippian church (Phili. 4:2).

Although economically successful with a household of her own, Lydia was probably of the low social status to which workers and traders in textiles usually belonged. But she acquired status through economic independence. It is significant that the first church in Europe met in the house of a woman and was supported by a woman. At the probable risk of a loss of business, Lydia courageously received the dissidents Paul and Silas back into her home after they were released from jail.[142] If she took the risk of extending her hospitality to people who had just been in jail, and thus remained suspect in the eyes of the police, she was indeed a woman of uncommon fortitude and character.[143]   Lydia, very interested in Christian faith, led all her household to that faith, hosted the church, and most probably gave leadership to the house-church. She also used her economic independence for patronizing the church and missionaries. Her economic independence gave her leadership role in her household and the power of determination. Her voice was respected and obeyed by the members in her household. After all, her experience reveals that even slaves could attain economic self-sufficiency, status and honour and come to the forefront of the society.

Summary

The search for the economic status of women in the book of Acts with the help of an exegetical study reveals certain relevant facts. Firstly, women possessed private property and income. They collected income from their landed property, or they conducted profitable business. Secondly these wealthy women gave financial support to the apostles and travelling missionaries. Thirdly they owned spacious houses on their own and were free to receive even male guests and host house-churches. Fourthly they were free to handle their income according to their will and pleasure. Fifthly, they shared equal authority in their husband's property by the privilege of their *ketubah* and their consent was needed to sell any property that their husband owned. Sixthly, wealthy women were free to give alms and do charity works for widows and the needy. Seventhly, single/divorced, widowed and married women had economic security and independence. Eighthly, their economic independence enabled them to acquire status and influence, which was otherwise formally denied to them in public life. The institution of patronage was open even to freed women slaves and they could patronize persons or movement, and this boosted their social status also. Thus, many wealthy women- named and unnamed- patronized Jesus movement and later Christian enterprise. They boldly received this 'illicit' gospel, led their household to the new faith, hosted churches and supported financially.

To sum up, there were a considerable number of rich and influential high-standing women who patronized Jesus movement. They even dared to host 'convicts' without fearing society or political opposition; their wealthy disposition gave them confidence to do what they deemed right and valuable. In the family they had the authority to handle their resources, in society they could travel or follow what seemed best to them, and after all majority of them had independent sources of income. They had decision-making capacity and they implemented their decisions without any hindrance from patriarchal authorities. Therefore, the assumption that most of the women in the book of Acts had economic independence and freedom to handle it according to their priorities can be concluded beyond doubt.

Endnotes

[1] Jerome H. Neyrey, ed., *The Social World of Luke-Acts* (Peabody: Hendrickson Publishers, 1991), x.

[2] Will Durant, *The Story of Civilization, Part III, Caesar and Christ A History of Roman Civilization and of Christianity from their beginning to AD 325* (New York: Simon and Schuster1944),134-135.

[3] Everett Ferguson, Backgrounds of Early Christianity, 2nd ed. (Grand Rapids: William B. Eerdmans, 1993), 73.

[4] Sarah B. Pomeroy, Goddesses, Whores, Wives, and Slaves Women in Classical Antiquity (New York: Schocken Books, 1975), 62.

[5] Pomeroy, Goddesses, Whores, Wives, and Slaves ,63.

[6] "Spartan Women,"," *Encyclopaedia of Women in the Ancient World* (California: ABC-Clio, Inc., 2001): 330.

[7] Elaine Fantham , et al., *Women in the Classical World* (New York: Oxford University Press, 1994), 64.

[8] Pomeroy, *Goddesses, Whores, Wives and Slaves*, 38.

[9] Lynn H. Cohick, *Women in the World of the Earliest Christians* (Grand Rapids: Baker Academie, 2009), 43.

[10] "Roman Women," *The Encyclopaedia of Women in the Ancient World*, 304.

[11] *Tutelage* means the supervision of a man- father, brother, husband, son, or a guardian- without whose consent a woman could not marry or dispose of property. See Will Durant, *The Story of Civilization*, Part III, 87.

[12] In a *sine manu* marriage a woman remained attached to her former family, retained her own property and she had the freedom to divorce her husband. She was not a legal member in the husband's family nor an heir to her husband's inheritance. But in practice, husbands and wives increasingly disregarded the legal strictures and willed property to each other, but the ambiguity continued, because it was economically and socially advantageous to a woman's *familia* to keep her as a member. See Deborah F. Sawyer, *Women and Religion in the First Christian Centuries* (New York: Rutledge, 1998), 19; Carolyn Oseik, "The family in Early Christianity: "Family Values" Revisited," *CBQ*, 58/1 (January 1996): 10.

[13] Sawyer, *Women and Religion in the First Christian Centuries*, 19.

[14] Cohick, *Women in the World*, 42.

[15] An emancipated woman, legally *sui iuris* or her own person, could own and dispose of her property.

[16] Carolyn Oseik and David Balch, *Families in the New Testament World Households and House Churches* ,57.

[17] Myrtle Pellew, *Women Leaders in Ministry* (USA: Xlibris Corporation,2011),16.

[18]Wayne A. Meeks, *The First Urban Christians The Social World of Apostle Paul* (New Haven and London: Yale University Press, 1983), 24.

[19] See P. Garnsey, "Grain for Rome", in *Trade in the Ancient Economy*, edited by P. Garnsey, K. Hopkins, and C.R. Whittaker (Los Angeles: University of California, 1983), 124-126, cited by Arlandson, *Women, Class and Society,*77.

[20] John C. Lentz, *Luke's Portrait of Paul*, Society for NT Studies Monograph Series, 77 (Cambridge: Cambridge University Press, 1993), 10.

[21] John Lobo, "Marriage Law: New Perspectives," *Asian Journal for Priests*, 50/1(January 2005): 28.

[22] Carol Meyers, "Procreation, Production, and Protection: Male-Female Balance in Early Israel", *JAAR,* 51/4, 573.

[23] Eckhard J. Schnabel, *Early Christian Mission*, vol. 1 Jesus and the Twelve (Downers Grove: Inter Varsity Press, 2004), 573.

[24] James Malcolm Arlandson, *Women, Class, and Society in Early Christianity Models from Luke-Acts* (Peabody: Hendrickson,1997), 37.

[25] John Stambaugh and David Balch, *The Social World*, 115; see also Will Durant, *The Story of Civilization*, Part III, 221-222.

[26] Grace I. Emmerson, "Women in Ancient Israel," in *The World of Ancient Israel*, edited by R. E. Clements (Cambridge: Cambridge University Press, 1989), 382.

[27] Families headed by fathers.

[28] John J. Pilch, "Marriage," *The Bible Today,* 40/5 (September 2002): 316.

[29] C. Meyers, "The Roots of Restriction: Women in Early Israel," *BA* 41(1978): 91-103, cited by Grace I. Emmerson, "Women in Ancient Israel," 383.

[30] Joseph Blenkinsopp, "Family in First Temple Israel," in *Families in Ancient Israel*, edited by Leo G. Perdue, et al. (Louisville: Westminster John Knox Press,1997), 60.

[31] K. C. Hanson, "The Herodians and Mediterranean Kinship," Part III: Economics, *BTB*, vol. 20/1 (Spring, 1990): 10.

[32] K. Grosz, "Bride-wealth and Dowry in Nuzi" in *Images of Women in Antiquity*, edited by A. Cameron and A. Kuhrt (Detroit: Wayne State University Press, 1983), 193-206, see Joseph Blenkinsopp, "Family in First Temple Israel,"60.

[33] Carol Meyers, "The Family in Early Israel," *Families in Ancient Israel,* edited by Leo G. Perdue, et al. (Louisville: Westminster John Knox Press,1997),25-26.

[34] B. S. J. Isserlin, *The Israelites* (Minneapolis: Fortress Press, 2001), 182.

[35] Isserlin, *The Israelites,* 102.

[36] Isserlin, *The Israelites,* 99-100.

[37] Collins, "Marriage, Divorce, and Family in Second Temple Judaism," in *Families in Ancient Israel,* edited by Leo G. Perdue, et al. (Louisville: Westminster John Knox Press,1997),146.

[38] The money given to bride's father by the bridegroom.

[39] M. Keuboth 6:5, Danby, *Mishna,* 253-4.

[40] Aramaic documents from the Jewish settlement at Elephantine in Egypt, dated firmly to the Persian period, include marriage contracts belonging to Jewish women. See Tal Ilan, "Women," *The Eerdmans Dictionary of Early Judaism,* 1347.

[41] M.J. Geller, "New Sources for the Origins of the Rabbinic Ketubah," *Hebrew Union College Annual* 49(1978):227-45, Collins, "Marriage, Divorce, and Family in Second Temple Judaism," 114.

[42] The term *ketubah* derives from *ketav*, which means a written document. Ketubah (plural *ketuboth*) refers to the marriage contract a groom gives to his bride at the time of marriage, and it also provides a settlement of a specified sum he is to make to her if he divorces her. The same settlement is to be made to her from his estate if he dies before her. See *The Talmud, Selected Writings*, translated by Ben Zion Bokser (New York: Paulist Press,1989),140.

[43]M. Ketuboth 1. 2, Danby, *Mishna,* 245.

[44] Lee A. Johnson and Robert C. Tannehill, "Lilies Do Not Spin: A Challenge to Female Social Norms," *NTS*, 56/4 (October, 2010): 481.

[45] Miriam Peskowitz, "Gender, Difference, and Everyday life," in *Religion and Society in Roman Palestine Old Questions, New Approaches*, edited by Douglas R. Edwards (New York and London: Routledge, 2004), 140.

[46] M. Yebam. 15:2; M.Eduyoth 1.12, Danby, *Mishna* ,241, 423.

[47] M. Ketub. 9.4, Danby, *Mishna* ,263.

[48] Cynthia M. Baker, "Imagined Households," In *Religion and Society in Roman Palestine Old Questions, New Approaches*, edited by Douglas R. Edwards (New York and London: Routledge, 2004), 117.

[49] Luise Schottroff, *Lydia's Impatient Sisters a Feminist Social History of Early Christianity* (London: SCM Press, 1995), 83-84.

[50] Ross S. Kraemer, "Jewish Women in the Diaspora World of Late Antiquity," in *Jewish Women in Historical Perspective*, edited by Judith R. Baskin (Detroit: Wayne University Press, 1998), 48.

[51] M. Ketub. 9:4, Danby, *Mishna,* 258.

[52] M. B. Bat. 8:5-7, Danby, The *Mishna,* 377-78.

[53] Richard Baucham, *Gospel Women: Studies of the Named Women in the Gospels* (New York: T&T Clark, 2002), 123.

[54] Baucham, *Gospel Women,* 123.

[55] M. Ketub. 9:4; 13:10-11;   M. Yebam., 15: 1, 2, 6,10, Danby, *Mishna* ,263, 242-3.

[56]Archives at Elephantine K 9: 3ff., K 9: 16ff., K 9:21; K 28; C5, 8, 9; C 13; C 14; C 15-17, cited by Linda Bennett Elder, "Judith," in *Searching the Scriptures A Feminist Commentary*, vol.2, edited by Elizabeth Schüsssler Fiorenza (New York: The Crossroad Publishing Company, 1994), 459.

[57] Halvor Moxnes, "The Social Context of Luke's Community," *Interpretation*, 48/4 (October, 1994): 385.

[58] Ross S. Kraemer, "Jewish Women in the Diaspora World of Late Antiquity," in *Jewish Women in Historical Perspective*, edited by Judith R. Baskin (Detroit: Wayne University Press, 1998), 48-49.

[59] Ben Witherington III, *The Acts of the Apostles: A Socio-Rhetorical Commentary* (Grand Rapids: Wm. B. Eerdmns, 1998), 335-336.

[60]Herbert Schneider, "Women in Early Christianity and the Institutionalization of Charisma," *EAPR*, 44/2 (2007): 166.

[61] Witherington III, *The Acts of the Apostles*, 335-336.

[62] Barbara H. Geller Nathanson, "Toward a Multicultural Ecumenical History of Women," in *Searching the Scriptures A Feminist Commentary*, vol.2, 277-78.

[63] Pheme Perkins, *New Testament Introduction* (Mumbai: St. Paul's, 1997), 166.

[64] Robert W. Wall, "The Acts of the Apostles," *The New Interpreter's Bible*, vol. 10 (Nashville: Abingdon Press,2002), 95.

[65] In the OT Hananiah is Daniel's friend who was given the name Shadrach by Nebuchadnezzar. There are two other persons named as Ananias in Acts; a believer (9:10-17; 22:12) and high priest (23:2; 24:1).

[66] C. K. Barrett, *The Acts of the Apostles, A Critical and Exegetical Commentary*, vol.1 (Edinburgh: T&T Clark, 1994), 70.

[67] C. K. Barrett, *The Acts of the Apostles, I-IX*, 264.

[68] Ben Witherington, *Jesus & Money* (London: SPCK,2010),103.

[69]Beverly Roberts Gaventa, *The Acts of the Apostles*, Abingdon New Testament Commentaries (Nashville: Abingdon Press, 2003), 102.

[70] In 1QS 6:24-25: "If there be found in the community a man who consciously lies in the matter of (his) wealth, he is to be regarded as outside the state of purity entailed by membership, and he is to be mulcted of one fourth of his food ration." In Qumran community there was sacral judgment through blessing and cursing (1QS 2:4-18; CD 19:13). See Hans Conzelmann, *Acts of the Apostles* (Philadelphia: Fortress Press, 1987), 37.

[71] J. Albert Harrill, "Divine Judgment against Ananias and Sapphira (Acts 5:1-11): a Stock Scene of Perjury and Death", *JBL*, 130/2 (Summer, 2011): 352.

[72] John Gillman, *Possessions and the Life of Faith: A Reading of Luke-Acts* (Collegeville: The Liturgical Press, 1991), 98.

[73] Gail R. O' Day, "Acts," in *The Women's Bible Commentary*, edited by Carol A. Newsom and Sharon H. Ringe (Great Britain: SPCK, 1992),309.

[74] This information is indebted to Ivoni Richter Reimer, *Women in the Acts of the Apostles A Feminist Liberation Perspective*, translated by Linda M. Maloney (Minneapolis: Fortress Press, 1995), 3-23 who depends on Elizabeth Koffman, *Die Doppelurkunden aus der Wüste Juda*.

Recht und Praxis der jüdichen Papyri des 1.und2. Jahrhunderts n.Chr. samt Übersetzung der Texte bund deutscher Übersetzung. Studies on the texts of the Desert of Judah 5. Leiden, 1968.

[75] These duplicate documents are papyri on which the same text is written twice, one version beneath the other. The upper writing was then rolled up, tied and sealed while the lower text was simply folded together in order to read easily.

[76] Richard Baucham, *Gospel Women*, 130.

[77] Ivoni Richter Reimer, *Women in the Acts of the Apostles*, 23.

[78] Prema Vakayil, *Women Shall Prophecy (Joel 2:28) Anna, The Prophetesses (Lk.2:36-38): a Study in Luke's Feminist Perspective* (Bangalore: Asian Trading Corporation, 2007),50.

[79] Barrett, *The Acts of the Apostles, A Critical and Exegetical Commentary,* 70

[80] Clarice J. Martin, "The Acts of the Apostles," in *Searching the Scriptures A Feminist Commentary*, vol.2, 779.

[81] "David A. Fiensy, "The Composition of Jerusalem Church," *The Book of Acts in its First Century Setting,* vol.4 *Palestinian Setting*, edited by Richard Baucham (Grand Rapids: Wm. B. Eerdmans Publishing Company, 1995), 229.

[82] F.F. Bruce, *The Book of Acts*, NICNT (Grand Rapids: Wm. B. Erdmans, 1983), 212.

[83] Parvey, "The Theology and Leadership of Women in the New Testament," in *Religion and Sexism Images of Woman in the Jewish Christian Traditions,* edited by Rosemary Radford Reuther (New York: Simon and Schuster, 1974),144. Cf. also Witherington III, *The Acts of the Apostles*, 332.

[84] The masculine form maqhthv~ is used in the sense of disciple for the first time by Luke in Acts 6:1. When Luke intends to mean the Twelve he uses do'deka (Acts 6:2) cf. Joseph Puthenkulam, "The Significance of 'Widow' in Luke-Acts: THE WIDOWS OF JOPPA (Acts 9,36-42)- An Exegetical Study," BB 40/2 (June,2014): foot note no. 15.

[85] C. K. Barrett, *The Acts of the Apostles*, 482.

[86] This is a common custom in antiquity, but this is not mentioned elsewhere in the NT. The inclusion of this intimate detail here provides one of several indications of Tabitha's significance in the community of

believers. See Beverly Roberts Gaventa, *The Acts of the Apostles*, 160.

[87] Ivoni Richter, *Women in the Acts of the Apostles*, 34.

[88] Keener, *The IVP Bible Background Commentary New Testament*, 349.

[89] Craig L. Blomberg, *Neither Poverty nor Riches, A Biblical Theology of Possessions*, NSBT 7 (Downers Grove: IVP,1999),170.

[90]Joseph Puthenkulam, "The Significance of 'Widow,' 88.

[91] This historically reliable source, Jerusalem-Caesarean source, can possibly be traced back to the evangelist Philip. See Joseph Puthenkulam, "The Significance of 'Widow' in Luke-Acts,"88, foot note no. 10.

[92] Joseph Puthenkulam, "The Significance of 'Widow' in Luke-Acts," 89.

[93] Joseph Puthenkulam, "The Significance of 'Widow' in Luke-Acts," 88.

[94] Beverly Roberts Gaventa, *The Acts of the Apostles*, 159.

[95] Ben Witherington III, *The Acts of the Apostles A Socio-Rhetorical Commentary* (Carlisle: Paternoster Press, 1998), 331.

[96] Ernst Haenchen, *The Acts of Apostles A Commentary* (Philadelphia: The Westminster Press, 1971), 339.

[97] Stählin, "Xhra," *TDNT*, vol.9, 451-52.

[98] Clarice J. Martin, "The Acts of the Apostles," 782.

[99] F. D. Bacon, *Women in the Church* (London: Lutterworth Press, 1946), 16.

[100] Jane D. Schaberg and Sharon H. Ringe, "Gospel of Luke," in *Women's Bible Commentary*, 507.

[101] Asher Finkel, "Women in the Jewish-Biblical Tradition," in *Women and Worship: Perspectives from World Religions*, edited by Augustine Thottakara (Bangalore: Journal of Dharma & Dharmaram Publications, 2000), 112.

[102] Ivoni Richter, *Women in the Acts of the Apostles*, 241.

[103] Arlandson, *Women, Class and Society*, 139.

[104] M. Yebam. 7:1; Danby *Mishna*, 227-28; see also K.C. Hanson, "All in the Family: Kinship in Agrarian Roman Palestine," in *The Social World of the New Testament* edited by Jerome H. Neyrey and Eric C. Stewart (Peabody: Hendrickson, 2008), 35.

[105] Keener, *The IVP Bible Background Commentary New Testament* (Downers Grove: IVP,1993), 356.

[106] Cf. Col.4:10 with Acts 4:36-37.

[107] Keener, *The IVP Bible Background Commentary New Testament*, 356.

[108] Keener, *The IVP Bible Background Commentary New Testament*, 356.

[109] "David A. Fiensy, "The Composition of Jerusalem Church," *The Book of Acts in its First Century Setting*, vol. 4 *Palestinian Setting*, edited by Richard Baucham (Grand Rapids: Wm. B. Eerdmans Publishing Company, 1995), 229.

[110] Richard Baucham, *Gospel Women*, 116.

[111] Frank E. Gaebelein, ed. *John-Acts*, The Expositor's Bible commentary (Grand Rapids: Zondervan Publishing House, 1981), 410.

[112] Clarice J. Martin, "The Acts of the Apostles," 783.

[113] C. K. Barrett, *The Acts of the Apostles, A Critical and Exegetical Commentary*, 583.

[114] Keener, *The IVP Bible Background Commentary New Testament*, 368.

[115] 1Macc. 10:62.

[116] Nancy M. Tischler, *Men and Women of the Bible A Reader's Guide*, (London: Greenwood Press,2002), 155.

[117] Barrett, *The Acts of the Apostles,* A Critical and Exegetical Commentary, 184, 252.

[118] Wayland Barber, *Women's Work: The First 20,000 Years, Women, Cloth, and Society in Early Times* (New York: W.W. Norton & Company, 1994), 150.

[119] John C. Lentz, *Luke's Portrait of Paul,* Society for New Testament Studies Monograph Series 77 (Cambridge: Cambridge University Press,1993), 11.

[120] Mary Ann Getty-Sullivan, *Women in the New Testament* (Collegeville: The Order of St. Benedict Inc.,2001), 246.

[121] See Isa. 66:19.

[122] Pliny the Elder, *Natural History* 5:10, cited by Luke Timothy Johnson, *The Acts of the Apostles*, Sacra Pagina series, vol.5 (Collegeville: The Liturgical Press, 1992), 292.

[123] F. F. Bruce, *The Book of the Acts,* Revised, NICNT, 311.

[124] Ivoni Richter Ivoni Richter Reimer, *Women in the Acts of the Apostles*, 93.

[125] Barrett, *The Acts of the Apostles,* in A Critical and Exegetical Commentary, 252.

[126] Gerd Theissen, *The Social Setting of Pauline Christianity: Essays on Corinth,* translated by J. H. Schültz (Philadelphia: Fortress Press, 1982), 86.

[127] Richard R. Losch, *All the People in the Bible* (Grand Rapids: Wm. B. Eerdmans, 2008), 264.

[128] Keener, *The IVP Bible Background Commentary New Testament,* 368.

[129] Keener, *The IVP Bible Background Commentary New Testament,* 368.

[130] Everett Ferguson, *Backgrounds of Early Christianity* (Grand Rapids: Wm. B. Eerdmans, 1987), 58.

[131]   Witherington III, "Women (NT)", *ABD,* Vol. 6 (New York: Doubleday,1992), 958.

[132] Nancy M. Tischler, *Men and Women of the Bible A Reader's Guide,* 154.

[133] Halvor Moxnes, "The Social Context of Luke's Community," 385.

[134] Keener, *The IVP Bible Background Commentary New Testament,* 368.

[135] Beverly Roberts Gaventa, *The Acts of the Apostles,* 237.

[136] Karen Jo Torjesen, *When Women were Priests: Women's Leadership in the Early Church and the Scandal of their Subordination in the Rise of Christianity* (New York: Harper Sanfracisco, 1993), 14.

[137] Ernst Haenchen, *The Acts of the Apostles* (Oxford: Basil Blackwell, 1971), 499.

[138] Karen Jo Torjesen, *When Women were Priests,* 15.

[139] Mini S. Johnson, *Women in Christianity* (Delhi: Mittal Publications, 2005), 28.

[140] Clarice J. Martin, "The Acts of the Apostles," 784.

[141] Mimi Haddad, "Social History as a Window into Paul's View of Women," in *Side by Side: Gender from a Christian Perspective,* edited by Beaulah Wood (Bangalore: SIACS Press,2007),128-129.

[142] Mini S. Johnson, *Women in Christianity,* 28.

[143] Samuel Terrien, *Till the Heart sings: A Biblical Theology of Manhood and Womanhood* (Grand Rapids: Wm. B. Erdmans,1985), 154-155.

Implications of Postmodernism in Pastoral Care and Counselling Practice

L.V. Bipinlal

INTRODUCTION

Pastoral counseling and pastoral care means "Explanation, clarification and guidance of human life, both individual and corporate at the experiential and behavioral levels through a theological perspective"[1]. Before Christianity pastoral care was a significant aspect of Israelite community's life and its tradition. Out of which the Old Testament or Jewish scriptures emerged. In recent years, postmodernism has emerged as an influential intellectual movement in various disciplines, including the field of counseling. Postmodernism is a philosophical framework that holds that knowledge is socially constructed and language based. The postmodern perspective is to be contrasted with traditional modernist conceptions that endorse an objectivist approach. Numerous counseling models have been developed in keeping with a postmodern perspective. This paper deals the implication of postmodernism in the pastoral care and counselling practice.

DEFINING POST MODERNISM

The term postmodernism became pervasive in European and North American culture in 1970's. It was the high period of capitalism marked by media consumption, consumerism, and 'globalization'. Postmodernism emerged out of the context of Marxism's failure to provide alternatives to the capitalistic scenario. The post-war period saw the emergence of various new social movements such as ant-war initiatives, ecological, feminist movements, and de-colonizing movements of Asians, Africans and Afro-Americans. They challenged the unitary notions of the project of modernity for being Euro-centric, andro-centric and colonial in content.[2]

To arrive at a single definition of postmodernism is possible. Of course post moderns do not believe in a single 'neutral' definition. Postmodernism meant different things for different people. Its supporters and critics are unanimous only in the matter of its plurality of definitions. 'Social space', 'social position' and 'subjectivity' are postmodern categories. It demands and points to an epistemic shift.[3] David Harvey is a respected geographer defines postmodernism as a condition. He does not call it as an "ism" nor even an "era". He identifies postmodern change as a "sea change".[4] "Postmodern" has become a gregarious adjective, and can often be seen in the company of such respectable terms as "literature," "philosophy," "architecture," "art," "history," "science," "cinema" – and, yes, even "biblical studies" and "theology."[5]

DIFFERENT VIEWS OF THE WORD "POSTMODERN"

Diogenes Allen of Princeton Theological Seminary identified five ways in which people see postmodernism: as theology that follows Karl Barth, as an existential-hermeneutical approach that trace back to Heidinger and Schleiermarcher, as a "deconstructionalist" approach that goes to Heidiger and Derrida; as a process theology that traces to Whitehead, and as a scientific world view that goes back to Planck and the development of Quantum theory.[6] For the American literary critic Ihab Hassan (1982), it is a 'new aesthetic formation'. Charles Jencks calls it as a 'condition'. Steven Connor (1997) considers it as a 'culture', while Fredric Jameson (1983) defines it as a 'cultural dominant'. For Jean Baudrillard (1975), Francis Fukuyama (1991) and Gianni Vattimo (1988), it is a period in which we have reached the 'end of history'. Terry Eagleton (1990) calls it as 'an illusion', while Alex Callinicose (1989) defines it as 'a reactionary political formation'.[7]

MODERNISM AND POSTMODERNISM

Postmodernism is a epistemological turn. It fills the epistemological gaps created by modernism. Postmodernism is related to modernism at least in its difference. The 'post' in the postmodernism indicates not a mere succession of modernism rather a new direction from the previous one.[8] Modernism is a world view that has developed out of the seventeenth century Galilean-Cartesian-Baconian-Newtonian science. Modernity established an epistemic break with the traditional world view. Unlike the traditional world view, modernity provided as anthropocentric worldview. The rationalist philosophical world view of Rene Descartes, the main exponent of modernity, led to the modern conception of epistemology and anthropology.

Descartes placed 'the authoritative mind' and a 'reason-endowed subject' at the center of knowledge. But by critiquing the pure reason of reason of Descartes, Immanuel Kant took *a priori* categories of the mind as the basis for knowledge. Knowledge so constituted is universal. Human self is perceived as universal. Modernity was a quest for a universally valid, epistemological foundation.[9] A postmodern philosopher, Jurgen Habermas, opines that at the heart of modernity there is a universalistic philosophical anthropology. On one hand, it implies the commitment to the unity of humankind and on the other; it attempts to manage human diversity in a hierarchical ordering.

Postmodernism is an epistemic shift. It fills the epistemological gap created by the project of modernity. Postmodernism as it emerges out of these quests for 'alternative knowledge' is a collection of 'contested epistemologies' and thus envisages epistemological and anthropological pluralism.[10] It was the Linguistic Turn that first marked the epistemological shift from modernity. Modernity defined the person as an autonomous individual with rational consciousness, which transcends one's particular place in culture, language, history and gendered body (Cartesian self).

THEORETICAL FRAMEWORK OF POSTMODERNISM

Three theoretical pillars support the postmodern approach-social constructionism, constructivism and poststructuralism.

Social Constructionism

Social constructionism argues that perceived reality is socially constructed by people in the same culture who interact dialectically with each other. The primary concern of social constructionism is to understand how we interpret the world around us and assign meaning to life events and social realities and how these social meaning influence us. Furthermore, the process of social construction is an ongoing, dynamic process in which socially constructed reality can be reconstructed in a new way.[11]

Constructivism

From a social constructionalist perspective, reality is socially constructed, while in the light of constructivism, reality is personally constructed. In other words, each individual authors his or her own meaning system to make serfs of his perceived reality. According to Rosen, there are as many realities as there are perceivers because reality is not a unitary, objective phenomenon.[12]

Poststructuralism

Poststructuralism asserts that all phenomenona including the self and mind are themselves nothing but texts and therefore all phenomena allegedly in linguistic or literary constructions created by readers/observers.[13] To borrow Derrida's words, "there is nothing outside the text".[14] Derrida further argued that language is an essentially self-referential system in which true meaning is, therefore, endlessly deferred.[15]

Another important figure of Poststructuralism, Foucault, argued that by distinguishing what is normal from what is abnormal, the institutionalized professional discourse generates power.[16] From this perspective, in the professional client relationship, the locus of power lies in professionals, who are believed to have expert knowledge, while clients are, regarded as passive recipients of help.

In summary, postmodernist philosophy suggests that truth and reality are individualized and contextualized in socio-cultural forces, language and narratives. For postmodernists there is no objective reality that can be observed and discovered; only subjective realities exist.

BIBLICAL MODEL FOR PASTORAL CARE AND COUNSELLING

Historically and within the Christian community pastoral care is in the care of souls a tradition. Bible is the most reliable source regarding the beginning of pastoral care. The care of the community of people who worshiped the one God, Yahweh required assignment of leadership role to certain individuals. The earliest pastoral care ancestors are the Israelite priests as their spiritual ancestors[17]. Three classes of such leaders are the priests, a hereditary class that had particular responsibility for worship and ceremonial life, the prophets who spoke for Yahweh in relation to moral issue, sometimes rebuilding the community. Political leaders and the wise men and women who offered counsel of all short of concerning issues of the good life and personal conduct[18]. During the period of Amos, Jeremiah and authors of the Isaiah were the dominant voice in giving moral guidance to the community. Later the scribes and rabies emerged as vocational groups who carried on the functions of wise men and women and priests. They became dominant force in providing pastoral leadership to the Hebrew community.

The coming of Jesus, recordings to John's gospel, identifies himself as "the good shepherd". The shepherding image takes its place as a primary grounding image for ministry. The ministry of Jesus incorporates the wisdom expressed in certain of the parables and the Sermon on the Mount, his priestly leadership in relationship to his followers, but also elements of prophecy such as is found in the story of Jesus cleansing of the temple and his confrontation with the Pharisees and Sadducees. Early Christian times the image "shepherd of the flock" has persisted as a prototypical image applied institutional church. These images again and again appear in the writings of the early church father[19]. God calls different people to different sorts of ministry "some apostles, some prophets, some evangelists, some pastors and preachers" (Eph: 4: 11)

HISTORICAL DEVELOPMENT OF PASTORAL CARE AND COUNSELLING

Historical development of pastoral care and counselling are given below

THE PRIMITIVE CHURCH

During the earliest period of Christian history, the care of the nascent tradition by which Christians were identified was influenced by the anticipation of the immanent and cataclysmic *parousia*. The care of the community of Christians involved concern for the purity of the congregation in a non-Christian, pagan culture.

THE AGE OF PERSECUTION

In the second and third centuries of the Christian era the immediacy of the expectation of the return of Christ to usher in the new kingdom gradually diminished. Christians began to adapt to the necessity of sustaining its faith into an indefinite future. Same time the community's imperial Roman cultural context became more hostile. At first sporadic and then more frequent persecution of Christian believers placed

Christian community was under intense and Terrifying pressure conformity to the state cultic practices was increasingly demanded and by the faithful refused. Many Christians were inevitably compromised detections and temporary lapses into pagan allegiance to the emperors became common. Care and protection of the community became a dominant concern of the Christian pastoral leaders; in that situation of cultural conflict and uncertainty. Christians who failed to meet the expectation of the church became a dominant pastoral concern. Pastoral care for the community and care of individuals were combined in modes of discipline members of the community who failed to follow the Churches rules of worship and behavior. Reconciling those who had remained steadfast to the faith with those who failed to do so likewise became a pre-occupying problem.

Two important aspects greatly affected pastoral practices during this persecution period were the Greek concepts of 'Metanoia' (repentance) and 'exomologesis' (confession)[20] The earliest known Latin theological writer, Tertullian (160-220 CE) strongly developed the concepts of repentance and confession as pastoral requirements of the Christian community that were designed to make reconciliation possible. As pastoral care historians William Clebsch and Charles Jaekle writes, "confession thus became a kind of medicine of humiliation possessing power to make better (person) and better Christian and as such demonstrating God's mercy[21] During this period, the Church emphasized discipline on the authority of the pastoral leader and enforces behavioral boundaries for members of the community, and other hand, emphasized the pastor's role as reconciler and healer of the wound of the people.

THE FALL OF THE ROMAN EMPIRE AND THE SPREAD OF CHRISTIANITY ACROSS EUROPE / MEDDLE AGES

It is important to recognize that the fourth and fifth centuries were a time of considerable fomentation and controversy within the Church regarding the proper care and interpretation of the Christian theological tradition. It was the time of Arian and Nestorian controversies, the council of Nicea and numerous other events and struggles that established the shape of orthodoxy in regard to theology in the Church. All these controversies and decisions had their effect on the ways in which pastoral and communal care developed. Gregory the great established the medieval model of pastoral care practice. Thomas Oden argues that, if Augustine set the tone for medieval theology, Gregory established the basic Christian community.[22] Gregory emphasis on the regulation ordinary life through the practices of prayer, meditation and spiritual discipline. For Him each person and his or her particular situation in life demanded individual, contextually relevant attention.

Two other interpretative connections between modern pastoral practice and the pastoral care developed in the early Middle Ages need to be noted. First, there developed ways of thinking about human spiritual needs and disciplines that focused on analogies between the care of the soul and the care of the body. Such terms as *spiritual health* and *spiritual sickness* were common. Priest became as the physician of the soul. Second, during the early middle ages, healing of spiritual problems such as guilt despondence through anointing with ritual oil and ointments was widely practiced.[23]

THE REFORMATION

Reformation of the church in 15th and 16th centuries a new understanding of the ministry developed. The rules about celibacy and other differences which separated the clergy and laity were ended the ordained leaders began to live more closely with their people. Martin Luther, stressed the doctrine of the universal priesthood of all believers for him repentance means "coming to one's sense; a change in our heart and our love as response to God's grace". Secondly the authority to bind loose sin being restricted to priest Calvin emphasized on dependence and it reflected on his pastoral approach. According to him "embraces the soul's progressive appropriation of the obedience, holiness and goodness that mark the restoration man's lost or obscured image of God. Luther's concern for justification by faith, the priest hood of all believers and his commitment to cure soul was important.[24]

PASTORAL CARE IN MODERNITY / ENLIGHTENMENT

The enlightenment was an age marked by the rise of secularism: the belief that human history as well as contemporary life can be understood without speaking of God or assuming divine activity in human affairs. In response to this new age of human thought and practice, pastoral care practices likewise opened a pathway toward a more scientific "practical" mode of operation. Among the writings that developed these new ways of understanding the work of the pastor, *The Reformed Pastor,* published in 1656 by Richard Baxter, an English Presbyterian priest and John Bunyan's *Pilgrim Progress.*[25]

This period received an important model for moral and ethical concern. In many ways they combined the ancient priestly, prophetic and wisdom roles of the pastor by being acutely sensitive to the issues of morality in the lives of those in their care. With the primary purpose of pastoral care practice becoming the fostering of the culture of the self, the way opened towards a full-blown appropriation of the rapidly developing psychological science. By the end of the nineteen century, two highly significant developments had taken place: one in the style of pastoral presence and the other in the style of congregational life. A second development that transformed the context of the Church's caring ministry took place within the life of the congregation.[26]

Psychology of Religion Movement

The most significant developments in pastoral care at the beginning of the twentieth century were in continuity with the turn toward the self that emerged from the rapid developing privatization of religion in the nineteenth-century west. Religion had become closely associated with self-development. This was the case whether one found affinity with mainline liberal theology, an evangelical theology of salvation by acceptance of Christ as personal Savior, or the moral honing of the self by means of pietistic holiness practice.

The Self and the Recovery of Pastoral Healing

Psychological Science's move to the forefront of pastoral attention at the beginning of the twentieth century came a renewed interest in pastoral healing. Psychology, particularly psychology sees as therapy for the beleaguered self, offered the possibility of enhancing pastoral ability to minister to troubled person in Christian congregations.[27]

Freud and the Freudian Psychoanalysis continued to have a major influence on the establishment of pastoral care as a psychologically oriented discipline through the early and middle twentieth century, as it does even today.

CHANGING PATTERNS IN THE CARE OF THE TRADITION: PASTORAL CARE AND COUNSELLING AND POSTMODERN THEOLOGIES

The twentieth-century pastoral care movement was not only influenced by consciousness-alerting socio-cultural changes during the 1960's, 1970's and 1980's; it was also influenced by changes taking place as the disciplined care of the Christian tradition moved ever deeper into essentially postmodern ways of evaluating and interpreting traditional thought. For some pastoral theologians this meant that the models pastoral care rooted in the liberal humanism symbolized by Rogerian and other humanistic methods empathizing the embodiment of the Christian gospel in pastoral relationships were no longer adequate. Their apparent avoidance of Christian language in pastoral care interactions came under suspicion. The substitution of psychological for theological language seemed to these pastoral theologians to be evidence of a loss of an essential critical edge grounded in Christian understandings of the human conditions.[28]

David Lyall in his article "Pastoral counselling in a postmodern context" gives brief analysis of the postmodern context's implication to pastoral counselling;

1) The growth of the counselling movement itself is understandable in the context of postmodern society.

2) In the context of the postmodern world of competing narratives, the Christian narrative has its own integrity and in relation to pastoral counselling.

3) In the context of the counselling relationship, the Christian narrative may be expressed in ways that stir the imagination (i.e. Parabolically and poetically.[29]

EFFECTS ON COUNSELLING THEORIES

Hansen has identified three primary corollaries of postmodern epistemology for the role of counselling theories[30]:

Theory as Narrative Structures:

All theories have to be entwined in culture, politics and language, thus it is "epistemically naive" to "assert the inherent superiority of one over another"[31]. Theories are narrative structures for rhetoric purposes and for persuading suffer to construct experience from a different perspective. Successful counselling outcomes are determined by counsellor's abilities to select new narratives that will be in tune with particular clients and of counselors, skills at internalizing these new story lines into clients.

In postmodern thinking, forms of language and the use of language in stories create meaning. There may be as many meanings as there are people to tell the stories. Each of these stories expresses a truth for the person telling it. Every persons involved in a situation as a perspective on the "reality" of that situation, but the range of truth is limited due to the effects of specific historical events and the language uses the dominate particular social contexts. In practice range of possible meaning is not infinite.[32]

The collaborative partnership in the therapeutic process is considered more important than assessment or technique. Understanding narratives and deconstructing language processes (linguistic) does the focus for both understanding individuals and helping them construct desired change. Individuals construct the meaning of life in interpretive stories, which are then treated as "truth." Because of the power of dominant culture narratives, individuals tend to internalize the messages from these dominant discourses. It often works against the life opportunity of the individual.

In the process of counselling and psychotherapy, it is more than the applying skills than it creates climates that encourage clients to see their stories from different perspectives. A series of "maps" of narrative conversational trajectories can help give structure and direction to a therapeutic conversation. The approach is also an expression of an ethical stance, which is grounded in a postmodern framework.[33] It is from the conceptual framework that practices are applied to assist clients in finding new meaning and new possibilities in their lives.

Theoretical Truth as Pragmatic Utility

Postmodern pragmatism claims that the best interpretation of events is the most useful one. Theoretical truth is redefined as local, utilitarian and pragmatic utility. Thus the theory selection should be based on whether a theoretical orientation is instrumental in meeting the objectives of a particular counselling situation. In postmodern world in which truth and reality are often understood as points of view bounded by history and context rather than as objective immutable facts.[34] By adopting a postmodern, narrative and social constructionist view sheds light on how power, knowledge and "truth" are negotiated in families and other social and cultural contexts. In which therapy is the reestablishment of personal agency from the oppression of external problems and the dominant stories of larger systems.

Externalization and deconstruction are the main process of healing methods. Therapists believe it is not the person that is in the problem, but the problem that is the problem.[35] These problems often are products of the cultural world or of the power relations in which this world is located. Living life means relating to problems, not being fused with them. For this purpose, therapists help clients deconstruct these problematic stories by disassembling the taken-for-granted assumptions that are made about an event, which then opens substitute possibilities for living. Externalization is one process for deconstructing the power of a narrative. This process separates the person from identification with the problem. When the clients view themselves as "being" the problem, they are limited in the ways can effectively deal with the problem. Then opens up space for new stories to emerge.

An Egalitarian Counselling Relationship

The counsellor is expected to be an equal partner with the client to construct narratives rather than an expert enlightening the client. These narratives can be helpful to the meaning construction process. From a postmodernist perspective, "the process of constructing meaning within the counselling relationship" is at the top of agenda.

The postmodern therapist adopts a social constructionist viewpoint, assuming that how people process and construct information about themselves and their world is central to their existence. Rather than conceptualizing progress as a departure from and rejection on the past. Postmodernism draws on the past to serve the present.[36] People's experience of emotions depends on the names that they give to these emotions. People's beliefs about their relationship affect how they interpret the reactions of others and how they respond to them. Personal behaviour results from theses cognitive processes and is therefore open to change or it can be rewritten.

Problem-free talk is used to enhance relationships. It often reduces anxiety and guilt if an individual finds that the therapist enquires about their successes and interest as well as the problems. It is helpful in widening the conversation away from the problem and hence indirectly encourages thinking about solutions.[37] The therapist adopts a non-expert or 'not-knowing' posture, in which the personage and not the therapist select goals and means to meet these goals. A therapist may negotiate goals with the attendee, if the goals are unrealistic.[38]

In postmodern approach interview (Counselling sessions) will contain certain exact basics. 'What do you want to get out of being here today?' or 'What are your best hopes for this sessions?' begin the process of collaboration between therapist and attenders. Problems and goals are defined in practical terms that enable the attenders to focus on solutions. It is a nonjudgmental relationship. In therapeutic relationship therapists believe that every word spoken is important and has significance. Clients are viewed as experts preferring about their own lives.

EFFECTS ON COUNSELLING PRACTICE

Some of the counselling modalities have changed their developmental trajectories because of incorporating postmodernist ideas and concepts. Nystul has noted that postmodernism brings a paradigm shift to **cognitive behavioral counselling** shifting its focus from intrapsychic causation to an appreciation of the effect of contextual factors on human functioning. It is more concerned with the counsellor and client constructing new narratives and less involved in addressing "internal cognitive deficits"[39] **Narrative therapy** is to facilitate clients to "deconstruct dysfunctional narratives (from the dominant culture) and reauthor new more functional narratives".[40] **Feminist Family therapy** is to help family systems to overcome oppression from social forces and enhances and enhance mutual respect, egalitarianism and gender sensitivity between the male and the female. It seeks to reconstruct patriarchy related narratives and reconstruct narratives that accommodate gender differences and special needs of the female in all dimensions of living. Valuing femininity and a positive attitude towards the female, it attempts to empower the female with the context of an egalitarian family.[41]

STRENGTHS OF POSTMODERN COUNSELLING

Some strengths are identified as follows.

AN EGALITARIAN COUNSELLOR-CLIENT RELATIONSHIP

It is understandable that the postmodern counselor treats the client as an equal partner and an expert, given that nobody can claim to capture the absolute truth. This kind of egalitarianism will encourage that client to unfold his or her stories from his or her own perspective and will help the counsellor gain an empathic understanding of the client. Particularly, an egalitarian relationship will enable the counselor and the client to co-tap the deeper meanings of the client's lived experiences.[42]

AN EMPHASIS ON PHENOMENOLOGICAL UNDERSTANDING

Recognizing multiple realities and refraining from labeling, stereotyping and using pathological language, the counsellor can better understand the client from a phenomenological perspective. This will help the counsellor gain insight into how the client constructs his or her personal meanings and how the client perceives his or her storied life. Furthermore, the use of narratives will enable the client to verbalize and ventilate his or her emotionally charged problems.[43]

FREEDOM FROM THEORETICAL BONDAGE

Embracing a nonjudgmental position and endeavoring to avoid preconceived theories, the postmodern counsellor tries to embark on counselling without ideological baggage and theoretical regalia. This may emancipate the counsellor from the bondage of preconceptions and prevent the counsellor from jumping to a conclusion prematurely.[44]

CONTEXTUALIZATION

Based on the argument that reality is contextualized in socio-cultural, politico-economic and linguistic forces as well as other forces that shape personal views of reality, postmodern counselling can help clients identify the negative and oppressive effects of mainstream culture and dominant societal forces on their personal life, thus minimizing their self-blame and enhancing their self-esteem. It can also enable the counsellor to consider a constellation of factors that might contribute to problems.[45]

LIMITATIONS OF POSTMODERN COUNSELLING

Although postmodern counselling is gaining momentum, a care full examination of it would reveal its limitations and pitfalls. Postmodernism is trapped within relative, idiographic and particular realities, thus failing to see absolute, monotheist and universal truths. So it tends to fall victim to relativism, solipsism and nihilism.

However, overemphasis on the relational self may turn us into a pawn of social factors and a passive receptor of external stimuli. It may also give us a moratorium on addressing intrapersonal issues and on appreciating the ultimate worth of a holistic person, thus short-circuiting the opportunity to achieve wholeness.

Postmodernism tends to be reductionist insofar as it is likely to reduce everything to language, a narrative or a story. Consequently, it may deter us from capturing the full range of realities and truths; it may turn us into a machine, a bundle of narratives or a carrier of text.

CONCLUSION

Postmodernism is an effective tool for client empowerment. First, postmodernism can facilitate the counsellor's understanding of strengths-related concepts such as empowerment, healing, resiliency and holism. Understanding and applying such concepts will prevent the counsellor from viewing the client as an "ugly duckling"; rather, it will help both parties find out the "white swan" (human capital and social capital) inside the client. Second, establishing an egalitarian counsellor-client relationship will help the client foster a sense of power and assertiveness and will enable counsellor and client to co-dig out meaning nuggets from client's narrative bonanzas. Third, counsellor can employ postmodernism to help client's deconstruct negative narratives and reconstruct empowering narratives.

BIBLIOGRAPHY

Adams, E Jay, *A Theology of Christian Counseling.* USA: Zondervan Publishing House, 1979.

Allen, J Joseph. *The ministry of the Church image of pastoral care* New York: St. Vlademir's Seminary Press; 1986.

Best, Ron. "Pastoral care and the millennium" Una M. Collins and Jean McNiff ed. *Rethinking Pastoral Care* New York: Routledge, 1999.

Carr, Wesley. *Hand Hook of Pastoral Studies Learning and preaching Christian ministry,* London: SPCK, 1997.

Clebsch, William A. and Charles R. Jaekle *Pastoral Care in Historical Perspective* New York: Jason Aronson, 1975.

Clinebell, Howard. *Basic Types of Pastoral Care and Counseling.* Nashville: Abington Press; 1992.

Cobb, B John. *Theology and Pastoral Care.* Philadelphia: Fortress Press, 1977.

Corey, Gerald. *Student Manual for Theory and practice of Counselling and Psychotherapy*, Australia: Thomson Learning, 2001.

______________. *Theory and Practice of Counseling and Psychotherapy Nineth Edition.* Delhi: Cengage, 2019.

Derrida, J. "The play of substitution" in W. Anderson ed., *The truth about the truth: De-Confusing and re-constructing the postmodern world* New York: Putnam, 1995.

Emerson, James G. *The effective Parish in the Twenty-First Century A Pastoral Response in Mission to the Postmodern World* Delhi: ISPCK, 2001.

Foucault, M. *Power/Knowledge: Selected interviews and other writings, 1972-1977.* New York: Pantheon, 1980.

Gergan, K. *The Saturated self: Dilemmas of identity in contemporary life* New York: Basis Books, 1991.

Gerkin, Charles V. *An Introduction to Pastoral Care* Nashville: Abington Press: 1997.

Hansn, J. T. "Thought on knowing: epistemic implications of counselling practice." *Journal of Counselling and development* 84/7 (2006), 291-298.

Held, B. *Back to reality: A Critique of postmodern theory in Psychotherapy* New York: Norton, 1995.

Jones, Richard Nelson. *Theory and Practice of Counselling and Therapy 5th Edition*. New Delhi: SAGE Publications, 2011.

Liyotard, Jean-Francois. *The Postmodern Explained* Minneapolis: University of Minnesota Press, 1992.

Lines, Dennis. *Spirituality in Counselling and Psychotherapy* New Delhi: Sage Publications, 2006.

Lyall, David. "Pastoral Counselling in a Postmodern Context" Gordon Lynch ed. *Clinical   Counselling in the Pastoral Settings* New York: Routledge, 1999.

Minn, R.M Mark. Psychology, *Theology and spirituality in Christian Counseling*. hestne: Cyndrle House Publishers; 1990.

Nichols, Michael P. *The Essentials of Family therapy Fourth edition* Sydney: Pearson, 2009.

Nystul, M.S. *Introduction to Counselling: An art and science perspective* 3rd ed. Boston: Allyn and Bacon, 2006.

Purnes, Andrew. *Theological Reflection, The New Dictionary of Pastoral Students edited by   Wesley Carr Grand Rapids*. Michigan: William B Eerdmans Publishing Company, 2002.

Raj, Y.T. Vinaya. *Re-imaging Dalit Theology Post Modern Reading* Thiruvalla: CSS, 2002.

__________. *Re-Visiting the other Discourses on Postmodern Theology* Thiruvalla: CSS, 2010.

Rodney J Hunter. *Dictionary of Pastoral Care and Counseling* Bangalore: Theological Publications in India, 2007.

Taylor, Harold. *Tend My Sheep Applied Theology -2* London: SPCK, 2002.

Thomas, Oden. C. *Care of Souls in the Classic Tradition* Philadelphia: Fortress Press, 1984.

Van, Deborah & Deusen Hunsinjer, *Theology and Pastoral Counseling. A new interdisciplinary Approach* Secunderabad: OM Books, 2001.

Vanhoozer, kevin J. "Theology and the condition of postmodernity: a report on knowledge (of   God)" ed. by Kevin J. Vanhoozer

The Cambridge Companion to Postmodern Theology New York: Cambridge University Press 2003.

Endnotes

[1] Deborah Van Deusen Hunsinjer, *Theology and Pastoral Counseling. A new interdisciplinary Approach* (Secunderabad: OM Books, 2001),1.

[2] Y.T. Vinaya Raj *Re-imaging Dalit Theology Post Modern Reading* (Thiruvalla: CSS, 2002), 17.

[3] Y.T. Vinaya Raj *Re-Visiting the other Discourses on Postmodern Theology* (Thiruvalla: CSS, 2010), 15.

[4] James G. Emerson, *The effective Parish in the Twenty-First Century A Pastoral Response in Mission to the Postmodern World* (Delhi: ISPCK, 2001), 37.

[5] Kevin J. Vanhoozer "Theology and the condition of Postmodernity: a report on knowledge (of God)" ed. by Kevin J. Vanhoozer the Cambridge companion to postmodern Theology (New York: Cambridge University Press 2003), 3.

[6] Kevin J. Vanhoozer "Theology and the condition of Postmodernity: a report on knowledge (of God)" ed. by Kevin J. Vanhoozer the cambridge companion to postmodern theology…, 38.

[7] Y.T. Vinaya Raj Re-imaging Dalit Theology Post Modern Reading…, 17-18.

[8] Jean-Francois Liyotard, *The Postmodern Explained* (Minneapolis: University of Minnesota Press, 1992), 76.

[9] Y.T. Vinaya Raj *Re-imaging Dalit Theology Post Modern Reading…*, 18.

[10] Y.T. Vinaya Raj Re-imaging Dalit Theology Post Modern Reading…, 18.

[11] K. Gergan, *The Saturated self: Dilemmas of identity in contemporary life* (New York: Basis Books, 1991), 41.

[12] K. Gergan, *The Saturated self: Dilemmas of identity in contemporary life…*

[13] B. Held, *Back to reality: A Critique of postmodern theory in Psychotherapy* (New York: Norton, 1995), 58.

[14] J. Derrida, "The play of substitution" in W. Anderson ed., *The truth about the truth: De-Confusing and re-constructing the postmodern world* (New York: Putnam, 1995), 89.

[15] J. Derrida, "The play of substitution" in W. Anderson ed., *The truth about the truth: De-Confusing and re-constructing the postmodern world...*

[16] M. Foucault *Power/Knowledge: Selected interviews and other writings, 1972-1977.* (New York: Pantheon, 1980), 65.

[17] Charles V Gerkin, *An Introduction to Pastoral Care* (Nashville: Abington Press: 1997) 25.

[18] Charles V Gerkin, *An Introduction to Pastoral Care...*, 23.

[19] Charles V Gerkin, *An Introduction to Pastoral Care...*, 27.

[20] Charles V Gerkin, *An Introduction to Pastoral Care ...*,30

[21] William A. Clebsch and Charles R. Jaekle *Pastoral Care in Historical Perspective* (New York: Jason Aronson, 1975), 95.

[22] Oden. C. Thomas, *Care of Souls in the Classic Tradition* (Philadelphia: Fortress Press, 1984), 43-44.

[23] Ron Best, "Pastoral care and the Millennium" Una M. Collins and Jean McNiff ed. *Rethinking Pastoral Care* (New York: Routledge, 1999), 16-17.

[24] Harold Taylor. *Tend my Sheep applied theology -2* (London: SPCK, 2002) 23.

[25] Charles V Gerkin, *An Introduction to Pastoral Care...*, 44-45.

[26] Charles V Gerkin, *An Introduction to Pastoral Care...*, 53-54.

[27] Wesley Carr *Hand Hook of Pastoral Studies Learning and preaching Christian ministry* (London: SPCK,1997), 179.

[28] Charles V Gerkin, An introduction to Pastoral Care..., 76.

[29] David Lyall "Pastoral counselling in a postmodern context" Gordon Lynch ed. *Clinical Counselling in the pastoral settings* (New York: Routledge, 1999), 12.

[30] J.T. Hansn, "Thought on Knowing: epistemic implications of counselling practice." *Journal of Counselling and development* 84/7 (2006), 293.

[31] J.T. Hansn, "Thought on Knowing: epistemic implications of counselling practice." .....

[32] Gerald Corey, *Theory and Practice of Counseling and Psychotherapy Nineth Edition.* (Delhi: Cengage, 2019), 361.

[33] Corey, *Theory and Practice of Counseling and Psychotherapy Nineth Edition.*, 378.

[34] Corey, *Theory and Practice of Counseling and Psychotherapy Nineth Edition.*, 361.

[35] Michael P Nicholas, *The Essentials of Family Therapy 4th Edition* (Boston: Pearson, 2009), 255.

[36] Richard Nelson Jones, *Theory and Practice of Counselling and Therapy 5th Edition* (New Delhi: SAGE Publications, 2011), 5.

[37] Jones, *Theory and Practice of Counselling and Therapy 5th Edition*, 377.

[38] Corey, *Theory and Practice of Counseling and Psychotherapy Nineth Edition.*, 361.

[39] M.S. Nystul, *Introduction to Counselling: An art and science perspective* 3rd ed. (Boston: Allyn and Bacon, 2006), 269.

[40] M.S. Nystul, *Introduction to Counselling: An art and science perspective* 3rd ed....293.

[41] M.S. Nystul, *Introduction to Counselling: An art and science perspective* 3rd ed....

[42] Wesley Carr, *Handbook of Pastoral Studies Learning and Practicing Christian ministry...*,73-74.

[43] Gerald Corey, *Student Manual for Theory and Practice of Counselling and Psychotherapy* (Australia: Thomson Learning, 2001), 82.

[44] Dennis Lines *Spirituality in Counselling and Psychotherapy* (New Delhi:Sage publications, 2006), 159.

[45] Michael P. Nichols *The Essentials of Family Therapy Fourth edition* (Sydney: Pearson, 2009), 233.

Contributors

Rev. Dr. L.V. Bipinlal is a presbyter of CSI, South Kerala Diocese and currently a faculty member of K.U.T.S. teaching Counselling and also Treasurer of FFRRC, Kottayam.

Rev. Ninan Jacob is a presbyter of CSI Madhya Kerala Diocese and currently Teaching New Testament at Kerala United Theological Seminary.

Rev. John Davidson Johnson is a presbyter of CSI Kollam-Kottarakara Diocese and currently a faculty member of K.U.T.S. faculty teaching Theology and Ethics.

Rev. Ebenezar Shinekumar is a presbyter of CSI South Kerala Diocese and was on the faculty of K.U.T.S. teaching Religions and Culture.

Dr. K.B. Jayasree is a faculty member of Kerala Theological Seminary, Kottarakara and Ebenezer Theological Seminary, Ayur, teaching New Testament.

Rev. Prof. Dr. C.I. David Joy is a presbyter of CSI South Kerala Diocese and currently principal of Kerala United Theological Seminary, Kannammoola, Trivandrum and a board member of Society for Biblical Studies, ICI

Dr. Sajitha Varghese is a faculty member of Kerala Theological Seminary, Kottarakara, teaching New Testament.

Dr. Supongmayang Longkumer is Academic Dean at SIBS, Bangarapet teaching New Testament.

Shri. M.A. Baby is a politburo member of CPI(M) and was a minister of the Kerala State.

Dr. Prof. Donald Schweitzer is a professor of Theology at St. Andrew's College, Saskatoon, Canada and a minister of United Church of Canada.

Rev. Prof. Dr. V.V. Thomas is a professor at United Theological College, Bangalore.

www.ingramcontent.com/pod-product-compliance
Lightning Source LLC
LaVergne TN
LVHW091445170726
843492LV00001B/47